Transmedia and Public Representation

Cultural Media Studies

Leandra H. Hernández and Amanda R. Martinez
Series Editors

Vol. 3

The Cultural Media Studies series is part
of the Peter Lang Media and Communication list.
Every volume is peer reviewed and meets
the highest quality standards for content and production.

PETER LANG
New York • Bern • Berlin
Brussels • Vienna • Oxford • Warsaw

Transmedia and Public Representation

Transgender People
in Film and Television

Magalí Daniela Pérez Riedel, Editor

PETER LANG
New York • Bern • Berlin
Brussels • Vienna • Oxford • Warsaw

Library of Congress Cataloging-in-Publication Control Number: 2021027589

Bibliographic information published by **Die Deutsche Nationalbibliothek**.
Die Deutsche Nationalbibliothek lists this publication in the "Deutsche Nationalbibliografie"; detailed bibliographic data are available on the Internet at http://dnb.d-nb.de/.

ISSN 2641-1415 (print)
ISSN 2577-6231 (online)
ISBN 978-1-4331-7032-4 (hardcover)
ISBN 978-1-4331-7033-1 (paperback)
ISBN 978-1-4331-7034-8 (ebook pdf)
ISBN 978-1-4331-7035-5 (epub)
DOI 10.3726/b15735

© 2022 Peter Lang Publishing, Inc., New York
80 Broad Street, 5th floor, New York, NY 10004
www.peterlang.com

All rights reserved.
Reprint or reproduction, even partially, in all forms such as microfilm, xerography, microfiche, microcard, and offset strictly prohibited.

Contents

Acknowledgments   vii

Introduction: Rewind or Fast Forward? Transgender Representation on Screen   1
    Magalí Daniela Pérez Riedel

Part I Representations, Change, and Progress?

1. The Construction of Transnormativity: Whiteness, Wealth, and Deviance   15
Sarah F. Price, Sim Butler, Richard Mocarski, Robyn Myers,
and Debra Hope
2. "I'm Not Your Adventure": Trans Fetishism on Contemporary Television   37
Charles Goehring
3. Hollywood and the Pathologization of Trans Identities   55
Patricia Di Risio

Part II From Irrelevance to Stardom, or Vice Versa

4. Beyond Tipping Points, Trauma, and Trailblazing: *Adventure Time*
and the Transordinary   77
Emma A. Jane

5. Performing as a Trans Reality Star: Chaz Bono and Isis King   97
   Erika M. Thomas

Part III Trans Narratives and Their Spectators

6. Trans, White, and Privileged: The Public Framing of Caitlyn Jenner on Twitter   121
   Nathian Shae Rodriguez, Jennifer Huemmer, and Mary E. Brooks

7. *Her Story*, Educating a Mainstream Audience   141
   Katerina Symes

List of Contributors   161
Index   165

Acknowledgments

To the Universidad Nacional de Quilmes, for giving me the foundations, the skills, and the training I needed to publish a second book.

I would like to thank my colleagues and friends, Pablo Scharagrodsky and Nancy Diaz Larrañaga, for working beside me for many years, encouraging me to become a better researcher.

To the team of the outreach project "Prácticas de comunicación y educación por la desobediencia sexo-genérica" [Practices of communication and education for sex-gender disobedience] from the Universidad Nacional de Quilmes, for their continuous effort to make schools more inclusive spaces.

To Francisco Perales Pérez and Alfredo Martínez-Expósito, for the discussions and work we did in Australia.

I would also like to thank Liora Elias and Raechel Tiffe for building this project many years ago, and for trusting me to take over the project when you could not continue with it.

To the reviewers and the series editors Leandra H. Hernández and Amanda R. Martinez, for your comments and feedback on the book. To the team of Peter Lang, for the ongoing administrative support and assistance to complete this book.

To the contributors of this volume: Charles, Debra, Emma, Erika, Jennifer, Katerina, Mary, Nathian, Patricia, Richard, Robyn, Sarah, and Sim. I am particularly thankful to each and every one of you for your time, patience, dedication, and commitment. Without you, this book would have never seen the light of the day.

To my family, Estela, Daniel, and Damián, for their love and support throughout these years.

To my chosen family, Leonel and Berenice. Thanks for always being there and helping me keep my feet on the ground.

To all and everyone of you, thank you.

Magalí D. Pérez Riedel
Manchester, United Kingdom

INTRODUCTION

Rewind or Fast Forward? Transgender Representation on Screen

BY MAGALÍ DANIELA PÉREZ RIEDEL[1]

Anzaldúa (2009) defines homophobia with a metaphor, saying it is the fear of going home. Then, it could be argued that transphobia is the fear of transformation or change: discrimination against trans folks is a way to protect gender hierarchies and boundaries. According to Darryl B. Hill (2016), transphobia is "the set of beliefs and values, the psychological motivation, for anti-trans discriminatory behavior and attitudes," and "it is clearly related and bolstered by cisgenderism" (2016, 1273). Transphobic and homophobic representations in media and other spheres have precluded the advancement and equal recognition of the rights of LGBTQ people. According to Thompson (1998), mediated representations have historically spread moral panics and promoted social anxieties, using homosexual persons as scapegoats to term what was normal. Thompson suggests that the media portrayed gays as criminals and promiscuous sexual deviants, saying they were mentally ill and carried sexually-transmitted diseases like HIV/AIDS. These "sexual deviants" were said to be a menace to the traditions and hegemonic values of the "normal" members of society, who were under threat. These fears were (and are still used) to marginalize transgender people (Pérez Riedel 2019). Following that logic, the exclusion and the violence against those "perverts" is a

---

1 Magalí Daniela Pérez Riedel, Ph.D. Lecturer and researcher, former co-director of LGBTQ outreach project at Universidad Nacional de Quilmes, Argentina. Email: mdpr88@gmail.com

justified and reasonable measure to remain safe from the dangers that LGBTQ people are said to represent.

The rights of LGBTQ people, and particularly those of transgender people, are constantly under threat. Serrano Amaya and Ríos González (2019) claim that "anti-rights movements have found in the buzz-word 'gender ideology' a connecting point to push back advances in gender and sexual rights" (2019, 378). Conservative governments are questioning the legitimacy of transgender subjectivities and challenging their inclusion in many spaces such as the military. Hate crimes are primarily taking the lives of Black transgender women, for example, in the U.S. (Martinez and Law 2019). In this context, mediated representations of non-cisgender and non-heterosexual people are slowly starting to proliferate and evolve. LGBTQ movements and advocacy groups have been fighting to halt discrimination and violence. Cultural texts are evidence of the recent changes and progress in terms of rights and protections of the transgender population in some Western civilizations. The growing visibility of transgender people in mass media accompanies the processes of social, political, and cultural transformations that demand the democratization and equal recognition of the human rights of vulnerable sectors, including transgender people.

Reading mainstream texts with transgender and gender-nonconforming characters allows us to interpret the mechanisms that support the heterosexist and cisnormative *status quo*. Here, we use the term "transgender" broadly and in an inclusive way, following Spencer's (2015, xii) suggestion to avoid using strict and fixed definitions. The authors of this volume and I often use "transgender" as an umbrella term to refer to the multiplicity of identities and subjectivities that distance themselves from the cisgender norm. Additionally, we use the term "mainstream media" to refer to popular and commercial products that disseminate and perpetuate hegemonic meanings, which can be either negotiated or challenged (Williams 1977). Communication is a meaning-making process that occurs within a culture, where people interpret and make sense of the actors and the processes that are part of their lives (Martín Barbero 1987). Even though discussions from this volume focus on media representations and the relationships among producers, cultural texts, and their audiences, communication cannot and should not be reduced to the media. Instead, it should focus on the mediations and the meaning-making processes (Martín Barbero 2008). Nonetheless, mediated communication is a fundamental point of entry to examine hegemonic ideas, values, and representations in a specific society at a given time (Orozco Gómez 2001).

The contributors of this volume reflect upon the role of television and film portrayals of transgender people in a context where there is a growing number of transgender and gender-diverse characters in the public eye. The authors analyze mainstream and independent productions where transgender people were cast or featured as main or secondary characters. Investigating transgender representation in cultural texts is an increasingly important topic in transgender media studies. The changes experienced by increased transgender visibility over the past decade remain unprecedented: now more than ever, transgender narratives are widely broadcast across network and cable television, on-demand streaming services, and even web series. In light of these recent events, it is becoming difficult to ignore the key role of transgender portrayals to understand broader social structures and cultural processes.

The contributing authors of this book answer the following questions: (1) how are transgender people represented in television and film? (2) how do recent transgender portrayals differ from the ones from the previous decades? and (3) how does the public respond to the films and programs that include transgender people and characters? Their investigations make progress in a growing field of literature that is concerned about the changes and challenges posed by the eruption of transgender folks into the mainstream.

LITERATURE REVIEW

There is an emerging area of interest in transgender studies and communication that recognizes the importance of studying transgender representation in television and film (Spencer 2015). A considerable amount of literature has been published on how portrayals of transgender women reinforce notions of cisgender normativity. A seminal study in this area is the work of Miller (2015), who identifies that transgender character constructions in popular film comedies "are constructed to support the system of cisnormativity" (2015, 128). Miller defines cisnormativity as the "systemic expectation that there are only two mutually exclusive genders and the gender of all members of a society will match the sex assigned to them at birth, [labeling] those who do not, transgender and queer individuals, as deviant" (2015, 127). She adds:

> Analysis of transgender representation in film and other media continues to be important, and future research must continue to bring attention to the myriad ways transgender people are distanced by these representations, but the privileging of cisnormativity in all films also works to maintain separation between transgender and cisgender people. (Miller 2015, 142)

The author concludes that transgender and non-transgender characters are not presented as equals, and transgender identities are presented in comedy movies to be laughed at.

In another major study, Serano (2007) finds that the marginalization and (mis)representation of transgender women in media are both rooted not only in transphobia but more in what the author calls "transmisogyny," a term coined by Serano to refer to the ridicule, fear, suspicion, and fetish attributed to female transgender characters. Transmisogyny targets trans women because they are transgressing gender norms and because femininity is seen as inferior to maleness and masculinity. Conversely, in an analysis of contemporary scripted television series from the United States, Capuzza and Spencer (2017) claim that televised representations of transgender folks are more sympathetic toward their transgender identities and expressions. The authors also observe that transgender men and genderqueer identities are largely absent from television, while transgender women are more prominent. However, there is still little research that particularly examines representations of transgender men and gender-nonconforming people, other than a few exceptions (Gazzola and Morrison 2014; Mocarski et al. 2013; Willox 2003). The lack of gender-diverse people in media also needs to be addressed, although there could be more nuanced investigations in the future, should more gender-diverse mediated portrayals become available.

According to Ford (2016), mainstream cultural texts released by video on-demand services like Netflix are making progress to tackle transphobia. As Ford points out, "while the online screen world moves forward at a rapid pace in its representations of gender-diversity, the world of the mainstream theatrical release cinema lags behind such cultural trends" (2016, 67). The author provides an in-depth analysis of the portrayal of *Dallas Buyers Club*'s (2013) secondary character Rayon, a transgender woman with AIDS who wants to undergo gender-confirmation surgery. Rayon, played by cisgender male actor Jared Leto, is a sex worker who also sells drugs for a living and dies due to AIDS-related causes near the end of the film. In this case study, Ford notes that Rayon's identity as transgender is linked to notions of amorality, sexual deviance, crime, disease, and death. Thus, trans representations in Hollywood remain problematic and display a one-sided and cisnormative view of transgender subjectivities. Ford concludes:

> Until there are an equal number of screen texts produced that show trans people as successful, healthy, loved, cherished, with adequate money that does not have to be earnt in marginalized settings, and characters that are alive at the end of the narrative, the problematics of the representation of Rayon in *Dallas Buyers Club* will remain. (Ford 2016, 82)

Overall, three important themes emerge from the studies discussed so far: (1) transgender women are more largely represented than other transgender and gender-nonconforming identities, (2) the increasing inclusion of transgender and gender-nonconforming people and fictional characters in television and film is not free of problems and disputes, and (3) research must continue to identify how mediated representations of transgender folks both reproduce and resist hegemonic and oppressive representations. Together, these studies indicate that transgender visibility in media has traditionally reinforced cisnormative notions of gender identity and expression while disseminating alternative and counter-hegemonic representations that challenged and transgressed gender boundaries and problematized the gender binary.

However, these studies remain narrow in focus dealing only with representations of transgender women and only with mainstream media. There remain several aspects of transgender representation about which relatively little is known, such as transgender portrayals in on-demand video streaming services and independent and non-commercial film and television productions; transmasculine representations and genderqueer identities; representations of underage transgender folks; and transgender and gender-nonconforming identities and their intersection with categories of age, religion, class, (dis)ability, health, sexual orientation, race/ethnicity, nationality, and socioeconomic status, to name a few. This collection sets out to fill in that gap through the examination of trans representation in past and contemporary screen texts with a critical lens. But we also adopt an intersectional lens (Crenshaw 1989) to understand the intersecting and often overlapping forms of oppression that affect transgender communities.

AN OVERVIEW

The book offers a vast array of nuanced interpretations of recent audiovisual texts featuring trans actors, narratives, and characters. It reflects upon hegemonic representations of trans people in the media by inviting trans voices and bodies into the scene to illustrate the complications and conundrums behind such representations and the roles they play in mainstream television and cinema today and in the recent past. It features local and foreign lecturers and early-career researchers who perform several textual and extra-textual analyses to demonstrate the characteristics and the impact of transgender representation in mainstream and independent television shows and commercial films.

The study of representational practices is the main topic of the first section, "Representations, Change, and Progress?" It begins with an overarching analysis of critically-acclaimed popular television shows. In Chapter 1, Sarah F. Price et al. analyze the first seasons of the most recent and prominent series and television programs featuring transgender and gender diverse characters: *Orange Is the New Black* (2013–2019), *I Am Cait* (2015–2016), *Transparent* (2014–2019), *I Am Jazz* (2015–2020), and *Sense8* (2015–2018). The authors study how the programs' depictions of trans characters represent a step toward progress and also forms of stagnation. They find that these shows have created and redefined transnormativity through the reinforcement of stereotypes that limit the understanding of what it is to be trans. These scholars explore the hegemonic transnormative narrative through the categories of race, socioeconomic status, sexuality, and deviance.

Their findings show that the transgender characters from their sample are mostly white and middle or upper-class, and they rarely take part in any romantic or sexual encounters. There were also occasions in which a character played by a transgender person of color was associated with crime and other deviant behaviors. Although these representations put trans characters at the forefront of the televisual landscape with more sympathetic and authentic portrayals, they do so in a way that presents them as freaks and denies them the possibility to be socially accepted and to even belong to the human race. Transnormative character constructions erase all the aspects that can threaten the gender *status quo*. Thus, trans representation remains within the scope of what it means to be intelligible as a trans person, inside of the boundaries of normative forms of gender, sex, and sexuality.

In the subsequent chapter, Charles Goehring centers his research on the hyper-sexualization of the transgender body. Goehring studies episodes from U.S. series *Transparent* (2014–2019) and British comedy show *Catastrophe* (2015–2019). He finds that transgender women are fetishized in ways that appeal to the cisgender heterosexual (and mostly male) gaze and fantasy. Using the category of agency, he observes that trans characters in *Transparent* are given more agency than their British counterparts. However, evidence suggests that some of the portrayals of these characters are transphobic since they are still tied to ideas that present trans people (especially women) as sexual deviants. If the fetishization of the transgender body serves both series as a narrative theme, it follows that increased visibility does not necessarily mean an improvement in the representation of trans folks. Goehring argues that it is necessary to carefully examine plotlines involving trans issues to problematize the implications of such representations. He suggests that nuanced interpretations ought to be considered when studying transgender representations.

Similarly, in Chapter 3, Patricia Di Risio discusses the representations in Hollywood in the past three decades. Using Foucault's definition of perverse implantation, Di Risio analyses four canonical films, *The Crying Game* (1992), *Boys Don't Cry* (1999), *Transamerica* (2005), and *The Danish Girl* (2015). While these movies depart from traditional negative tropes that blatantly depict transgender people as murderous, they are still far from representing them in a positive light. Di Risio demonstrates that cinematic representations of transgender people reinforce the "wrong body" discourse and reproduce outdated notions and stereotypes that are pathologizing. Because all four transgender characters in the sample want to undergo gender confirmation surgery, the experiences of non-fictional transgender individuals are reduced to a medically-oriented understanding of their bodies, identities, and desires. Di Risio concludes that even the most recent Hollywood films embrace yet fail to represent transgender identities in a progressive way.

Together, these three chapters offer readers a set of critical narrative analyses of popular cultural texts that are widely disseminated in the United States and other Western countries. Their authors conduct nuanced interpretations of those representational practices to identify trends and disruptions in the mediated portrayals of transgender and gender-nonconforming people. Since the beginning of the second millennium, prime time broadcast and cable television shows, on-demand streaming services, and Hollywood have been releasing movies and shows with visibly transgender individuals and fictional characters. While some of these contemporary representations seem progressive, they still struggle to break free from traditional representation regimes.

The second section, "From Irrelevance to Stardom, or Vice Versa," sets out to critically scrutinize these hegemonic transgender tropes in animated series and reality television shows. In Chapter 4, Emma A. Jane provides an in-depth account of the past and present regimes of mediated representation of transgender people. The two central tropes that the author identifies are the tragic trope, which shows trans folks as victims of traumatic events, crimes, or mental health problems; and the trailblazer trope, which celebrates trans people for their success and special achievements. In her examination of the 10 seasons of Cartoon Network's *Adventure Time* (2010–2018), Jane finds that another option is possible and argues for the "transordinary." The children's cartoon depicts transgender folks as ordinary people in everyday situations in a fictional universe that is made up of many transgender and gender-nonconforming people, where their identities, bodies, and gender expressions are irrelevant within the storylines and the character structure.

This decentering of trans identities is the opposite of what occurs in popular reality television shows. In Chapter 5, Erika Thomas highlights that the inclusion of transgender women and men as stars, celebrities, and fashion models can be problematic, especially when trans folks are allowed to be in the spotlight to reinforce gender norms. In her analysis of one season of *America's Next Top Model* (2008) and *Dancing with the Stars* (2011), Thomas describes how these reality shows frame the performances of transgender contestants Isis King and Chaz Bono. The author's application of performance theory as a theoretical and methodological framework allows for the examination of the discourses and framings of both participants. Thomas observes how King and Bono are "making it" since their performances, modeling, and dancing conform to gender roles and expectations. However, she identifies that the performances of King and Bono reinforce hegemonic notions of femininity and masculinity. They are not entirely successful in their attempts to "break" or transgress gender norms. Moreover, King and Bono are mostly depicted in a positive light, although hosts, judges, and other participants treat them both as childlike, or as if they were "faking" or failing to be a legitimate woman or a man, respectively.

The author suggests that these were possibly the grounds for their dismissal from the competitions.

Taken together, these two chapters indicate that the identities of transgender people and fictional characters who are trans, as well as their gender performances, can either be acknowledged and validated, or called into question by other characters, participants, judges, and members of the audience. These chapters are key to understand the traditional and current regimes of representation, and how they broadcast the acceptance, celebration, or disapproval of transgender and gender-diverse people.

The last section, "Trans Narratives and Their Spectators," accounts for the audiences and their role in the meaning-making process. In Chapter 6, Nathian Shae Rodriguez, Jennifer Huemmer, and Mary E. Brooks address the reception and framing of the televised "coming out" of Caitlyn Jenner through social media research. With an intersectional and queer approach, the authors move from television to Twitter and perform a textual analysis of a sample of 1,000 tweets of 160 words each. While the positive portrayals were supportive of her publicized "coming out" and transition, users mostly presented Jenner in a negative way and criticized her because of factors such as her age and male privilege. Interestingly, users identified that Jenner's celebrity status, wealth, and whiteness afford her privilege that other trans people do not have. Nonetheless, a positive aspect of Jenner's "coming out" and her participation in the reality television show *I Am Cait* (2015–2016) is that her televised appearances helped educate audiences to familiarize themselves with transgender issues at the same time that Jenner was educating herself on such topics.

Shifting the focus to less commercial productions, in Chapter 7, Katerina Symes theorizes about the educational role of television shows with transgender and queer characters. In her analysis of the independent web series *Her Story* (2016), Symes studies the pedagogical role of this production, which the author defines as a queer crossover program. *Her Story* depicts many queer and transgender people having discussions about everyday issues, such as disclosing one's trans identity while dating, the acceptance of trans women among lesbian groups, and discrimination within the LGBTQ population, to name a few. *Her Story* is a series made by queer and transgender individuals in an attempt to challenge conventional understandings of gender and sexuality. The author maintains that its character proxy structure serves a pedagogical function to educate LGBTQ and non-LGBTQ viewers on the struggles and complexities of life as a transgender person. Despite casting a trans woman in a leading role and featuring other trans people on screen and behind the camera, implicit in the series is a tacit fetishization and pathologization of trans folks. Moreover, transgender stories are narrated via the cisgender character in an attempt to educate cisgender heterosexual audience members.

Overall, the chapters from this section center on the relationship between transgender people and characters and their presumably cisgender spectators. The authors identify that these productions address issues in a way that may prove to be educational and informative by disseminating sympathetic portrayals of transgender people facing everyday situations and issues. While some of these depictions repeat outdated stereotypes and are not representative of transgender and gender-nonconforming communities, they challenge hegemonic readings by putting trans voices in the forefront, and by placing transgender people and characters in relatable situations and scenarios.

IMPLICATIONS AND LIMITATIONS

The aim of this chapter was to examine current trends and challenges in transgender media studies. The findings from this book contribute in several ways to the current literature on transgender representation and LGBTQ studies. First, it provides one of the first comprehensive assessments of commercial and non-commercial productions across different channels and genres. Second, it adds to the growing body of literature on the topic by shedding light on the representation of a myriad of transgender identities and experiences. Third, it brings together communication scholars from different areas and theoretical backgrounds and traditions. And finally, it reports on transgender representations on a transnational level, including contributions from Australia, Canada, the United States, and the United Kingdom.

The major limitation of this book is the absence of cultural texts from non-English speaking countries. A second limitation is the lack of diversity of non-fiction genres, as it could have included news reports or user-generated online content. Another weakness of this book is that the generalizability of the results is subject to certain limitations. For instance, the portrayals of the experiences of a Black transgender woman in a U.S. prison are hardly similar to the ones of a White middle-class transgender woman. Similarly, the depictions of the issues faced by a transgender man who is a celebrity may differ from the ones of a transgender female adolescent. Notwithstanding these limitations, the collection offers valuable insights on how diverse and complex the experiences and struggles of fictional and non-fictional transgender people on screen can be.

Further work needs to be done to establish the extent to which transgender representation improves in the years to come. One of the productions that fell outside of the scope of this book due to temporary constraints is U.S. drama *Pose* (2018–), which features transgender people of color. A further study could assess the effectiveness of including Black transgender characters and narratives on television to fight sexism and racism. Another study might explore the representations of drag culture in non-competition reality television shows. A greater focus on transgender masculinities and genderqueer identities could produce interesting findings that account for more nuanced interpretations and representations of transgender folks.

The challenge now is to examine to what degree popular texts with transgender people are enabling or resisting the recognition of the rights of transgender and gender non-conforming people. We hope that this book will make a contribution not only to the field but also to the betterment of the lives of trans folks in the United States and the rest of the world.

REFERENCES

Anzaldúa, Gloria. 2009. "Miedo a volver a casa: homofobia." In *Manifiestos gays, lesbianos y queer: Testimonios de una lucha (1969–1994)*, edited by Rafael M. Mérida Jiménez, 207–8. Barcelona: Icaría.

Capuzza, Jamie C. and Leland G. Spencer. 2017. "Regressing, Progressing, or Transgressing on the Small Screen? Transgender Characters on U.S. Scripted Television Series." *Communication Quarterly* 65, no. 2: 214–30.

Crenshaw, Kimberlé. 1989. "Demarginalizing the Intersection of Race and Sex: A Black Feminist Critique of Antidiscrimination Doctrine, Feminist Theory, and Antiracist Politics." *University of Chicago Legal Forum* 1, no. 8: 139–67.

Ford, Akkadia. 2016. "Whose Club Is It Anyway?: The Problematic of Trans Representation in Mainstream Films—'Rayon' and *Dallas Buyers Club*." *Screen Bodies* 1, no. 2: 64–86.

Gazzola, Stephanie B. and Melanie Ann Morrison. 2014. "Cultural and Personally Endorsed Stereotypes of Transgender Men and Transgender Women: Notable Correspondence or Disjunction?" *International Journal of Transgenderism* 15, no. 2: 76–99.

Hill, Darryl B. 2016. "Transphobia." In *The SAGE Encyclopedia of LGBTQ Studies*, edited by Abbie E. Goldberg, 1272–3. Thousand Oaks: SAGE Publications.

Martinez, Gina and Tara Law. 2019. "Two Recent Murders of Black Trans Women in Texas Reveal a Nationwide Crisis, Advocates Say." *Time*, June 12, 2019. https://time.com/5601227/two-black-trans-women-murders-in-dallas-anti-trans-violence/

Martín Barbero, Jesús. 1987. *De los medios a las mediaciones*. Mexico: Gustavo Gilli.

———. 2008. "De la experiencia al relato. Cartografías culturales y comunicativas de Latinoamérica." *Anthropos. Huella del conocimiento* 219: 21–42.

Miller, Lucy J. 2015. "Becoming One of the Girls/Guys: Distancing Transgender Representations in Popular Film Comedies." In *Transgender Communication Studies: Histories, Trends, and Trajectories*, edited by Leland G. Spencer and Jamie C. Capuzza, 127–42. Lanham: Lexington Books.

Mocarski, Richard, Sim Butler, Betsy Emmons, and Rachael Smallwood. 2013. "'A Different Kind of Man': Mediated Transgendered Subjectivity, Chaz Bono on *Dancing with the Stars*." *Journal of Communication Inquiry* 37, no. 3: 249–64.

Orozco Gómez, Guillermo. 2001. *Televisión, audiencias y educación*. Buenos Aires: Grupo Editorial Norma.

Pérez Riedel, Magalí D. 2019. "Improper Subjects: Thoughts on Discrimination Bills and Online Discrimination against LGBTIQ People." *About Gender* 8, no. 15: 364–78.

Serano, Julia. 2007. *Whipping Girl: A Transsexual Woman on Sexism and the Scapegoating of Femininity*. Emeryville, CA: Seal Press.

Serrano Amaya, José F. and Oriol Ríos González. 2019. "Introduction to the Special Issue: Challenges of LGBT Research in the 21st Century." *International Sociology* 34, no. 4: 371–81.

Spencer, Leland G. 2015. "Introduction: Centering Transgender Studies and Gender Identity in Communication Scholarship." In *Transgender Communication Studies: Histories, Trends, and Trajectories*, edited by Leland G. Spencer and Jamie C. Capuzza, ix–xxii. Lanham: Lexington Books.

Thompson, Kenneth. 1998. *Moral Panics*. London: Routledge.

Williams, Raymond. 1977. *Marxism and Literature*. New York: Oxford University Press.

Willox, Annabelle. 2003. "Branding Teena: (Mis)Representations in the Media." *Sexualities* 6, no. 3–4: 407–25.

PART I
REPRESENTATIONS, CHANGE, AND PROGRESS?

CHAPTER ONE

The Construction of Transnormativity: Whiteness, Wealth, and Deviance

BY SARAH F. PRICE, SIM BUTLER, RICHARD MOCARSKI, ROBYN MYERS, AND DEBRA HOPE[1]

INTRODUCTION

In 2011, Chaz Bono became the first openly transgender person to be on U.S. network television during prime time with his turn on *Dancing with the Stars* (*DWTS*). Before Bono, representations of transgender and gender diverse (TGD) people were scarce, with only a few appearances by TGD persons on daytime operas (Morrison 2010) and a few negative portrayals on daytime talk shows (Gamson 1998). In the intervening years since Bono's *DWTS* appearance, representation of TGD individuals in media has significantly expanded, including reality television (Morse 2017), dramas, comedies (Capuzza and Spencer 2017),

---

1 Sarah F. Price. Assistant Professor of Communication, Florida Gulf Coast University. Email: sprice@fgcu.edu
Sim Butler, Ph.D. Assistant Professor of Communication Studies, University of Alabama. Email: butle027@crimson.ua.edu
Richard Mocarski, Ph.D. Assistant Vice Chancellor for Research and graduate faculty of Communication at the University of Nebraska at Kearney. Co-Founder of Trans Collaborations. Email: mocarskira@unk.edu
Robyn Myers. Graduate Student in Counseling and School Psychology, University of Nebraska at Kearney. Email: robynk@ymail.com
Debra Hope, Ph.D. Aaron Douglas Professor, University of Nebraska-Lincoln. Director of the Rainbow Clinic and co-Founder of Trans Collaborations. Email: dhope1@unl.edu

news (Capuzza 2015), and documentaries (Booth 2015). This increase coincides with a change in the television delivery landscape with the streaming services of Amazon and Netflix becoming prestige destinations for content, and both producing award-winning shows with TGD characters. While visibility and representation of TGD persons progress from complete erasure, these constructions are not without issues, as even representations with many positive elements leverage hegemonic norms as the keystone of mainstream representation (Mocarski et al. 2013). As Caitlyn Jenner explains on *I Am Cait*, the reality television show that follows her coming out as a transgender woman, "What I feel like we're really trying to do here is normalize this as much as we can" (season 1, episode 2). Normalizing may make the TGD form more palatable for conservative audiences, but it also has specific implications for denoting gender expressions deemed acceptable on the gender spectrum. This chapter explores how television representations of TGD persons have created and changed transnormativity in ways that limit the breadth of the TGD communities while promoting positive and negative stereotypes. This development of normativity creates a specific identification of what becomes the hegemonic transnormative narrative. We theorize about transnormativity and narrative through the categories of race, socioeconomics, sexuality, and deviance. A working concept of transnormativity is sketched across multiple representations, and the nuanced issues of current representation and the fluid nature of hegemonic heteronormativity is addressed.

From CBS to Netflix to TLC to E!, a wide breadth of representation is taking shape for TGD characters within the realm of television. As is often the case when underrepresented identities are suddenly brought to the forefront, representation is both negative and positive in its portrayal of the TGD communities as there are many aspects yet to be studied. Here we focus on the representations within the first seasons of *Orange Is the New Black* (2013–2019), *I Am Cait* (2015–2016), Transparent (2014–2019), *I Am Jazz* (2015–2020), and Sense8 (2015–2018) in an attempt to give a sense of the diversity, and simultaneous lack of diversity within the portrayals of TGD characters and the dominant narrative these representations create. These shows were selected due to their cultural importance and, in turn, visibility. Both *Orange Is the New Black* and *Transparent* are considered prestige dramas and have garnered many awards and accolades. Furthermore, *Transparent* is a show where the lead character is TGD, while *Orange Is the New Black* has a TGD community member portraying a TGD character. *I Am Cait* rose to public visibility thanks to its star, Caitlyn Jenner, who is part of the Kardashian entertainment empire and an Olympic gold medalist. She also released the show after a coming-out tour. Finally, teenager Jazz Jennings won a GLAAD Media Award for *I Am Jazz* and launched other cultural artifacts such as children's picture books that aimed to introduce TGD persons to the rest of the world.

For the analysis, we selected the first season of each of these series, where the main characters are introduced to the audiences. Typically, the first season of a television show spends time presenting their main characters, while subsequent seasons expect a level of familiarity. We look at how TGD identities and narratives work across the shows to form a larger view of what it means to be TGD by constructing a portrait of transnormativity through the current representations on mainstream television. Additionally, we examine how these representations are consistent and inconsistent across the programs. In looking at these series together, significant trends in how television portrays TGD characters emerge, as well as differences that conform to genre or stem from the unique circumstance of each show.

LITERATURE REVIEW AND THEORETICAL UNDERPINNINGS

Power and Discourse

Systems of power that control members through omnipresent yet invisible, unquestioned norms are hegemonic systems, also called discourses of power (Foucault 1972, 1977). The rules of these discourses of power are understood by its members but not stated; rules are transmitted via cultural institutions and norms. These are governing rules, and they make the dominant discourses regulatory. The true power of discourse is its ability to be invisible. Governing rules are not meant to be exclusionary; they are meant to bring people in so that the power system perpetuates itself. These rules are passed down through societal norms, and they project the appearance of autonomy to members of the system (Foucault 1977). Those who do not conform to the discourses of power are rebuked to coerce them back into the system or are outcast by the hegemony (Brown and Alderson 2010; Preston and Stanley 1987). These rules thereby dictate what is acceptable and unacceptable within the hegemonic narrative of marginalized identity.

Gender is one of the most pervasive discourses of power in Western culture, and its current configuration, which values men over women, is what establishes and perpetuates gender bias. Being a man, or specifically, a white, heterosexual, cisgender man, is the norm by which all other people are defined, and the absence of any of these traits marks people as the "other" (Connell 1990). In Gender Trouble (1990), Judith Butler outlines how the heterosexual white male is the default to which everyone is compared. She posits that the white heterosexual male is our culture's optimal state of being. To be anything different is to be lesser. Thus, anyone who does not fit this default is an outsider. This puts a person in a position of weakness or subordination to the default. These "others" then face added obstacles to gain the same status as those they are defined by; this is the genesis of gender bias. Butler stripped gender bias to its roots by isolating the core assumptions and preferences of our society and deconstructing the ways they function, primarily through sexuality.

Crenshaw's (1989) theory of intersectionality further elucidates the overlapping and contradictory systems of power placed on TGD subjectivity. As these characters represent TGD identity within an arena that dictates the normative TGD performance as that which is acceptable to the "cisgender gaze" (Thomas 2019), the characters' identities are mandated by dominant norms of gender, race, sexuality, and socioeconomic status, flattening the diversity of TGD identities within hegemonic expectations of gender presentation and performance. The statement by the Combahee River Collective (1986) explains the interlocking nature of the forces of race, sex, gender, and class oppression, as these societal markers perpetuate systems of power meant to divide and isolate those who are deemed "other." Therefore, the TGD characters' identities are subsumed by their TGD label as defined by the cisgender hegemonic norm, erasing and ignoring the layers of stigmatization and oppression TGD people face as a result of their gender identity, as well as the dominant systems of race, sexuality, and class.

Gender Performativity

Butler (1990) deconstructs the discourses of gender and power and illustrates that gender is fluid through her exploration of gender transgressors, but the norms embedded in culture stagnate fluidity to make sure gender is not free. This ties into Foucault's theorization of hegemonic systems as discourses, with a power that is related to their ability to remain hidden. Since gender is inculcated as a natural binary from birth, the constructed nature of gender is invisible, becoming a powerful ordering force.

Butler furthers her investigation by reconstructing the agency of the individual through what she calls the performance of gender or doing gender. Each person can act how they want to act in all regards. Within gender, people can make their own ways without strict binary gender ties. However, as Butler points out, we are positioned within our culture, and there may be consequences against those who perform in taboo ways that upset the gender binary. Despite that, the ability to act a gender can be liberating. While Butler's construction did not attend to TGD persons in the language of today, her work is still vital to understanding the ways TGD people challenge gender norms in ways that can and do cause hegemonic system retribution. As Judith Butler (1993) later articulates in *Bodies That Matter*, willful transgressions of the heterosexual matrix are not possible because the domains of performativity are unintelligible and bound by their history. A willful transgression can be interpreted as the involuntary reification of the very domain which the transgression is aimed at, by being the definition of the negative. Nevertheless, taboo performances are possible, even if they are not purely taboo. In the context of TGD persons, as it will be documented in the analysis later, dominant understandings of gender have ways of co-opting what, on its surface, is a direct affront to gender norms in TGD subjectivities. Thereby, these characters and the transnormative narrative they construct both fight against and work within hegemonic constructions of gender and performativity.

Hegemonic Gender

Heteronormativity (Warner 1991) and hegemonic masculinity (Connell 1990) share the same socially constructed worldview as Butler's gender performance theory. In a hegemonic masculine worldview, gender is artificially comingled with biological sex. The artificial codes of gender are transmitted from a multitude of cultural institutions beginning with the relationship between father and son (Connell 1990). Since gender norms are embedded in pervasive institutions like health agencies (Foucault 1978), media (Shugart 2003), or even language (Lakoff 2000), these codes seem natural and are free from questioning. Hegemonic masculinity is a more focused look at the white heterosexual male standard, that Butler touches on, by which all other gender norms are judged against. Trujillo (1991) outlined five tenets of this standard: (1) physical control and power, (2) occupational achievement, (3) familial patriarchy, (4) frontiersmanship, and (5) heterosexuality. Any masculinity in violation of these tenets is viewed as lesser by the system. In defining hegemonic masculinity, Connell (1990) defines those left out, the feminine, by their absence. While those masculinities that are not the ideal hegemonic form are lesser, femininity is even more subordinated. This hegemonic ordering sketches out the binary logic of gender and its seemingly inescapable links to both biological sex and sexuality. This hegemonic ordering of gender with these artificial norms shape the discourse that suppresses TGD subjectivities. If gender is fluid, sex is different from gender, and sexuality is not tied to gender, then it follows that TGD subjectivities are a threat to the hegemonic gender ordering.

Media Narratives and Transnormativity

Media is a powerful tool to disseminate discourses of power (Steel 2017). In modern times, television is widely available and consumed by most of the populous (Seiter et al. 2013). As such, television is an important platform to study how dominant norms are broadcast. Furthermore, it is vital to document the challenges to these norms that appear on television to better understand how fluid they are and how this fluidity manifests. In terms of gender as a dominant norm, television has been an essential site of analysis to study hegemonic masculinity

(Hanke 1990; Hatfield 2010; Myers 2012; Scharrer and Blackburn 2017; Vavrus 2002). Scholars have shown how hegemonic masculinity is not static or uniform, with challenges to traditional tenets including metro-sexuality, race, and sexual orientation, among others (Watson and Shaw 2011). This type of fluidity has also been displayed within the realm of heteronormativity. For instance, the rise in portrayals of gay characters on television challenged heteronormativity on its surface. However, dominant discourses have ways of incorporating these challenges, as in the case of gay characters. Helene Shugart (2003) analyzed the character Will Truman on the primetime network television show *Will and Grace*; he was the first openly gay main character in a network show. Nonetheless, while Will was portrayed positively, his representation created a homonormativity that was upper-class, white, unsexed, and that had heterosexual access to other characters. This normalization of gay characters continues today, with several examples of this type of pigeonholing (Avila-Saavedra 2009; Kies 2016; Martin 2014; Papacharissi and Fernback 2008). Even in the case of homosexuality, which has years of a head-start on representation on television, the normalization of otherness is strong. This is even true for shows that break out of the homonormative mold in some ways, such as race (Martin 2015). These representations of marginalized people, therefore, create the normative narrative within the dominant culture. Transnormativity follows a similar logic.

ANALYSIS

The television shows *I Am Cait*, *Transparent*, *I Am Jazz*, *Sense8*, and *Orange Is the New Black* were analyzed using critical rhetorical analysis. Our method includes careful readings of the artifacts under investigation through a critical theory lens. These analyses were based on narrative analysis, hegemonic gender orderings, and normativity. Texts were studied with close readings that revealed the components of this particular lens. They were then read again through this interpretive lens to gather evidence to support a theory of transnormativity. All the episodes of the first seasons of the shows were viewed and discussed by the researchers while paying close attention to how narratives of identity were constructed and performed regarding hegemonic transnormativity. Despite different formats and genres, several patterns emerged across the shows, making visible the normative representations of TGD people.

Our findings are that TGD characters are portrayed as white, wealthy women who have chosen to undergo gender confirmation surgery. These characters are almost always transgender women, and although their genders may be discussed regularly within the series, the characters tend to be lacking in sexual relationships and portrayed largely as non-sexual themselves, except Nomi from *Sense8*. There is little to no discussion of their sexual desires or interests, even when surrounded by the sexual exploits of others, and they are often connected to the deviance of others, or directly credited with said deviance. The major themes that we are discussing in this manuscript are race, socioeconomic status (SES), sexuality, and deviance; however, it is important to note that none of these representations are constructed in a vacuum. The themes present within the shows interact, intersect, and intertwine with each other along with other, less consistent elements of identity construction. The analysis below highlights the emphasis of each significant theme while positing how the intersections of systemic oppression and identity construction bear social and cultural consequences on those couplings.

In this analysis, the racial depiction of TGD characters is generally white, with the exception of Sophia Burset from *Orange Is the New Black*, played by TGD actress Laverne Cox. The main characters of these shows are white and fraternize with largely white casts, which contributes to a white normative representational lens. However, the introduction of non-white characters underscores that whiteness is the default. For example, in *Transparent*, Maura is an older adult transitioning from male to female. She has three adult children, and her daughter Ali has a relationship with a Black man, a personal trainer named Derek. While they partake in heavy drug use, Ali tries to arrange a threesome with Derek and his roommate, also a Black man. This instance highlights the ways in which non-white representation is introduced as deviant. While the two Black men begin to go along with Ali's fantasy, they cast her aside when she suggests, at the moment, that the two men engage in intercourse while she watches. Between the drugs and vitriol displayed once Ali's suggestion is aired, these men are shown as stereotypes and characters whom the audience never gets to know. This particular scene, which we claim demonstrates the whiteness of the show, also demonstrates issues with SES, sexuality, and race—the three other constructs we highlight in our construction of transnormativity. Here, we see Ali, an economically privileged white woman, engaging in acts the show portrays as deviant with men from a different SES class. This SES distinction is demonstrated through the juxtaposition of their small, shared apartment compared to Ali's childhood home, which is upper-middle class. Furthermore, Ali tried to blur the lines of sexuality by asking the men to engage in sexual acts with each other while she watches. She is rebuked for this and is then cast aside and later shown to be in a state of self-loathing. In short, the show displays these different intersectional values in a complex web, which reifies the normative construction of hegemonic gender and sexuality (Hill Collins and Bilge 2016), while providing a small space for a new hegemonic and acceptable transnormativity.

It should be noted that Ali is not the main character of the show or TGD. However, her sexual behaviors, along with those of her siblings, are implicitly linked to their childhood and the behaviors of Maura as she tried to figure out her gender identity. Both the white-leaning portrayals of TGD identities and the intersectional nature of race shown in this scene are also prevalent in *I Am Cait* and *I Am Jazz*, as characters of color are both sparse in these series and mostly in the background. Some, mainly in *I Am Cait*, are clearly shown to be of a different SES status.

In contrast, *Orange Is the New Black* has more racial diversity in the cast, with the only TGD person of color in the sample. Yet, even the construction of Sophia Burset regarding race is problematic due to her status as an inmate in Litchfield Prison. Prison as a setting inherently creates a separation from the outside or "normal" world and gives space for the representation of non-white characters. The prison creates a bubble in which the normal rules of race and sexuality in television no longer apply, thereby nullifying the inclusion of diversity in race and ethnicity. This nullification is built on the foundation that prison is both apart from the outside world and is a place that automatically characterizes all its inhabitants as deviant. Through this logic, the producers of *Orange Is the New Black* can bend the rules as to what is "normal" for a TGD character. Although she lives in the area of the prison termed the "ghetto" with the other Black inmates, she does not overly interact with people of her own race, except during particular episodes, or in moments of doing their hair, as she is the top hairstylist of the prison—another TGD and person of color stereotype. Unlike the majority of the other characters who mainly associate solely with their racial group, Sophia does not strictly identify with any of the racial groupings, instead forming a close bond in the third episode with an elderly white former nun, Sister Ingalls, reinforcing the erasure of her race (Thomas 2019). For the most part, Sophia is utterly isolated and cut off from any racial identification. Sophia is shown as isolated from both white and Black groups. This is an important decision the show makes as, simultaneous to her isolation, she lives in the part of the prison known as the "ghetto," which houses the people of color, and is shown in a negative light. One reading of this isolation is an intersectional perspective that factors in both her gender and sexual identities (Hill Collins and Bilge 2016). While the history of racial ghettos is beyond the scope of this chapter, the way *Orange Is the New Black* treats the ghetto is as a space for a non-preferred racial group. When the show's main character, Piper, runs afoul of those in charge of the prison, her punishment is to be banished to the ghetto. Piper, as the show's white protagonist, navigates and gentrifies the space for the audience. By being the viewer's docent in the ghetto, the audience is introduced to the characters in the space in a hegemonic white-centric manner.

In all the other shows, the TGD characters are white. This creates a false homogeneity within the narrative of the TGD community. Representation of solely white characters portrays a privilege of narrative identity and denies the intersectionality of transgender experiences and overlapping systems of oppression between differences of race, socioeconomic status, sexuality, and gender, especially those that interact with TGD persons differently. As described above, even in *Orange Is the New Black*, Sophia, as a Black woman, is left without a racial identification among the other characters, defining her transgender identity as separate from her race. Essentially, the characters in the show interact with Sophia's transgender identity far more than they do with her racial identity, isolating her from the most recognizable cliques, groups, and alliances within the prison. Much of the show is built on how these distinct groups interact, negotiate, and feud with each other, but Sophia's intersectional identification as a transgender Black woman removes her from these experiences. Later in the series, Sophia is attacked by both the Latina and Black communities, further denying her identification within their racial affiliations. Racial isolation or denial is compounded with SES, as white and upper-middle status become emblematic of the TGD identity, even if the character herself is not white. Therefore, race and SES status become synonymous within the developing trans narrative as those who are racially diverse are either categorized within a lower SES, or their race is erased by the series' characterization of TGD identity.

An upper-middle-class SES is demonstrated as inherent, as few of these series discuss in-depth the economic realities of being TGD, particularly if those identifying as such embark on a medical transition. Much of this discussion is circumvented by the high SES of the transgender characters. The most salient examples are Caitlyn Jenner and Jazz Jennings. When these shows discuss the economic burdens of being TGD, we see several trends develop. The most extreme case is Caitlyn Jenner in *I Am Cait*. Her wealth and privilege are so significant that they become the themes of many episodes, as other trans people openly address her wealth and celebrity status, help her avoid the paparazzi, and purposefully introduce her to other community members with less financial means. Despite efforts to draw attention to Jenner's wealth and the privilege her wealth affords, Jenner's SES quickly becomes commonplace and normalized throughout the series. For instance, in episode two, a group of trans women, tasked with teaching Jenner about TGD culture, decide it would be good for her to visit the Human Rights Council in San Francisco in order to hear stories from some trans women whose means are scarcer. Then, Jenner rents a luxury RV for them all, and before and after a stop at the Human Rights Council building, they spend several days in luxurious rented homes in the mountains in wine country. The privilege enjoyed by the members of the show seems immediately acceptable as it affords comfort and isolation, and simultaneously sidesteps more in-depth and involved discussion on the SES of those outside of the series. Jenner utilizes her wealth and status throughout the show to "do something" without actually engaging in efforts toward systemic change. After this exchange, the conversation is dropped and very little effort is made on the part of Jenner or the series to deepen the discourses surrounding the socioeconomic equalities faced by the majority of TGD people as a result of discrimination and stigma. After her moment of grace toward the trans women she met at the Human Rights Council, there is no further impact or work done to break apart the systemic and cultural problems that reinforce these economic disparities or those TGD people who find themselves at the lower end of the SES ladder.

Jenner's wealth and fame become the avenues through which she can most actively generate TGD activism. Listening to the stories of other TGD individuals who describe losing jobs because of their identities and gender journeys, Jenner is moved to tears. After hearing one particular story of a person named Blossom rejected from nursing school because of her gender, Jenner pulls her producer in front of the camera and makes a plan to help her out. The plan involves calling comedian and television presenter Ellen DeGeneres, getting Blossom on *The Ellen DeGeneres Show*, and Jenner paying for Blossom's nursing school. No one questions how, precisely, Jenner's sponsorship in nursing school or an appearance on *Ellen* will suddenly reduce the stigmatization that barred Blossom's acceptance in school so far. Instead, Jenner's wealth is appreciated as a necessary part of being TGD. So, while the show attempts to address the significant income gap between Jenner and others, high socioeconomic and celebrity status are heralded as the means to acceptance, not a hindrance to it.

Another aspect of socioeconomic privilege involves the discussion of the medical expenses associated with transitioning. *I Am Cait* and *Transparent* do not address these medical procedures or the costs. As noted above, Caitlyn Jenner's wealth is well known. In *Transparent*, Maura is also portrayed as well-off in terms of both finances and prestige, as a professor of some acclaim. She has a picturesque home that she readies for sale to move quickly into a new house and buys a new wardrobe and other markers of wealth. Furthermore, in her new apartment, she is forced to see those who are financially less fortunate than her and displays discomfort with the situation. The source of Maura's wealth is mostly unexplained and may play upon stereotypes of the Jewish community or may play into the larger narrative in media that academics are social elites and therefore wealthy. The source of her income is inconsequential, but her wealth and social status are vital to her ability to transition easily.

While socioeconomic status is often ignored in these representations, several of the shows talk, in detail, about gender confirmation procedures. The fact that these shows ignore the financial implications of these procedures is problematic, as it creates a world where those represented in television have very different realities than the majority of those watching. *I Am Jazz* takes viewers through the different steps with Jennings' transition. Multiple episodes show her going to the doctor to check on her hormonal levels, and bottom surgery is even discussed throughout the first season. Jennings provides in-depth information about the transition, expressing feelings of nervousness about the finality of gender confirmation surgery, which she describes as life-altering, while also stating, "I don't want to die a virgin" (season 1, episode 1). This statement links gender confirmation surgery with sexuality, as Jennings believes that without the surgery, she will not be able to engage fully in a sexual relationship. Therefore, SES and sexuality become linked in that without this surgery these characters are unable to engage to any extent in sexual relationships. This is further problematized by the fact that the characters are generally portrayed as sexually deviant, or they are portrayed as non-sexual.

The lack of focus on the economics of gender confirmation solidifies a representation where binary gender logic is the only available option. We find that each show in our sample has a main character whose goal is to switch sides of the hegemonic gender binary, erasing gender-nonconforming individuals or those with other identities. These portrayals also fail to represent those who identify as transgender within the gender binary but do not wish to undergo surgical or medical transition. Moreover, the selection of binary TGD persons as representatives of the community avoids creating dissonance for a hegemonic binary audience of largely non-TGD persons. Hence, the viewers do not have to think about the actual journeys of these characters because they are often at the end of their transitions, and their finish line is a hegemonic gender within the binary. These journeys also play into the characters being wealthy. Since costs of surgeries are often prohibitive, transnormative representations exclude those who wish to transition but cannot afford to do so.

The exception that confronts the public with the costs of these procedures is the character Sophia Burset, from *Orange Is the New Black*. In the third episode of the first season, where we learn about Sophia's backstory, the prison reduces her estrogen dose by half because of alleged budget cuts. Sophia spends much of the episode trying to convince the prison administrators to put her back on the correct dosage. In a discussion with other inmates, she explains the repercussions of the change in her hormonal levels as akin to going through menopause. Later, in episode four, she befriends Sister Ingalls in an attempt to steal her hormone pills.

Revisiting her past, right after top surgery, it is disclosed that Sophia's wife had asked her not to undergo bottom surgery, saying, "I'm fine with the rest of it. Just please keep your penis. For me" (season 1, episode 3), further relating confirmation surgery to sex and romantic relationships. Sophia subsequently has bottom surgery, bragging later in prison that she designed her vagina herself, stating "I had plans drawn up and everything" (season 1, episode 4), as she teaches the rest of the female inmates about the structure of a vagina. The processes of these surgeries or hormonal supplements are never discussed. Periodically, Sophia makes references to the changes she has made, but the processes and costs are entirely left out of the discussion.

Sophia is in prison because, during her course of duty as a firefighter, she stole credit card information from fire damaged homes in order to pay for her surgery. Though theft could point audiences toward the idea of high medical costs, the storyline is complicated by the character's wealth and spending choices. From episodes that reveal Sophia's backstory, she, her wife, and her son Michael were by no means destitute. The clips within their home show a well-furnished, large house, and within one of her reflective scenes, Sophia is seen buying a $300 pair of tennis shoes for her son. Although the viewers are not aware of whether this is a reasonable expense for her family, it is clear that money is not an issue. So, in the one opportunity to address the costs of transition, audiences are left wondering if Sophia's theft was necessary for medical treatment or part of a pattern of overindulgence and frivolous spending.

Within *I Am Cait*, *Transparent*, *Sense8*, and *I Am Jazz*, the costs associated with the procedures and hormonal injections are never addressed, as those characters and individuals who transitioned or are transitioning had the means to make it happen or do not discuss it. This is doubly problematic, as these representations ignore the lived experiences of many within the TGD community faced with the high costs of medically transitioning while not providing context for audiences unfamiliar with these matters. Throughout these series, all the characters undergo gender confirmation surgery. Their transitions may be discussed in-depth, but for the most part, they are discussed retrospectively once the process is complete or before it even began, rather than giving the audience a full story while the transitions take place. All in all, there is very little allusion to the process, the cost, or the pain that this surgery entails, as well as the alternatives or the narratives of those who cannot afford or have no interest in medical and surgical transition.

Even when significant themes of race, class, and, as we discuss later, deviance, overlap with the sexuality of characters in these series, the focused construction of the sexuality and gender of the TGD characters remains problematic. Although gender and sexuality are the central themes in many of these series, the sexuality of the TGD characters is rarely ever mentioned, which leaves issues of sexual activity vague or explicitly denied. Almost none of the characters in the series are part of sexual relationships or engage in sexual activities with the other characters, and their sexual desires are left unspecified and ignored. While it is not unprecedented for a television show to ignore the sexuality of its characters, what is notorious is that the absence of sexual activity seems to be isolated only within the construction of the TGD characters. *Transparent* is a prime example of this dichotomy between the TGD character and the supporting cisgender characters. The program is sexually charged and explicit, showing each of Maura's adult children in sexual relationships and encounters. These relations, as will be discussed in the deviance section, are often not healthy and are certainly not always mainstream, which makes the absence of sexuality for Maura even more troubling. Furthermore, Maura is older than the other characters of the sample, and while her age provides possible reasoning behind her lack of sexuality in comparison with that of her children, her inability to comment upon her sexuality or sexual desires further reinforces the absence of sexuality within TGD persons of all ages. *Transparent* demonstrates that it is willing to break heteronormative boundaries in sexual relationships with its characters but refuses to give Maura a hint of sexuality.

In the reality television show *I Am Cait*, Jenner is regularly questioned by others about a potential relationship with another transgender friend. Moreover, while some characters openly talk about who they are in sexual relationships with and what type of person they are attracted to, Jenner has a hard time expressing attraction. At the same time, Jenner's relationship with her former wife, Kris Kardashian, fizzled when Jenner came out. Thus, Jenner is left without a hint of sexuality that she can explain. This persistent representation of a lack of sexuality denies the variety of sexual identifications within the transgender community. These characters set up a stereotype that, after transition, sexuality no longer exists.

Another example of this lack of sexuality with TGD characters comes from *Orange Is the New Black*. Just like in *Transparent*, *Orange Is the New Black* has many characters whose sexuality is fluid, with each episode discussing some aspects of at least sexual exploits, relationships, desires, and love of sex. For most of the characters in *Orange Is the New Black*, prison acts as a space where women can explore their sexuality in new ways within the confines of the "prison bubble." Yet, Sophia is the only character that is left out of this dialogue, which even includes a former nun. There is an abundance of same-sex couples; however, the characters themselves are portrayed solely on a gender binary, as men or women. Even the characters with more stereotypically masculine characteristics adamantly identify as solely female. Sophia then is again on the outside of discussions of gender as well as sex. She is portrayed as overtly stereotypically female in her presentation of self, but she is not permitted to join in the discussions of sex and desire, despite, as previously discussed, open discussions of genitalia and sexual organs. Although it is clear that before her transition, she and her wife had a son and, therefore, at one point she participated in sexual activities, her desire is never discussed throughout the series, and sex is never mentioned. The closest the audience gets to seeing Sophia as having a sexual preference is in a discussion with an abusive prison officer. While eating a sandwich, he tells Sophia that she can "suck it out of my dick," to which Sophia responds, "I don't do sausage in my breakfast sandwich" (season 1, episode 3). This, paired with the fact that she is married to her wife Crystal, gives the viewers a slight indication that Sophia prefers women to men.

Also, worth noting in this exchange is the intersection of race within the expression of sexuality, particularly as it pertains to interracial relationships. The exchange referenced above is one of several in which interracial sexual relationships are suggested and rejected. For instance, Piper, the white main character in the show, becomes the love interest of a Black character called Crazy Eyes. Though this relationship does not have the authoritative overtones of Sophia's interaction with the white guard, Piper's avoidance and rejection of Crazy Eyes' advances add layers of racial overtones to who is sexual, and with whom, in prison. Nonetheless, Sophia's sexuality is disregarded to the extent that within the first season, Sophia is even convinced to give her wife permission to begin dating other people. She is the only inmate who is expected to make these allowances for a partner outside of prison, as all the other inmates expect their partner to be faithful or they end the relationship.

Further problematizing Sophia's lack of sexuality is the fact that she is a transgender woman that has been placed in a prison of cisgender women, something that rarely happens outside of television. Placing her in a women's prison, especially within the sexual setting of this show, creates an opportunity to open discussions around gender diversity and sexuality. However, the show pointedly overlooks what Sophia's presence could contribute to these discussions and leaves her without sexual agency or desire. Because of her status as a transgender woman, Sophia is not allowed sexual desires or preferences and is simultaneously expected to make allowances to accommodate the sexual desires of others.

From a different perspective, Jazz Jennings is a teenage girl who is trying to figure out her sexuality. She emphasizes that she is interested in love and being in love, but that she is not "boy crazy" because she does not currently have feelings for anyone. Being a transgender female in middle school hinders Jazz from exploring and learning more about her sexuality. Jazz's mom sees this and worries about Jazz because boys stay away from her and are not kind to her. The mother emphasizes the importance of exposing Jazz's transgender identity before dating. Many people have been physically harmed when they have not told their partner about their trans identities before intimacy. To explore the idea of dating and sexuality, Jazz visits a therapist as well as a transgender support group. The therapist asks Jazz if she ever thinks about being sexual, to which Jazz replies "not really, I just want love in general" (season 1, episode 3). Jazz also indicates that she is willing to fall in love with anyone, just as long as they are the right person. "I'm still exploring my sexuality. I don't even know who I'm attracted to" (season 1, episode 7). Although *I Am Jazz* acknowledges that trans sexuality exists, it highlights there are many steps and choices to consider when becoming sexually active.

A case that deviates from this rule of lost sexuality is Nomi in *Sense8*. In the first scene that she appears in, she is having vigorous sex with her girlfriend.

Throughout the series, they regularly discuss both gender and sexuality in conjunction with each other and separately. They periodically engage in healthy sexual relations, including a couple of metaphorical and psychological group orgies with the other main characters through their psychic link.

In sum, sexuality is repressed for most TGD characters in our sample, except Nomi in *Sense8*. The remaining shows mimic the desexualization of some of the first TGD characters in leading roles on television, creating a hegemonic transnormative narrative in which TGD people are segregated from sexuality and sexual identification. Furthermore, gender and sexuality surrounding these characters are constructed as deviant through how these characters interact with and influence others.

Finally, these characters are portrayed through a lens of deviance. Throughout the series, there is a consistent trend of illustrating the interactions and relationships of the TGD characters as different and separate from the norm. These characters are presented as the negative side of society who made personal choices to deviate from the expected societal gender norms. Even though they are created as representations of transnormativity, they are still not normal within societal standards. From a hegemonic transnormative perspective, the idea that each TGD character represents deviance is not unexpected. One of the most salient findings from the critical rhetorical analyses of the referred discourses is that sexual deviance is often associated with the TGD person in some way or another, which can perpetuate stigmatizing representations and narrative. For example, in *Transparent*, the three adult children of Maura display non-normative and destructive relational and sexual relationships. While the show does not explicitly link these deviances to the TGD parent, that is a reading available to the viewers.

Another representation of deviance comes from *I Am Cait*, who has several conversations with TGD activists, authors, and friends about being seen as a "freak." At one point, Caitlyn Jenner expresses that part of the reason she wants to have her show is to prove that TGD people are not "freaks," to which a queer activist replies "but you are a freak" (season 1, episode 2), signaling that Jenner must embrace her abnormal side. TGD voices on the show encourage Jenner to express her difference with pride, while many of the cisgender voices on the show express how much she is the same person. These perspectives are not presented as dichotomous, but we do see Jenner attempting to reconcile her break and isolation from society and family in part because of her difference, with the freedom of her living a more authentic life as Caitlyn. This struggle within deviance highlights the pull of embracing a gender binary. She talks about who has and who has not "met" Cait as if Cait is a new person who was born from the physical and medical transition. Jenner makes comments about how much better she was at tennis and golf as a man, and is routinely doing hair, make-up, and trying on clothes, which speaks to the comfort Jenner feels in the gender stereotypes of being a female.

Thus, Jenner's struggle with deviance, expressed in being seen as a freak of nature, is mitigated by reinforcing the gender binary.

Another stereotypical trope of deviance comes from *Orange Is the New Black*. Sophia Burset is in prison for stealing credit cards to pay for her gender confirmation surgery. Her decision to transition is directly linked to criminal activities, not only criminalizing the act of stealing credit card information from burned houses but the actual act of her transition. Her incarceration in prison and the poor decisions she made inside are directly linked to her transition and deviance from the expected norm of a cisgender man and a father. Sophia's incarceration is not solely a situation in which she happens to be transgender, but instead a direct result of her decision to undergo surgery. Her inclusion in the show is a positive revelation, especially since Laverne Cox is a transgender woman of color. Since representations of a TGD people of color are rare, their deviant behavior reinforces many of the transnormative trends of whiteness and class associated with being TGD. While most characters on the show are criminals, Sophia's portrayal is more complicated in terms of representation because it reinforces the deviance narrative of the TGD community. Conversely, crimes of the main character, Piper, are contextualized as a phase, preserving her status as the viewer's innocent surrogate, while also reinforcing the stereotype of deception for the greater queer community since her ex-girlfriend is the direct reason for her incarceration.

Unlike the more stereotypical deviance tropes within many of the shows, *I Am Jazz*'s adherence to deviance is particular to her age. Jazz's transition started when she was just five years old. But, according to the show, even before that, Jazz would wear her sister's high heels and purses, which the parents saw as "just a stage." However, as soon as Jazz developed verbal comprehension and vocabulary skills, she communicated to her parents that she was a girl. This shows the audience the struggles within the family, as the parents and the child may be reading the situation very differently.

All the characters within our sample feature individuals whose development has reached maturity and, thus, can make medical, social, and political decisions without parental oversight. Jazz breaks from this mold; she is portrayed as a child in control of the decision-making elements typically reserved for adults. Regardless of whether or not audiences believe a child has the ability to understand their gender, much less identify as TGD, audiences of *I Am Jazz* witness the performance of persuasion between the child and the parents that involves life-changing decisions. Jazz's rebellion from heteronormativity and the gender she was assigned at birth, and her persistence as to her TGD identity, mirrors narratives of teenage deviance centered on rebellious, spoiled, and entitled youth controlling their over-accommodating parents. Thus, another aspect of transnormativity within the hegemonic narrative is deviating from normative family power structures and decision-making processes.

Even as Jazz's parents articulate the reasoning behind her empowerment, to maintain her happiness and mental health, they choose to support their child, which feeds into the flexibility of the deviance of the spoiled child. This double bind is a crucial example of the flexibility of transnormativity as a hegemonic power structure. Jazz's mother often refers to the number of people with depression and the rates of suicide among the transgender community. She claimed that these statistics supported their choice of allowing Jazz to transition at age five, but the framing of who is making what decisions are still centered on Jazz's feelings and gender articulation. It should be underscored that Jazz's parents support her transition and this is rare. Many TGD youth do not have support from their families and communities, which can lead to devastating impacts. Conversely, the support Jazz receives can often feel like it is a reaction to prevent potential negative impacts, instead of support for Jazz herself. Thus, transnormativity claims deviance within both supportive and empowering families like Jazz's, as well as in situations where individuals are not supported by their families.

Sense8 takes this deviance a step further by introducing superhuman mental links between the eight main characters, of which TGD Nomi is a member. These subjects are mentally and emotionally connected, and they can transfer themselves into each other's consciousness. Nomi, already considered deviant by her family for her transition, is now further separated from normalcy by these special powers. She and the other seven are seen as the next step in evolution, presenting a portrayal of a transgender person who is above the average. They are beyond the prejudice of gender norms, while stuck in a world that still largely adheres to them. Nomi's status as transgender is acceptable within this group because she is beyond the norm of humanity, and therefore not human.

CONCLUSIONS

If television is one of the primary vehicles for storytelling in our society, and characters are vehicles for identification, current TGD characters make place for identification for mainstream audiences. Transnormativity allows TGD representations that are not threatening to dominant norms because it erases most of the non-intelligible aspects of what it can mean to be TGD. It follows that a story serves as rhetorical method for keeping the normative modes of gender, sex, and sexuality as dominant and coupled. As representations of TGD persons proliferate across the media landscape, the diversity of these representations will grow. Therefore, representational diversity and authenticity are vital to the continued progress of acceptance for TGD persons.

It is important to continue to understand how these representations rely on hegemonic genders as a shorthand, how they limit possibilities for identity articulation, and how they challenge hegemonic gender norms. Scholars and audiences need to pay attention to the narrative constructions that go along with representation and how stereotypes and hegemonic normativity shape the characters. While our work highlights emerging patterns in transnormative character constructions, often they rely on overlapping and intersecting hegemonic constructions that have nothing to do with being transgender. Sophia's role in the prison as a hairdresser can easily be playing on existing tropes within the broader LBGTQ community. Maura's wealth, as a Jewish person, fits with stereotypes involving religion, and discussions about sex with both the older characters, and the younger persons overlap with ageist conceptions about who audiences want to think about as sexual beings.

Intersectionality within the construction of transnormativity presents both positive potential and negative ramifications. Intersectionality as a framework (Cho, Crenshaw, and McCall 2013) demonstrates this duality and complex web of societal structures that constrain and minimize TGD subjectivity to that of binary gender. In terms of constructing well-rounded, relatable characters whose journeys and conceptions of identity can be both diverse and buoyed by identities that are not based on gender, intersectionality can serve for better media representations of TGD people and likewise serve to deconstruct hegemonic stereotypes and constrictions of gender performance. By presenting TGD characters with intersecting identities through the incorporation of discourses surrounding race, gender, sexuality, and SES, these representations have the power to deconstruct hegemonic dictations of the cis-centric normative.

In these shows, TGD characters are represented through the "cisgender gaze" (Thomas 2019), making their gender identity seemingly palatable to dominant audiences. These normative dictations are demonstrated through the physical appearance and gender identification within the gender binary, wealth, and the erasure of both racial diversity and sexuality. While it is encouraging to see an increase in TGD representation as a whole, limiting the diversity of these characters to a singular narrow conception of TGD identity has the potential to further reinforce limited stereotypes of TGD people. These stereotypes become representative of the whole of TGD experience within a cisgender, dominant world and, in turn, inform political policy and medical gatekeeping on a national scale.

These representations furthermore present a duality of power as they are both constricted by and breaking from the hegemonic restrictions of identity and performance. These characters are presented both with and without agency as they navigate TGD narratives. Their TGD identities simultaneously dictate their actions and interactions, while also serving as a source of power in breaking free of societal understandings of gender identity. TGD people thereby challenge traditional gender norms; however, they do so within the hegemonic narrative of TGD identity, reinforcing a specific understanding of transnormativity.

Future research should focus on the instances where transnormativity is challenged. The television industry is becoming more active in casting transgender individuals to play fictional transgender characters. While this practice is still not universal, there are more transgender actors portraying transgender characters today than in the past. As this trend continues, important research questions need to be posed regarding viewers' reception of these portrayals, particularly in regard to perceived authenticity and attitudes toward TGD persons. Moreover, while reality television attempts to produce glimpses into the lives of specific TGD individuals, fictional TGD characters, played by TGD individuals, add a layer of nuance to performances of identity and narrative fidelity. With the airing of shows such as *Pose* and *Euphoria*, it is important that scholars continue to identify and analyze the dominant narratives of transnormativity projected through media representation. The construction of the genre in which representation happens should be investigated in more detail as well. In this manuscript, we focused on series that include dramas, comedies, and reality television shows. This excluded television documentaries, like Catie Kuric's *Gender Revolution*, and cartoons, like *Sailor Moon*, *Steven Universe*, and *South Park*.[2] As the genre of television changes, so do audiences' expectations of storylines, character construction, and portrayal. Each type of genre plays a role for the audience in terms of constructing and deconstructing hegemonic norms. Moving forward, careful attention should be paid to how shows featuring TGD characters and individuals navigate what qualifies as an acceptable portrayal, both for audiences and media executives, and will need to be continually critiqued through a transformative lens.

REFERENCES

Avila-Saavedra, Guillermo. 2009. "Nothing Queer about Queer Television: Televised Construction of Gay Masculinities." *Media, Culture and Society* 31, no. 1: 5–21.

Booth, E. Tristan. 2015. "The Provisional Acknowledgment of Identity Claims in Televised Documentary." In *Transgender Communication Studies: Histories, Trends, and Trajectories*, edited by Leland Spencer and Jamie Capuzza, 111–26. Lanham, MD: Lexington Books.

Brown, Tyler L. and Kevin G. Alderson. 2010. "Sexual Identity and Heterosexual Male Students' Usages of Homosexual Insults: An Exploratory Study." *Canadian Journal of Human Sexuality* 19, no. 1–2: 27–42.

Butler, Judith. 1990. *Gender Trouble: Feminism and the Subversion of Identity*. New York: Routledge.

———. 1993. *Bodies That Matter: On the Discursive Limits of "Sex."* New York: Routledge.

Capuzza, Jamie C. 2015. "What's in a Name? Transgender Identity, Metareporting, and the Misgendering of Chelsea Manning." In *Transgender Communication Studies: Histories, Trends, and*

---

2 Emma Jane (Chapter 4, this book) makes progress in this topic with her study on the portrayals of transgender and gender-diverse characters in children's cartoon *Adventure Time*. Ed.

Trajectories, edited by Leland G. Spencer and Jamie C. Capuzza, 93–110. Lanham, MD: Lexington Books.

Capuzza, Jamie C. and Leland G. Spencer. 2017. "Regressing, Progressing, or Transgressing on the Small Screen? Transgender Characters on U.S. Scripted Television Series." *Communication Quarterly* 65, no. 2: 214–30.

Cho, Sumi, Kimberlé W. Crenshaw, and Leslie McCall. 2013. "Toward a Field of Intersectionality Studies: Theory, Applications, and Praxis." *Signs* 38, no. 4: 785–810.

Combahee River Collective. 1986. *The Combahee River Collective Statement: Black Feminist Organizing in the Seventies and Eighties*. Albany, NY: Kitchen Table.

Connell, Raewyn W. 1990. "A Whole New World: Remaking Masculinity in the Context of the Environmental Movement." *Gender and Society* 4, no. 4: 452–78.

Crenshaw, Kimberlé. 1989. "Demarginalizing the Intersection of Race and Sex: A Black Feminist Critique of Antidiscrimination Doctrine, Feminist Theory, and Antiracist Politics." *University of Chicago Legal Forum* 1, no. 8: 139–67.

Foucault, Michel. 1972. *The Archaeology of Knowledge and the Discourse of Language*. Translated by Alan M. Sheridan Smith. New York: Vintage Books.

———. 1977. *Discipline and Punishment: The Birth of the Prison*. Translated by Alan M. Sheridan Smith. New York: Vintage Books.

———. 1978. *History of Sexuality. Volume 1: An Introduction*. Translated by Robert Hurley. New York: Vintage Books.

Gamson, Joshua. 1998. "Publicity Traps: Television Talk Shows and Lesbian, Gay, Bisexual, and Transgender Visibility." *Sexualities* 1, no. 1: 11–41.

Hanke, Robert. 1990. "Hegemonic Masculinity in Thirty Something." *Critical Studies in Media Communication* 7, no. 3: 231–48.

Hatfield, Elizabeth F. 2010. "'What It Means to Be a Man': Examining Hegemonic Masculinity in *Two and a Half Men*." *Communication, Culture and Critique* 3, no. 4: 526–48.

Hill Collins, Patricia and Sirma Bilge. 2016. *Intersectionality*. Malden, MA: Polity Press.

I Am Cait. 2015. Produced by Caitlyn Jenner. E! Network, 2015–2016.

I Am Jazz. 2015. Produced by Taylor Garbutt. TLC, 2015–2020.

Kies, Bridget. 2016. "First Comes Love, Then Comes Marriage: (Homo) Normalizing Romance on American Television." *Journal of Popular Romance Studies* 5, no. 2: 1–13.

Lakoff, Robin T. 2000. *The Language War*. Berkeley, CA: University of California Press.

Martin, Alfred L., Jr. 2014. "It's (Not) in His Kiss: Gay Kisses and Camera Angles in Contemporary U.S. Network Television Comedy." *Popular Communication* 12, no. 3: 153–65.

———. 2015. "Scripting Black Gayness: Television Authorship in Black-Cast Sitcoms." *Television and New Media* 16, no. 7: 648–63.

Mocarski, Richard, Sim Butler, Betsy Emmons, and Rachael Smallwood. 2013. "'A Different Kind of Man': Mediated Transgendered Subjectivity, Chaz Bono on *Dancing with the Stars*." *Journal of Communication Inquiry* 37, no. 3: 249–64.

Morrison, Eleanor G. 2010. "Transgender as Ingroup or Outgroup? Lesbian, Gay, and Bisexual Viewers Respond to a Transgender Character in Daytime Television." *Journal of Homosexuality* 57, no. 5: 650–65.

Morse, Nicole. 2017. "A Double-Take on Reality Television: Laverne Cox's Political and Pedagogical Gestural Humor." *Feminist Media Studies* 17, no. 2: 168–80.

Myers, Kristen. 2012. "'Cowboy Up!' Non-Hegemonic Representations of Masculinity in Children's Television Programming." *Journal of Men's Studies* 20, no. 2: 125–43.

Orange Is the New Black. 2013. Written by Jenji Kohan. Netflix, 2013–2019.

Papacharissi, Zizi and Jan Fernback. 2008. "The Aesthetic Power of the Fab 5: Discursive Themes of Homonormativity in *Queer Eye for the Straight Guy*." *Journal of Communication Inquiry* 32, no. 4: 348–67.

Preston, Kathleen and Kimberley Stanley. 1987. "What's the Worst Thing … ? Gender-Directed Insults." *Sex Roles* 17, no. 3–4: 209–19.

Scharrer, Erica and Greg Blackburn. 2017. "Cultivating Conceptions of Masculinity: Television and Perceptions of Masculine Gender Role Norms." *Mass Communication and Society* 46: 1–29.

Seiter, Ellen, Hans Borchers, Gabriele Kreutzner, and Eva-Maria Warth. 2013. "Introduction." In *Remote Control: Television, Audiences, and Cultural Power*, 1–16. New York: Routledge.

Sense8. 2015. Written by Lana Wachowski and Lilly Wachowski. Netflix, 2015–2018.

Shugart, Helene. 2003. "Reinventing Privilege: The New (Gay) Man in Contemporary Popular Media." *Critical Studies in Media Communication* 20, no. 1: 67–91.

Steel, John. 2017. "Media Control: News as an Institution of Power and Social Control." *European Journal of Communication* 31, no. 6: 710–3.

Thomas, Victoria E. 2019. "Gazing at 'It': An Intersectional Analysis of Transnormativity and Black Womanhood in *Orange Is the New Black*." *Communication, Culture and Critique*. doi.org/10.1093/ccc/tcz030

Transparent. 2014. Written by Jill Soloway. Amazon Video, 2014–2019.

Trujillo, Nick. 1991. "Hegemonic Masculinity on the Mound: Media Representations of Nolan Ryan and American Sport Culture." *Critical Studies in Mass Communication* 8, no. 3: 290–306.

Vavrus, Mary D. 2002. "Domesticating Patriarchy: Hegemonic Masculinity and Television's *Mr. Mom*." *Critical Studies in Media Communication* 19, no. 3: 352–75.

Warner, Michael. 1991. "Introduction: Fear of a Queer Planet." *Social Text* 29: 3–17.

Watson, Elwood and Marc Shaw, eds. 2011. *Performing American Masculinities: The 21st-Century Man in Popular Culture*. Bloomington, IN: Indiana University Press.

CHAPTER TWO

"I'm Not Your Adventure": Trans Fetishism on Contemporary Television

BY CHARLES GOEHRING[1]

INTRODUCTION

After decades of relative invisibility regarding mediated representation, we are now witnessing a surge of popularity surrounding transgender celebrities and pop culture products featuring transgender characters, themes, and storylines. Recent narratives and plotlines involving transgender issues have given rise to surprisingly varied depictions of characters, and yet discussion over the perceived power of increased visibility often neglects the complicated and sometimes problematic implications of representation. With this increased prominence of complex and empowered transgender characters on television, this research engages larger questions of visibility and representation to focus on an interesting development within several shows that feature transgender characters: the fetishization of the transgender body as a narrative theme. I examine the shift within some storylines away from viewing trans characters as abject (Chanter 2008), with disgust (Lester 2015), or of seeing "transgender people as an intriguing oddity or amusement" (Siebler 2015, 135), to a specific sexualized objectification of the transgender body, or the transgender individual as fetish. If, as McClintock suggests, the realm of fetishism is an "arena of contestation and negotiation" (2003,

---

1 Charles Goehring, Ph.D. Assistant Professor in the School of Communication at San Diego State University. Email: cgoehring@sdsu.edu

661), a closer examination of these plotlines is necessary in order to analyze how transgender fetishism is constructed, as well as how television shows contest and negotiate transgender relationships with cisgender characters.

Increased visibility is often simplistically perceived to equal empowerment, while invisibility is equated with disempowerment or marginalization (Brummett 2010). In contrast, this research identifies the "serious limitations to visual representation as a political goal" (Phelan 1993, 6) by challenging the notion that the increased visibility of transgender characters necessarily results in positive outcomes, and argues that particular nuance in the depiction of transgender sexualization is essential in order to avoid the trap of visibility. Hence, I begin this chapter with a discussion of the problems associated with representational practices and the politics of visibility to define and integrate the concept of fetishism. Next, I analyze narrative and visual features of the fetishization of transgender characters by cisgender characters in several episodes of popular contemporary television. To examine current narratives involving trans fetishism, I present case studies from the critically-acclaimed American series Transparent (2014–2019) and the British comedy series Catastrophe (2015–2019). As I explain, these fetishistic depictions of transgender individuals can serve as a critique of representational practices, but often fall into problematic traps. Many perceptions of trans identity, sexuality, and relationships are reflected through specific genres of pornography and other forms of media that perpetuate stereotypes, misconceptions, and simplistic understandings of transgender subjectivity. These mediated representations also shape perception and constitute our thoughts on what it means to be transgender. I end this chapter with implications for these particular narrative themes since what is at stake in the discussion of transgender representation, and the subsequent fetishization of the trans body is nothing less than the question of agency for trans individuals.

LITERATURE REVIEW

Representation and Trans Identity Politics

Representation continually conveys more than it intends, and it is never totalizing (Phelan 1993). There is always an excess that allows for multiple readings, whether resistant or not, and it constantly fails to represent reality accurately. Even seemingly positive representations must lack something; characters representing a particular subjectivity on TV can never totalize any identity category. Booth (2015) agrees, suggesting that televised representation functions as synecdoche, with any part representing the whole. Scholars that talk about "authentic" representation or "accuracy" in characters miss this point. Phelan (1993) provides four presumptions regarding identity politics that illustrate these mistakes. First, she says that physical resemblance provides a means of identifying the community. Identities are visibly marked so that the physical resemblance between a marginalized population and its depiction on television can be read by members of the same community. Second, there is a linear and mimetic relationship between representation and identity, leading to what can be categorized as "what one sees is who one is" (Phelan 1993, 7), and third, there is a belief that if one does not see their mimetic likeness represented, one is not being addressed and is therefore excluded. The fourth presumption is that this may lead to a growth in power and inclusion within society. Phelan adds that the problem is that these presumptions "reflect the ideology of the visible, an ideology which erases the power of the unmarked, unspoken, and unseen" (1993, 7). These four presumptions bolster the belief that increased visibility and better representation of specific identity categories are the goals of identity politics.

For all the supposed power that increased representation promises, it often comes with some complications. Representation is closely articulated with notions of visibility. Phelan (1993) adds that the standard liberal notion of increased visibility for marginalized populations may carry negative consequences. Following Lacan's caution that "visibility is a trap," Phelan says that more visibility can lead to "surveillance, and the law; it provokes voyeurism, fetishism, the colonialist/imperial appetite for possession" (1993, 6). While she notes the political appeal of visibility politics, she cautions that giving over the power of remaining unmarked is not without its consequences. That is, when a previously invisible identity is made visible, the image often becomes fixed, subject to categorization, and open to contestation. Brouwer (1998) has astutely used Phelan's theories to examine HIV/AIDS tattoos as a performance of visibility politics with both positive and negative potential.[2] Thus, while greater visibility and increased representation for marginalized perspectives is often perceived as indicative of political and social progress, particular identity categories, especially gendered bodies, often come under increased scrutiny and become the focus of cultural and political controversy.

Several scholars have noted that increased visibility regarding transgender representation on television has not always yielded revolutionary results. Booth argues, "Visibility is a risky prospect" (2011, 191) since more representation often confuses the public, and trans identities can easily be exploited for their commercial potential. Accompanying the rise in the televisual depiction of trans characters, Siebler contends there is a "cultural curiosity of trans identity [that]

---

2 Recent transgender bathroom bills and bans on transgender troops serving in the U.S. military are prime examples of how increased visibility has translated into cultural issues with negative legal and political ramifications.

permeates popular media" (2015, 135). Despite increased representation on more scripted and reality television shows, she found continued rigidity between gender categories: "Transgender bodies are discussed, displayed, and regulated" (Siebler 2015, 134) in reductive ways. Rather than queering notions of gender, evidence shows that transgender people and characters are discussed in terms of their masculinity or femininity, their maleness or their femaleness. That is, the trans stands for "transitioning" to a preconceived gendered norm rather than "moving outside systems defining sex and gender" (Siebler 2015, 133). The shorthand initialisms MTF (Male to Female) and FTM (Female to Male) function to simplify understanding and reduce the complex subjectivities of transgender people. MTF people are discussed in relation to hyper-feminine idealizations, and FTM are categorized as "trans men," erasing any notion of disruptions of the gender binary (Siebler 2015). The increasingly more common and accepted designations AMAB (assigned male at birth) and AFAB (assigned female at birth) are attempting to move outside this binary (Palczewski, DeFrancisco, and McGeough 2018).

In their sweeping analysis of scripted TV series featuring transgender characters, Capuzza and Spencer (2017) argue that in no way does increased visibility simplistically lead to representation of the wide diversity of transgender and gender non-conforming identities. Following scholarship that contends a dominant narrative about trans' lives, their research examines recent television depictions to determine alternative transgender experiences and subjectivities. While Capuzza and Spencer observe progress in many respects, such as smaller occurrences of "trans ridicule and violence" (2017, 226), they find limited visibility of the characters, particularly for trans masculine characters. Transgender men are few and far between on television, with transgender women remaining the primary focus. Additionally, they note that U.S. scripted television "regularly explored relationships between transgender and cisgender characters" (2017, 224), yet most of the shows they study eschew romantic or sexual relationships and focus on family interaction between transgender and cisgender characters. However, as I show, there are more plotlines involving fetishistic relationships between trans and cisgender characters.

Representation and the Problem with Fetishization

As I have stated before, scholars have described the risk in representational visibility, which often results in the fetishization of the image of whatever "other" of which we are speaking (Mulvey 1989; Phelan 1993). Fetishism is a difficult theory to grasp, largely due to its use within many different disciplines. For instance, from an anthropological perspective, the fetish is an object endowed with some sort of totemic or spiritual power. Marxist theory suggests a fetish is an object bestowed with economic power, which has serious implications for how we view (and often ignore) the labor and material resources that go into commodities (Sturken and Cartwright 2018). Fetishism, as Pietz argues, is a term "always threatening to slide" (1985, 5). Yet, for all its confusion and slippage, it is still a practical concept. As McClintock explains, fetishism "inhabits the border of the social and the psychological, [and] throws into sharp relief the invalidity of separating the realms of psychoanalysis and social history" (2003, 637).

Taking all these conceptualizations into account, it is within the field of psychoanalysis that fetishism gains a libidinal investment. Following the Freudian theory, fetishism is understood as the displacement of the sexual drive onto a substitute, whether another part of the body or another object. Such libidinal investment in an object is the result of a castration complex: males are threatened by a woman's lack of a penis, and, fearing castration, disavow the process by finding substitutions (Mitchell 1995, 170). The substitute, standing in for an absent phallus, is erotized with some type of sexual investment or desire for an object that cannot be directly accessed (Hall 2001). Feminist film scholars like Laura Mulvey (1989) provide a common example through the analysis of situations whereby women are fetishized to nullify the threat of castration. This displacement onto the represented figure turns the female into a reassuring character instead of a dangerous threat to masculinity.

However, McClintock's (2003) work has challenged the simplistic, Freudian emphasis on phallocentrism. She argues that fetishism is a "complex, historically diverse phenomenon" (2003, 637) constituted by race and class as well as gender. These understandings of the fetish follow Lacan's reconceptualization of Freud: the phallus functions as a signifier of desire, and since the phallus is only an imaginary symbol, the fetish can best be understood as any metonymic displacement (Wilden 1968). As Hall explains, the displacement and disavowal entail the simultaneous indulgence and denial of a tabooed desire or fascination, resulting in "a displaced form of representation" (2001, 267). He adds:

> Fetishism takes us into the realm where fantasy intervenes in representation; to the level where what is seen, in representation, can only be understood in relation to what cannot be seen, what cannot be shown. *Fetishism* involves the substitution of an object for some dangerous and powerful but forbidden force. (Hall 2001, 266)

From this perspective, fetishism is structured into representation itself.

In the case of transgender bodies, fetishism takes place primarily because of its difference and cultural exoticism. The trans body is hyper-sexualized and eroticized solely for its bodily anatomy, which is also the result of what is not shown and unknown, resulting in inevitable questions surrounding an individual's trans identity. It follows as well that fetishism can be understood as a space of liminality, like the transgender body in transition (Booth 2011; Dentice and Dietert 2015). Capuzza and Spencer suggest that "the struggle to move television away from objectification, fetishism, and ridicule of transgender people must continue unabated" (2017, 226), and it is within this spirit that this research begins.

READING STRATEGY

Using the concepts discussed regarding fetishism, my analysis utilizes a narrative approach to the study of three important episodes recently featured on the popular streaming service Amazon Prime. While *Catastrophe* largely follows heteronormative storylines, *Transparent* has been lauded as groundbreaking and a harbinger of cultural change regarding transgender representation in media (Bastanmehr 2014). I chose specific episodes from these popular shows as exemplars of contemporary discourse involving the theme of trans fetishism. A narrative approach acknowledges the important role of stories in constituting identity and shaping our reality. I engage in a symptomatic reading of the episodes, determining the objective of the particular theme in the narrative as a product of the cultural conditions out of which they arose. A theme is understood as the abstract general idea incorporated into and illustrated by the narrative (Abbott 2002). Whether implicit or explicitly presented to the viewer, themes are often designed to be persuasive or didactic in nature. I ask, then, what is the point of including the theme of fetishizing trans bodies in these episodes? Identifying themes in these television shows "can help enormously in establishing what a work is about and where its focus lies" (Abbott 2002, 88). I then evaluate the appropriateness of this theme in terms of its representation of trans lives, as well as to critique the specific ways the themes are addressed. My analysis proceeds by discussing several important elements of how the specific narrative is constructed. For instance, I engage aspects of the dialogue between specific characters for what it suggests about how the issue of trans fetishism is being rhetorically constructed. Additionally, I explain the function of the characters and theme in each episode, relevant for determining if that character is given agency. Thus, I examine whether the trans characters featured are simply subjected to the theme, or if they drive the theme itself.

ANALYSIS

Phelan's (1993) focus on questions of visibility and representation serves as the starting point for my analysis. With the increased visibility of transgender identities on television and within culture, we are seeing an increase of many negative byproducts, such as the exoticizing of the trans body. This results in a fetishistic gaze often imposed on those characters and actors. At stake is that these types of representations "affect a viewer emotionally more than words alone [and] often contribute to misinformed perceptions that have the weight of established facts" (Lester 2015, 144). In the case of fetishized transgender bodies, these plotlines deserve analysis because within the realm of representation, even fictional televisual persons and events "can never be completely divorced from political and ideological questions" (Mitchell 1995, 15).

Catastrophic Representation

I begin with a case study involving the television show *Catastrophe*. Set in London, this show features a cisgender couple, an American man (Rob) who is involved in a relationship with an Irish woman (Sharon). One notable storyline in *Catastrophe* depicts a friend of the couple, cisgender man Chris, leaving his wife Fran, a cisgender woman. In order to portray the difficulties experienced by Chris and Fran in negotiating their lives outside of their relationship, the show highlights Chris' fetishistic fantasy about sleeping with a transgender woman, which I suggest is a case of transphobia due to its dehumanizing characterization, its ridiculous plotline, and its function within the series.

Previously, Chris told Rob, "Sometimes, I find myself thinking that I'd like to have sexual intercourse with women who have penises." Rob reacted with a look of bewilderment. Then, in Episode 2.4 (2016), we see Chris lying in bed in his underwear talking on the phone. He is inquiring about how much his encounter will cost. His estranged wife walks in and he throws the phone down and chastises her for coming to his apartment. Later on, we see the interaction between Chris and Georgia, a transgender sex worker. Georgia (played by trans actress Nicole Gibson) is a tall blonde woman wearing skimpy lingerie. She is depicted as unintelligent and disinterested. She is constantly texting on her phone, laughing to herself, and barely acknowledges Chris. He begins the conversation:

> Georgia? Is, er, 30 minutes OK? 'Cause that makes it an even hundred. Is there somewhere I can charge my phone? [She gestures to a small table by the bed]. This is a bit weird for me. Not you, you're not weird, you're lovely. Just the situation is weird. For me.

His nervous mannerisms and obvious discomfort with the situation signify the taboo nature of the sexual interaction.

Because Georgia seems unresponsive and is attached to her phone, Chris asks, "Do you speak English?" With a lack of emotion or affect, she responds, "You're handsome, thank God." Again, Chris is nervous. Georgia comes closer, puts her head near his shoulder, and smells him. Chris quickly begins undressing, throwing his clothes on the floor. Clearly annoyed that he has thrown them in a heap, Georgia asks, "Do you want to put them on the chair?" Chris immediately apologizes and attempts to straighten the clothes and place them on the couch. He sits down next to her on the bed. She looks at him and says:

> Georgia: How many knuckles deep?
> Chris: How many what?
> Georgia: It's a joke.

After other scenes, we revisit Chris getting dressed and engaging in small talk while Georgia stares vacantly at her iPad:

> Chris: Nice place.
> Georgia: It's not mine.
> Chris: Right.
> Georgia: You're a wild man. I did not expect [it].
> Chris: Yeah, yeah, yeah.
> Georgia: We can try something else next time … Use a bigger vibrator, take a shower …
> Chris: No. I don't think so.

Georgia shifts the discussion to a show she is watching on the tablet. She asks Chris whether he knows the program. Chris says "no" and adds: "I'm just going to get back to, um … There's the extra $20 for the balls thing." While it may be possible to read Georgia's attitude as more positive, the scene is clearly depicted from the point of view of the male gaze. The whole exchange reinforces stereotypes. Georgia is almost completely dehumanized; her disinterested mannerisms and dialogue signify her as "weird," and she is portrayed as silly, inattentive, and devoid of emotion. Additionally, her statement that the room is not hers indicates a lack of agency.

What is particularly troubling about this episode's plotline is its cultural insensitivity amidst an increase in trans visibility and the general acceptance of transgender rights. The scene is a throwback to earlier types of stereotyping and "trans ridicule" (Capuzza and Spencer 2017), with the audience being expected to laugh at both Georgia and the situation. The fact that the character is a transgender sex worker is especially problematic for several reasons. In general, transgender people experience higher levels of poverty, homelessness, discrimination, marginalization, and a lack of resources (Fitzgerald, Patterson, and Hickey 2015); while there may be some who choose to participate in sex work, research shows that it often becomes the only option due to these issues (Nadal, Davidoff, and Fuji-Doe 2014). Such scenes may result in "victim-blaming" if the sex workers are subject to hate-motivated violence (Juang 2006). The plotline functions to show the difficulty that Chris is experiencing after leaving his wife, and no further interactions involving Georgia take place within the series. The scene is largely predicated on stereotypical notions of disavowal; it asks the audience to buy into a common argument for why cisgender males express interest in transgender women: homosexual disavowal. Chris is shown grappling with these homoerotic feelings and the way he deals with it is the stereotypical fetishization of the female transgender sex worker.

Traversing the Fantasy

In contrast to the awkward plotline from *Catastrophe*, I now turn to two moments from *Transparent* that tackle the issues of cisgender/transgender relationships in different ways. The first occurs in episode seven of season one, "The Symbolic Exemplar" (2014). Maura Pfefferman's daughter Ali goes on a date with a transgender man, Dale (played by trans actor Ian Harvey). Previously, when they met, he told her to dress in "high femme" clothes for their date. Later, Ali is seen shopping with her friend for an outfit to wear. She contemplates what "high femme" means. She chooses a retro outfit that shows off her breasts and waits on the street for Dale to pick her up. He arrives in an old truck and tells her, "You look good." They drive, and he says, "almost there, little lady." When they get to his house, Ali looks longingly at a rustic-looking cabin in the woods. Dale looks the epitome of masculinity with a full beard and wearing a plaid, long-sleeve shirt. As they enter the room, Ali appears in awe of her surroundings. She walks into a retro-mancave, complete with a Pabst Blue Ribbon neon sign, vintage television set, and a raging fire in the stone fireplace. Dale sits on the couch and opens a bottle of beer. Ali attempts to sit but immediately stands back up as Dale says, "Nobody said you could sit down." In a dominating tone, he tells her, "Don't talk, just let me look at you," and demands that she end every sentence with "Daddy." Here is a curious perspective, as the trans male gaze fetishizes Ali in her high-femme look. He tells her to take her panties off. When he questions her abundant pubic hair, she tells him that "big girls have bush, Daddy." Later, Dale shaves Ali's crotch using an old-fashioned shaving kit.

The next scene features Dale and Ali shopping for sex toys. He explains the best process for picking out a fake penis: "Just let the dick choose you." They buy a pink unicorn sex toy. Ali then takes Dale to see a performance by Maura, her trans mother. She brags to Josh and Sarah that her date is the "hot" trans guy. The three Pfefferman siblings discuss the ins and outs of bottom surgery. Ali explains that Dale has chosen not to have surgery. Ali must leave the performance because she is having a hard time dealing with Maura's transition. Dale comes on to Ali in the bathroom and tries to open the sex toy. He has difficulty due to the blister packaging. Once he opens it, he slathers it with lube. The toy then slips out of his hand onto the floor. Ali's mood is completely ruined, and she asks to leave. We cut to the ride back to Dale's house in the middle of a heated conversation:

Ali: "Chaser." What does that even mean, a "chaser"?
Dale: Just someone who likes trans people because they're trans.
Ali: Wait a minute. Are you calling me a "chaser"?
Dale: I'm just sayin' the timing's interesting. That's all.

The specific exchange regarding people who have been deemed "trans chasers" reflects nonfictional issues for transgender individuals negotiating the difficult road of relationships. Couched as admirers of transgender persons, these individuals have been well documented (Edison 2014; Reid 2016).

Ali is visibly disgusted by the assumption that she could be a "chaser." She pulls off the too-tight dress top and throws it out of the window. The car rolls to a stop, and while she is getting out of the car Dale asks, "Everything cool?" As she exits the vehicle the entire scene has changed. There is no longer a cabin, but an ordinary house. As she looks back at Dale, he is no longer in the macho truck, but in the driver's seat of a small, white sedan. They walk in and the interior of Dale's house is completely different. Instead of a rural, masculine vibe, it is instead a modern-looking, IKEA-inspired home. The fireplace has unlit candles rather than a raging fire. None of this matches her original fantasy. The scene cuts to Dale in the kitchen with a teapot in his hand, who asks if she would like some tea. The episode ends with a look of utter amazement on her face.

The audience is surprised to realize that a major portion of the plotline between Ali and Dale was an elaborate fantasy. By playing with what most viewers assume as a mimetic representation, the episode disrupts the realism of the show in order to illustrate the fetishism at work. The fantasy also has added significance. Ali desired the absolute epitome of manliness in Dale, and this scenario conveys the whole facade of masculinity as portrayed on screen. While the fantasy she constructs highlights the fetishization of a male transgender character, she is left disappointed as the image falls apart. Dale is provided a modicum of subjectivity, and his character engages in the objectification of Ali, leading to several important implications of this episode. First, this specific narrative is compelling given that most early understandings of fetishism, dominated by Freudian theory, have privileged a male-centered fantasy. In fact, most storylines feature a male cisgender character obsessing over female transgender characters. Yet Ali's fetishizing of Dale counters this narrative, even as Dale objectifies Ali in her "high femme" style. We are witness to a female-centered notion of the fetishizing of the trans male body. However, even this interpretation is subject to critique. As Jack Halberstam has theorized, the "transgender look" is a result of "complex problems of temporality and visibility" that complicates all processes of looking (2005, 76, 78). Second, the episode explicitly gives the lie to the fantasy that structures the logic of the fetish. Not only does this illustrate the issue of trans fetishism, but it also does so in a way that focuses the audience's attention on the articulation between fetishism and desire. Ultimately, though, the focus is largely on Ali's concerns and fantasies, and while Dale starts out as a transgender character with some agency, much of it is lost once the illusion of extreme masculinity is destroyed.

"I'm Not Your Adventure!"

The second important plotline featuring the fetishization of the transgender body occurs in episode six of season three of *Transparent*, "The Open Road" (2016). Previously, Maura's son Josh learned that his former babysitter, and mother of their child together, has killed herself. He decided to take an urn of her ashes to his teenage son. He first contacted his former girlfriend, who had no interest in rekindling the relationship that Josh ruined. The end of episode five shows Josh watching Shea (played by transgender actress Trace Lysette), a recurrent character who was dancing at her job in a strip club. Josh is depicted as emotionally fragile, staring at her with his head in his hands while she dances. In the following episode, the relationship between Josh and Shea is formed, and Shea shares information about her surgery, her HIV status, being stigmatized even within the trans community due to her having had bottom surgery, the dehumanization of her work, and the difficulties of dating while trans.

"The Open Road" begins with Josh driving. Shea is shown in the passenger seat. The camera pans between Josh driving and her sleeping. Josh stares at her sleeping next to him. The next scene features them both coming out from a motel. He asks her if her room was okay, then discusses waffles and breakfast. Once in the car, she talks about the fact that she needed to call to tell her boss she would be missing work. She hopes that she won't be fired, but states there are plenty of places to dance if necessary. Describing her job as an exotic dancer, she says, "It's actually way less crazy than everyone thinks. It's mostly just sad guys with cocaine problems." Another scene shows them walking into a coffee shop that is holding an open mic event. They engage in small talk as they sit and drink coffee and eat food. After watching an older man reading a narrative, Josh looks at Shea and decides to grab his guitar and perform. As he sings, the camera shifts from Josh, to Shea, and to other customers who are audience members. She smiles as he sings a song that features the lyrics "We can make it in another world," indicating he is specifically singing about Shea.

The relationship is being set up between Josh and Shea, a scene we have witnessed countless times on television, albeit with a difference. The visual elements of the scenes are highly romanticized. There are the obligatory landscape images featuring Shea's long hair blowing in the wind. The next scene features conversations initiated by Shea, who discusses past partners as she drives. She then delves into dating while trans, specifically discussing fetishization and gender confirmation surgery:

You know, dating while trans is a real shit-show. If you don't get the pussy, you're fetishized by a bunch of cock-hungry Johns. And if you do get it, you know, you're still stigmatized. It's like a no-win situation. All my girlfriends told me not to bother with bottom surgery. They said I'd be giving up my coin machine.

Troubled by this information, Josh says, "Jesus." She adds: "I even had a trans auntie tell me, 'Miss Shea, girl, don't you go get that pussy, darling. [Do] You know what they say? A chick with a dick is always paid.'" Attempting to be understanding, Josh says, "But that, that's assuming that you're gonna be, like, a sex worker. Like, forever. Or, whatever. I mean, what about, I don't know, maybe even having a family." While the idyllic, heteronormative future he discusses simultaneously reflects his experiences and neglects Shea's perspective, Shea's sharing of her issues and experiences disrupts Josh's more traditional understanding of sexual identity and relational arcs.

Shea later tells Josh that her foot is asleep. They pull over to switch positions and see an abandoned water park. Sneaking through a gap in the fence, they frolic through the park, laughing and running in a flirtatious manner. As they round the corner of an empty lazy river, the interaction continues:

Josh: I just had a notion.
Shea: What's your notion?
Josh: Um, like when a guy's having sex with a girl, he's like, always in the back of his mind, he's like, "I might get this girl pregnant." Not good. But, like, with you, it's like not possible, so, I don't know, you could just relax. Like, go all out.

Josh's comments about her anatomy reduce Shea solely to her sexuality. Shea's facial expression indicates that she's heard this line of reasoning before and is put off by it. The dialogue continues:

Shea: That's, I'm just ... that's fucked up.
Josh: Wait, why? I ... It's like a positive [thing].
Shea: That's what you go to? That's the positive?
Josh: It's a positive. I'm just tryin' to say ... It's like, I don't see why it would ever be a negative [thing] for anybody. It's, like, great. I mean, [he sighs] I'm sorry.

Josh is struggling and knows he has messed up. Shea tells Josh, "It's such a fucking stupid thing to say." He looks at her sheepishly and replies, "I'm a fuckin' idiot."

After apologizing, he begins to touch her arm, then her hair. While Shea is annoyed by what transpired, she is still attracted to Josh and the possibility of a relationship with him. They begin to kiss and Josh moves his hands over her body. She flirtatiously runs away, and he catches up to her. They again begin to kiss passionately. As Josh begins to take off her clothes, she moves away and divulges more information about herself:

Shea: Can you just stop for a second? There's just something I have to talk to you about. Look, I'm totally healthy and my viral load is undetectable, and there's really nothing to worry about, but I just have to tell you that I'm HIV positive. I have to. Just don't want you to find out later and hate me or murder me or something.

Being a victim of violence by withholding information such as HIV status, or being trans, is a troubling prospect for Shea, and it makes Josh uncomfortable.

Josh: I mean, we're just kissing, I mean, you can't get it from kissing, right?
Shea: No, you can't get it from kissing.
Josh: Um, I'm not gonna … I'm not gonna … I'm not gonna murder you. I'm not gonna hate you.

Coming out to him as HIV positive further troubles his "notion" about Shea's inability to get pregnant, and the "positive" aspects of her anatomy. This follows:

Shea: I have some condoms in the car.
Josh: Um, are condoms, like, 100 percent?
Shea: They work? Look, there's, uh there's this pill called PreP, and it pretty much eliminates any chance of you getting it if you want to …
Josh: Um, pretty much?
Shea: Well, they're still researching it.
Josh: You have it here with you?
Shea: Uh, no, I don't have it here. It doesn't work like that. It would be more like if you wanted to slow things down and figure out where this is going. Maybe we could see a doctor when we get back. Like, explore this more long term.
Josh: Long term? [He exhales heavily] It's just … that's a lot of build-up. I mean …
Shea: Let's just go.

Despite this being something that Shea has been looking for, Josh recoils when confronted with the possibility of a long-term relationship. Throughout the series, Josh has shown an inability to engage in deep, meaningful relationships, but there is added significance when it comes down to disappointing Shea. Josh asks, "Are you mad?" to which Shea replies, "Yeah, I'm mad."

Josh: At me? Why? Why? I'm, like, I've been totally cool with everything.
Shea: Yeah, you know, you deserve an award. What a hero.

Josh:	Okay, you just were about to fuck me, and, like, probably not give me HIV. Okay? I'm not allowed to ask some questions? I'm not allowed to, like, pause, and, like, feel weird?
Shea:	Why the fuck did you bring me here?
Josh:	I brought you here because it seemed fun. Like, this is fun.
Shea:	Fun?
Josh:	Yeah, you seem fun.
Shea:	Fun? Like a sex worker good time fun, Josh?
Josh:	No. Okay, well, now that you mention it, I did pay for all this.

Shea begins screaming at Josh: "I see right through you, and I'm not your fucking adventure! I'm a person! I'm not your fucking adventure! Grow up! You fucking child! Fuck you!" The scene cuts to Josh helping Shea into a taxi to drive her to the airport. He apologizes to her, stating that he doesn't know what he's doing. She looks at him but gets into the cab. The scene cuts to Josh in the car, alone.

I spend considerable time detailing this scene because it skillfully highlights several concerns many transgender people face in the real world while avoiding many of the pitfalls of other television shows. The plotline may begin with Josh's (and thus, the viewers') focus on Shea's body as she dances, but it develops into a more nuanced and complex conversation about trans relationships and other serious issues affecting the trans community. Several aspects of her identity, such as her HIV status and her job as an exotic dancer, could be considered problematic since so many shows stereotype trans characters as dealing with illness and in these roles. However, I argue the show largely avoids discrimination and a pathologizing of the trans body in the unique way the episode addresses them. The elements of the narrative explicitly expressed Shea's perspective, focusing on many of the experiences she has faced and continues to face regarding surgery, work, and romantic relationships. Rather than stereotyping, the show deftly tackles these issues that exist in the trans community. More importantly, this scene is the first in my examples that expressly provides the trans character with a strong sense of agency. Shea is given the opportunity to voice her opinion regarding life as a trans woman, she can be angry with Josh, and she asserts her standpoint.

While Shea thinks she is experiencing a genuine romantic connection with Josh, the narrative shows that he is not sure what he really desires, and yet he was excited by the possibility of the exotic and unknown. By the end of the episode, the whole exchange is negatively coded, and the audience is drawn to adopt the subject position of Shea. In doing so, *Transparent* portrays problems encountered by many transgender individuals and does so in a forceful way for the audience.

CONCLUSIONS

This research reiterates that increased visibility often results in problematic implications. In this case, the increased visibility of transgender characters has resulted in numerous plotlines that depict the fetishization of the transgender body, and each example analyzed provides a unique way to focus on the issue. The *Catastrophe* episode is a transphobic throwback to earlier stereotypes and misperceptions, and functions to garner laughs at the expense of trans sex workers. In contrast, the *Transparent* episodes I examined are much more complex in their representation of transgender/cisgender relationships. "The Symbolic Exemplar" episode of *Transparent* candidly addressed the issue of the fetishization of trans identity by a cisgender character, and even discusses the concept of "trans chasers." Additionally, the surprise scenario that structures the plot is important in illustrating how fetishism is predicated on a logic of fantasy. The plotline in "The Open Road" directly confronts audiences with the issue of trans fetishizing through a complicated trans character in Shea, who is provided a strong sense of agency that differs from many television depictions of trans characters.

Ultimately, the problem with fetishization is that it reifies the traditional gender binary. Reduced to its sexualized, anatomical parts, the transgender body is no longer a subversive or disruptive force in terms of gender identity. Even the more nuanced and complex representations, since they can never be totalizing, neglect the diverse identities and gendered subjectivities that encompass what it is to be transgender. For instance, one major critique of all of these examples is that they only feature white transgender characters. The lack of representation and visibility of transgender people of color can be damaging, especially given the number of crimes against trans women of color (HRC Report 2019). While positive strides have certainly been made in regard to transgender visibility and representation on television, especially in comparison to the history of transgender characters and storylines in the past, there is much to be done and much to be theorized. Indeed, the fact that fetishism is occurring in the first place is a testament to the increased visibility and acceptance of transgender individuals. However, given the systematic misrepresentation of trans persons within television and other forms of mass media, "a politics of recognition requires more than just disseminating positive images for a group" (Juang 2006, 244). Rather, such politics necessitates that more diverse and complicated gender experiences be portrayed on television.

My analysis of the select television narratives illustrates that representational aspects rely on stereotypes and simplistic generalizations about trans individuals, bodies, and relationships. In each show, the cisgender character realizes that their feelings for the trans characters have little to do with any romantic intentions. As I have explained, fetishism is not about love, but about a metonymic displacement that, in this case, involves the objectification and sexualization of the transgender body. Such representational forms may not be the visibility that transgender individuals need or desire. More varied and nuanced representations are necessary as the ideas of the viewers about gender nonconformity and trans issues are being shaped through these often problematic representations.

REFERENCES

Abbott, Porter. 2002. *The Cambridge Introduction to Narrative*. Cambridge, MA: Cambridge University Press.

Bastanmehr, Rod. 2014. "Is Pop Culture Having a Trans Moment?" *Vice*, November 2, 2014. https://www.vice.com/en_us/article/exm8bz/were-having-a-trans-moment-456

Booth, E. Tristan. 2011. "Queering Queer Eye: The Stability of Gay Identity Confronts the Liminality of Trans Embodiment." *Western Journal of Communication* 75, no. 2: 185–204.

———. 2015. "The Provisional Acknowledgment of Identity Claims in Televised Documentary." In *Transgender Communication Studies: Histories, Trends, and Trajectories*, edited by Leland Spencer and Jamie Capuzza, 111–26. Lanham, MD: Lexington Books.

Brouwer, Dan. 1998. "The Precarious Visibility Politics of Self-Stigmatization: The Case of HIV/AID Tattoos." *Text and Performance Quarterly* 18, no. 2: 114–36.

Brummett, Barry. 2010. *Techniques of Close Reading*. Thousand Oaks, CA: SAGE.

Capuzza, Jamie C. and Leland G. Spencer. 2017. "Regressing, Progressing, or Transgressing on the Small Screen? Transgender Characters on U.S. Scripted Television Series." *Communication Quarterly* 65, no. 2: 214–30.

Catastrophe. 2015. "Episode 2.4." Directed by B. Taylor. Written by Rob Delaney and Sharon Horgan. Avalon Television, April 8, 2016.

Chanter, Tina. 2008. *The Picture of Abjection: Film, Fetish, and the Nature of Difference*. Bloomington, IN: Indiana University Press.

Dentice, Diane and Michelle Dietert. 2015. "Liminal Spaces and the Transgender Experience." *Theory in Action* 8, no. 2: 69–96.

Edison, Avery. 2014. "I'm Trans and on Tinder, but I Am Not a Fetish for Your Sexual Bucket List." *The Guardian*, December 12, 2014. https://www.theguardian.com/commentisfree/2014/dec/12/trans-tinder-sexual-bucket-list

Fitzgerald, Erin, Sarah E. Patterson, and Darby Hickey. 2015. *Meaningful Work: Transgender Experiences in the Sex Trade*. National Center for Transgender Equality. December 2015. https://www.transequality.org/sites/default/files/Meaningful%20Work-Full%20Report_FINAL_3.pdf

Halberstam, Jack. 2005. *In a Queer Time and Space: Transgender Bodies, Subcultural Lives*. New York: New York University Press.

Hall, Stuart. 2001. "The Spectacle of the 'Other.'" In *Representation: Cultural Representations and Signifying Practices*, edited by Stuart Hall, 223–90. London: SAGE.

Human Rights Campaign. 2019. "A National Epidemic: Fatal Anti-Trans Violence in the United States 2019." November 2019. https://www.hrc.org/resources/a-national-epidemic-fatal-anti-trans-violence-in-the-united-states-in-2019

Juang, Richard M. 2006. "Transgendering the Politics of Recognition." In *Transgender Rights*, edited by Paisley Currah, Richard M. Juang, and Shannon Price Minter, 242–61. Minneapolis: University of Minnesota Press.
Lester, Paul M. 2015. "From Abomination to Indifference: A Visual Analysis of Transgender Stereotypes in the Media." In *Transgender Communication Studies: Histories, Trends, and Trajectories*, edited by Leland G. Spencer and Jamie C. Capuzza, 143–54. Lanham, MD: Lexington Books.
McClintock, Anne. 2003. "Imperial Leather: Race, Cross-Dressing, and the Cult of Domesticity." In *Feminist Postcolonial Theory: A Reader*, edited by Reina Lewis and Sara Mills, 634–66. New York: Routledge.
Mitchell, William John T. 1995. "Representation." In *Critical Terms for Literary Study*, edited by Frank Lentricchia and Thomas McLaughlin, 11–22. Chicago: University of Chicago Press.
Mulvey, Laura. 1989. *Visual and Other Pleasures*. Bloomington, IN: Indiana University Press.
Nadal, Kevin L., Kristin C. Davidoff, and Whitney Fuji-Doe. 2014. "Transgender Women and the Sex Work Industry: Roots in Systemic, Institutional, and Interpersonal Discrimination." *Journal of Trauma and Dissociation* 15, no. 2: 169–83.
Palczewski, Catherine H., Victoria P. DeFrancisco, and Danielle D. McGeough. 2018. *Gender in Communication: A Critical Introduction*, 3rd edition. Los Angeles: SAGE.
Phelan, Peggy. 1993. *Unmarked: The Politics of Performance*. New York: Routledge.
Pietz, William. 1985. "The Problem of the Fetish, I." *RES: Anthropology and Aesthetics* 9: 5–17.
Reid, Charley. 2016. "My Trans Identity Is Not a Fetish." *The Establishment*, March 31, 2016. https://theestablishment.co/my-trans-identity-is-not-a-fetish-1d6f2dc5d5a1
Siebler, Kay. 2015. "Transgender Transitions: Sex/Gender Binaries in the Digital Age." In *Gender, Race, and Class in Media: A Critical Reader*, edited by Gail Dines and Jean M. Humez, 132–42. Thousand Oaks, CA: SAGE.
Sturken, Marita and Lisa Cartwright. 2018. *Practices of Looking: An Introduction to Visual Culture*, 3rd edition. New York: Oxford University Press.
Transparent. 2014. "The Symbolic Exemplar." Directed by Jill Soloway. Written by Faith Soloway and Jill Soloway. Amazon Studios, September 26, 2014.
Transparent. 2016. "The Open Road." Directed by Jill Soloway. Written by Jill Soloway and Bridget Bedard. Amazon Studios, September 23, 2016.
Wilden, Anthony. 1968. *Lacan and the Discourse of the Other*. Baltimore, MD: Johns Hopkins University Press.

CHAPTER THREE

Hollywood and the Pathologization of Trans Identities

BY PATRICIA DI RISIO[1]

INTRODUCTION

This chapter explores how transgender people are distinguished as a subcategory in screen representations in spite of sensitive approaches to the portrayals in four canonical films, *The Crying Game* (Neil Jordan 1992), *Boys Don't Cry* (Kimberly Peirce 1999), *Transamerica* (Duncan Tucker 2005), and *The Danish Girl* (Tom Hooper 2015). The absence and under-representation of transgender characters are gradually being challenged with the release and box office success of such films. Despite the apparent progressive agenda of more recent representations of transgender characters, they tend to concentrate their attention on the desire for surgery, reducing the experiences of transgender people to this medically oriented understanding. Commercial cinema ultimately continues to perpetuate rather than reverse what Michel Foucault calls the "perverse implantation" (1976), frequently embracing yet pathologizing transgender identities:

> Through the various discourses, legal sanctions against minor perversions were multiplied; sexual irregularity was annexed to mental illness; from childhood to old age, a norm of sexual development was defined and all the possible deviations were carefully

---

1 Patricia Di Risio, Ph.D. Lecturer in media, film, and journalism at Monash College, Monash University, in Australia. Email: patricia.dirisio@monashcollege.edu.au

described; [...] moralists, but especially doctors, brandished the whole emphatic vocabulary of abomination. (Foucault 1976, 36)

I examine how transgender characters are often equated with the hermaphrodites and homosexuals that Foucault cites as examples of individuals who are cast as unnatural aberrations of the heterosexual norm. I demonstrate how the increasing attention from a medical perspective on transgender identity in cinematic representation functions to fuel the perverse implantation. I argue that film representation not only imposes this definition on transsexual identity but also on the overall experience of trans folks, facilitating their marginalization through the creation of a distinct social category that is inherently portrayed as entailing a medical condition. This occurs even though each film places the transgender characters at the center of the stories in ways that suggest a more sensitive and sympathetic approach to their representation.

THEORETICAL FRAMEWORK

Michel Foucault (1976) argues that the desire to read individuals as a straight man or woman is part of the dominant hegemonic discourse that shapes our legal, medical, social, and psychological frameworks. According to his theories, the open discussion and monitoring of non-procreative sexual practices by authority figures such as teachers, doctors, and clergy lead to the creation of subcategories of perverse individuals, such as the hermaphrodite and the homosexual. In his words, "This new persecution of peripheral sexualities entailed the incorporation of perversions and a new specification of individuals" (1976, 42). The homosexual is set apart from mainstream society through what he terms as the "perverse implantation." He suggests that alternative sexualities are often annexed into mental illness via psychoanalytical discourse, where homosexuality and transgender people have historically been sufferers of psychological disorders, sometimes resulting in their institutionalization or incarceration. Although there is evidence of greater tolerance of homosexual people in Western societies, they continue to struggle to gain acceptance.

As John D'Emilio (1993) points out, the expression and acceptance of alternative sexual identities is made possible through the economic freedom that capitalism perpetuates, although capitalist culture promotes a strictly heterosexual ideology through the establishment and recognition afforded to the nuclear family, upon which it relies. He adds: "How is it that capitalism, whose structure made possible the emergence of gay identity and the creation of urban gay communities, appears unable to accept gay men and lesbians in their midst?" (1993, 473). The same question could be asked about transgender individuals. Here I intend to consider the cinematic conflation of all transgender people with transsexuals (individuals who are seeking or have completed gender confirmation surgeries) and how this trend continues to create obstacles to social acceptance.

According to Coll-Planas and Missé (2015), the definition of transgender has increasingly taken on a more medically oriented definition, which does not reflect the experience of individuals who may not desire to undergo gender confirmation surgery. As Karine Espineira (2016) contends, the politics of the terminology employed to describe the experiences of transgender people is often debated within the trans population, which tries to resist confusing or conflating gender identity with sexual orientation. The experiences are very individual and may or may not reflect binary structures of gender and sexuality. Espineira adds that the media often ignores this debate. Although cross-dressing and transvestism can be a part of the transitioning process, these can also be very separate aspects of the transgender experience. I argue that commercial cinema has yet to develop the ability to capture these complexities and tends to reduce the transgender experience to transsexualism and the journey of gender confirmation surgery. This failure to accept the gender ambiguity of many transgender individuals has been especially exploited by post-classical Hollywood films, frequently representing them as sexually confused, psychotic, and even murderous. The most notable example of the cinematic equation between transvestism and a disturbed mind is the portrayal of Norman Bates (Anthony Perkins) in Hitchcock's *Psycho* (1960).

While more recent portrayals intend to provide more informed representations of the transgender experience, I argue that they continue to perpetuate Foucault's notion of perverse implantation to include transgender people. This can be seen in narratives that focus on gender confirmation surgery, which inevitably involve the medical profession. This particularly includes psychiatric discourses, which often frame transsexuals (and, by implication, transgender people) as an aberration. Unlike television screen representations where some shift has occurred toward greater diversity, in cinema the discourse which promotes the prevailing notion of the "wrong body" has yet to be dislodged. Despite the more varied and progressive stories they identify on television, Capuzza and Spencer (2017) argue that the invisibility of transgender characters on screen remains a problem. In this chapter I explore how commercial cinema's attempt to address this invisibility by investing in stories with transgender protagonists remains considerably limited in its scope and its ability to create a genuinely progressive agenda.

METHODOLOGY

This discussion outlines a problematic historical trajectory of trans representations in film before focusing on the four canonical films: *The Crying Game*, *Boys Don't*

Cry, Transamerica, and *The Danish Girl.* I demonstrate how these more recent films represent a progression in the narrative positioning of transgender characters but a regression in terms of a narrower understanding of the varying and complex nature of their experiences. The tendency to favor what Lucy Miller (2017) has identified as "cisnormative" ideology can be seen as a prevailing thread throughout these films. Miller argues that transgender identity is often characterized by stealth and deception which can instill fear in the audience, and that this is especially promoted through the horror genre. However, I explore how other genres can also perpetuate such notions in more subtle or surreptitious ways. The films have been selected based on their importance in terms of the history of cinematic representation of transgender identity and for their prominence in terms of their commercial status. Andre Cavalcante (2017) identifies both *Transamerica* and *Boys Don't Cry* as "breakout texts." He examines the impact such texts have had on transgender communities in instigating discussion and acknowledgment of trans identities. Nonetheless, as Cavalcante points out, "even as breakout texts make departures from a regime of representation, they are not necessarily ideologically 'pure,' […] or even liked by their viewers. By virtue of being early attempts at representing difference, they can lack imagination, complexity, and authenticity" (2017, 543). I consider each of the films under examination from this perspective.

The textual analysis of the films focuses on the characterizations of the protagonists but also considers how elements such as narrative structure, dialogue, cinematography, and *mise-en-scène* are employed to undermine the more progressive promise of the films. Additionally, the role of critical and theoretical responses to these texts are considered in terms of the part they can play in this tendency to reinforce ideas that support a traditional gender binary. The analysis questions the ideological agenda toward transgender identity that each film exhibits and whether the integrity of this agenda frames discourses about transgender identities in ways that promote Foucauldian notion of perverse implantation.

THE GOOD, THE BAD, AND THE EVIL: TRANS PEOPLE IN COMMERCIAL NARRATIVE CINEMA

Historically, representations of transgender individuals in cinema have been characterized by negative portrayals, despite the presence of sensitive examples such as the docudrama *Glen or Glenda?* (1953). A more daring exploration of gender identity can be found in the Hammer horror film *Dr. Jekyll and Sister Hyde* (1971). These two films were provocative in their suggestion of the kind of gender fluidity that later emerged through the discourse advanced in queer theory and politics (Butler 1990; Halberstam 1998). Wood, who has been described as the worst

Hollywood director in history[2] and who was himself a cross-dresser, made an appeal for greater tolerance. His film encouraged acceptance so that transgender individuals would not fear coming out of the closet. Wood attempts to demystify the sexual orientation of transgender people and, despite his particular and overly didactic approach, his film portrays a range of transgender identities. On the other hand, Baker's horror film ends tragically as the eventual transformation into Sister Hyde results in the death of the protagonist. Although these two early examples focus solely on male-to-female (MTF) transition (focusing on a male transgender experience at the exclusion of female-to-male, or FTM, experiences), they are the most salient commercial examples of the period. In particular, *Glen or Glenda?* addresses transvestism, cross-dressing, and transsexuality to capture a wide variety of lived experiences of transgender people.

Rebecca Bell-Metereau (1993) identifies a shift in the attitude toward cross-dressing which has also worked to subject transgender identities to the perverse implantation. Speaking about Hollywood's use of cross-dressing characters for comedic purposes, she says:

> Almost all cross-dressing films involve the relationship between authority and freedom—the extent to which the male is free to explore his female nature and the extent to which female characters are capable of establishing their own authority. These films also explore the individual's confrontation with "the other." Imitation of the otherness of the female arouses curiosity, desire, fear, and even loathing in the male characters within such films. When a film concentrates on the comic aspects, as did the majority of films before 1960, the ultimate movement is toward reconciling dichotomies between playful curiosity and obsessive fear. (1993, 3)

The exploration of gender identity as a playful and ambiguous social position in classical Hollywood is eroded by the increasingly negative associations that were aligned with transvestism (Bell-Metereau 1993, 118).

In the 1960s, references to homosexuality or transvestism in commercial cinema became more overt, but with a tendency to demonize and pathologize these identities. Vito Russo adds: "Lesbians and gay men were pathological, predatory and dangerous; villains and fools, but never heroes" (1987, 122). The tendency to conflate homosexuality with transvestism or transsexuality often resulted in casting such characters as dangerously disturbed subjects. This idea of a homosexual perversion is especially carried over to transvestism in *Psycho* and later in *Dressed to Kill* (1980). These films feature men who dress as women when they murder their victims. In *Dressed to Kill*, Michael Caine plays Dr. Robert Elliot, a cross-dressing psychiatrist who is blatantly pathologized. At the end of the film, when

---

2 In the 1980 book *The Golden Turkey Awards*, film critic Michael Medved described Ed Wood as the world's worst director.

he is placed in a psychiatric hospital, his doctor explains that Elliot harbored secret desires to become a woman, but his male side refused to allow him to proceed with an operation to complete the transition. This psychological profile is like that presented at the end of Hitchcock's film *Psycho*, to which *Dressed to Kill* pays homage. Much like Norman's impersonation of his mother, Elliot's cross-dressed persona, Bobbi, becomes dominant and emerges as murderous. This not only reiterates the idea of the demise of the individual when the female side takes over the "original" identity, as seen in *Dr. Jekyll and Sister Hyde*, but it also shows the emergence of a pattern of using gay and lesbian characters as villains, and this is accompanied by a tendency to use transgender characters as serial killers. This practice had become so entrenched in Hollywood that when the erotic thriller *Basic Instinct* (1992) went into production, the filming was picketed by various queer protest groups. Sharon Stone plays Catherine Trammel, a novelist and psychiatrist who is depicted as a lesbian and a murderer. As Yvonne Tasker (1993) notes, the more controversial aspect of the character is her bisexuality because it is laden with ambiguity both within and beyond the film *diegesis*.

The social angst that this kind of gender ambiguity triggers becomes particularly evident in the treatment of transgender characters, especially in the thriller genre. *The Silence of the Lambs* (1991) persists with the association between transgender identities and criminal behavior via the depiction of the serial killer, Buffalo Bill (Ted Levine). Female F.B.I. agent, Clarice Starling (Jodie Foster), is assisted by a former psychiatrist and serial killer, Hannibal Lecter (Anthony Hopkins), in her pursuit of Buffalo Bill, whose sexually ambiguous identity is represented as disturbed. Tasker (1994) argues that the character was mistakenly seen as gay:

> Reading the villain as gay is both possible and yet impossible, simultaneously inevitable and absurd. The disturbing sexual dysfunction that characterizes Bill's deviance lies in a wish to change his body. He hides his penis from view, seeking to transform his body into something else. Critics argued that such nuances would be missed by the popular audience who would simply read "gay man." (1994, 175)

I argue that what Tasker has actually noted is that gay and transgender identities have become cinematically conflated and that this fusion has facilitated the imposition of the perverse implantation on transgender identities. Homosexuality was associated with villainy, while gender ambiguity became identified with generating violent psychotic behavior. Thus, the perverse implantation results in a distinct shift in cinematic tolerance toward individuals who exhibit non-normative genders and sexual identities and became particularly hostile to transgender identities.

This tendency has persisted in screen representations and clearly remains an issue. According to Miller (2017), the prevalence of casting transgender characters as horrifying murderers creates a considerable obstacle to the legitimacy of transgender identities. Martin Lester (2015) goes so far as to suggest that this kind of demonization can result in a pornographic degradation of transgender identity: "Disgust as an emotional construct that includes hatred is important to consider as it can be linked to the commodification of violence against transpersons as entertainment, a form of visual pornography" (2015, 148). Thus, historically, cinema has fueled the perverse implantation by representing trans people as requiring medical attention which in turn accentuates the fear and loathing this can encourage. Foucualt's notion of the perverse implantation emphasizes the way in which sexual diversity is marginalized because it is depicted as requiring medical attention and correction, and commercial screen representations have particularly indulged in and, ultimately, profited from perpetuating this perspective. Whilst more recent commercial films have clearly challenged this trajectory, it is nonetheless imperative to examine the significant limitations to their more progressive agenda and to identify avenues for further and more meaningful improvement in these important creative practices.

ANALYSIS

The Crying Game

The release of *The Crying Game* in 1992 was an enormous commercial success in the United States.[3] In the film, I.R.A. terrorist Fergus (Stephen Ray) falls in love with Dil (Jay Davidson), the fiancée of British soldier Jody (Forrest Whitaker). Jody was held captive by the I.R.A. and died while being guarded by Fergus, who feels remorse for the part he played in the soldier's death. As a result, Fergus decides to honor Jody's dying request that he go to London and take care of his fiancée. Fergus is attracted to Dil and they become romantically involved, but then he discovers that Dil is a transgender woman. A significant amount of the critical discussion of the film is dedicated to the suggestion that this unmasking of Dil unveils a homosexual attraction between Fergus and Jody. Andrea Caloiaro (2015) assumes that Dil identifies as a man (casting the relationship with Jody as homosexual) and uses Jody's attraction to I.R.A. operative, Jude (Miranda Richardson), to conclude that Jody is bisexual.

---

3   According to Cormack (2014), *The Crying Game* hit $62 million at the box office in the U.S. and received six Oscar nominations, which contrasted with the negative reviews and poor box office performance of the film in the United Kingdom and Ireland because of the way it depicted the conflicts in the region of Northern Ireland.

In the second half of the film, Fergus asks Dil to wear Jody's cricket uniform after he understands they are now both I.R.A. targets. Fergus cuts Dil's hair and makes her wear the uniform as a disguise to protect her from the violence of his political affiliations. This gesture has especially been interpreted as evidence of a homosexual attraction (Chumo 1995). The revelation of Dil's penis creates an emphasis on the performativity of gender roles and the dubious notion of the authenticity of biological sex. However, this moment in the film is often treated as little more than a cinematic cross-dressing gesture aimed at shocking audiences.[4] The considerable amount of attention given to the presence of a homoerotic dynamic overshadows the existence of a transgender figure at the center of the film and undermines the subversive value of the unconventional gendered social space Dil occupies.

Dil never expresses a need for surgery, nor does she exhibit confusion over her identity. As Shantanu DuttaAhmed argues, the film's "revealing moment is not the evidence of her penis but rather her disbelief in Fergus' ignorance" (1998, 62). Dil is genuinely surprised that Fergus was unaware she is transgender as her relationships with men are normally predicated on this knowledge. This is seen in all her relationships with other men, such as her fiancé, Jody, her obsessive and violent admirer, Dave, and the friendly barman, Col. Dil fundamentally believes in the authenticity of the desire men feel for her and only appears in masculine attire under duress. Furthermore, in the critical response, Dil's ability to "pass" as a woman and her determination to live life as a woman elicit a difficulty in acknowledging Dil as a trans woman:

> What [film critic] Johnathan Romney aptly terms Dil's "fundamental indeterminateness" is reflected in the apparent difficulty critics have found in exactly describing "her." Dil is called "a transvestite" by [authors] Mark Simpson and Diane Sippl, "a transvestite man" by Sarah Edge, "a homosexual transvestite" by [philosopher] Žižek, a "transvestite," a "gay," a "black female," a "transgender," and a "transsexual" by [professor] Joy James, and an "effeminate transsexual" by [author] Jack Boozer; [Kristin] Handler covers various eventualities by referring to Dil's "homosexual/transgendered/feminine identity," while Lola Young, after worrying over whether Dil is a transvestite or a transsexual, opts for the analogously compound, "homo/transsexual." (Grist 2003, 7)

As Grist (2003) points out, Dil's own sense of gender identity is particularly called into question. This suggests that Dil's transgender identity has not been fully considered, especially in terms of the discussions of the motivations that draw Fergus to Dil. It is also evidence that such discussion is governed by an ideology of cisnormativity.

---

4   A gesture which could be seen as comparable to the removal of a wig in drag performance.

As a character, Dil is treated as comfortable and confident with her body and her identity, but this is not always supported through the *mise-en-scène*, where it is not contextualized and is deliberately disguised until later in the film. The obscuring of this aspect of Dil is evident, for example, in the scene in the Metro bar and the way it is represented. When Fergus first follows Dil into the bar, there is no indication that this may be a venue featuring drag performers. Both the exterior and interior shots suggest an ordinary corner pub. In the scene where Dil performs the song *The Crying Game*, the performer who precedes her is equally not visibly transgender. The patrons in the bar who are watching the performances are quite diverse and include men and women who generally appear to be cisgender. However, immediately after the revelation, Fergus returns to the bar and sees what it seems he had previously ignored. The first woman he encounters has a similar appearance to Dil. However, her masculine features are more visible and indicate a trans woman. As he gazes around the room, almost every person appears to be visibly transgender. He also notices a person at the bar is wearing a blonde wig, which has strong associations with drag performance. When the camera pans across to Dil drinking and smoking at the bar, she is virtually surrounded by individuals who can be more visibly identified as transgender, transvestites, transsexuals, and drag performers. The Metro is thus unmasked and this reinforces the impact of the earlier scene of the revelation of Dil's anatomy. The fear and disgust which have frequently dominated associations with transgender characters are also at play in evoking this shock value and further highlight the notion that transgender identity inevitably involves deception.

Representations of transgender protagonists offer the possibility to challenge the traditional use of gendered positions in Hollywood. However, Grist (2003) notices that the intensely ambivalent responses to films like *The Crying Game* and *M. Butterfly* (David Cronenberg 1993) reflect a deep social angst: "The undoubtedly transgressive resonances in these texts are, ultimately, problematically partial and compromised [in] that both texts implicitly uphold what they explicitly challenge" (2003, 3). In his analysis of *The Crying Game*, he concludes that the film's narrative closure re-establishes patriarchal authority, especially in reference to Fergus, where "a stable identity and his phallic masculinity [are] restored" (2003, 24). Such interpretations of the film's resolution obscure the experiences of trans people and their varied expressions of sexual desire. Helen Hanson provides a different and rarer assessment of the function of Dil's identity: "Dil retains her/his [sic] sexual and gender ambiguity and it is the phallus as a signifying figure that is called into question" (1999, 64). This debate highlights the way in which a conventional gender binary is prioritized in the critical discussion. This is also achieved by an association between transgressing gender boundaries and perversity through the portrayals of other key characters in the film.

Aisling B. Cormack (2014) argues that I.R.A. member Jude increasingly takes on masculine attributes through her clothes and femme-fatale appearance, while Fergus is feminized because he softens his ruthless persona when he develops a bond with his hostage. Fergus' bond with Jody is interpreted as a homosexual attraction, which fuels the notion that Jody is bisexual. This transition across one gender stereotype to the other is marked as unnatural and renders them weak or vulnerable: Jody's (supposed) bisexuality lures him into a death trap, Jude's attempt to assassinate Fergus fails when she is shot dead by Dil, and Fergus is imprisoned and weakened by his romantic attachment to Dil. His desire to protect her from the authorities also suggests that they are confined to a purely platonic relationship. Thus, the relationship may be preserved but cannot be depicted as including sexual intimacy. The author adds: "Although *The Crying Game* transgresses norms that tie biological sex to socially constructed gender, [it] nevertheless upholds conventional gender roles" (Cormack 2014, 173). I argue that this is predominantly achieved through a lack of consideration of Dil's position as transgender. The character is treated as a man who merely impersonates a woman, rather than someone who identifies and lives as a woman.

The Crying Game has an implicit agenda that contradicts its explicit one. On the one hand, it seeks to explore non-normative genders and sexualities, but there are elements of the film which ultimately reaffirm more traditional binary understandings of gender and sexual orientation. It continues to pathologize or repress their transgression while it simultaneously deconstructs and disturbs gender (Lugowski 1993; Handler 1994). Therefore, the perverse implantation is reinforced in the film and especially in the critical response, as they neglect the opportunities the film offers regarding questioning binary notions of sex and gender. Nonetheless, *The Crying Game* sets a precedent that Hollywood soon attempts to follow. However, this proves to be equally problematic when exploring the docudrama recounting the life and death of Brandon Teena.

Boys Don't Cry

Boys Don't Cry (1999) is based on the real-life story of transgender man Brandon Teena, who was murdered in Nebraska in 1993. Hilary Swank stars in the role of Brandon, and the film depicts his desire to transition from female-to-male (FTM) and how this results in his tragic death. He is portrayed as contemplating surgery to complete his transition and is also shown using a prosthetic penis in his sexual encounters. He develops a relationship with Lana Tisdel (Chloë Sevigny), a young cisgender woman whose family and friends uncover that Brandon is a transgender man. Later on, Brandon is violently targeted, raped, and murdered by Lana's step-father, John Lotter (Peter Sarsgaard), and his friend, Marvin Thomas Nissen (Brendan Sexton III).

Critical discussion points out how the film tends to cast Brandon as a lesbian rather than a transgender man. While Jack Halberstam (2001) argues that *Boys Don't Cry* establishes a transgender gaze, the film has been rejected as an example of queer cinema due to the mainstream treatment of the subject (Rich 2000). Despite Brandon's assertion that he was a man, it has been argued that the film undermines his gender identity by portraying him as a lesbian in denial (Willox 2003). Rachel Swan (2001) suggests that the film fails its own agenda as Brandon is inevitably positioned as a female (and, therefore, a lesbian) via diegetic and extra-diegetic strategies. She adds: "Our culture's neurosis with regard to sex-gender symmetry demands ultimately that Brandon be castrated and re-positioned in a female body" (2001, 51).

This reversal occurs despite the film's in-depth treatment of the dangers of not "passing," the fear of discovery, and the violence often perpetrated on transgender people.[5] The film portrays Brandon's experience as a trans person as risky and as often courting danger, thus illuminating an important aspect of a transgender gaze. For Brandon, the act of "passing" is portrayed in a variety of social spaces that frequently test the authenticity of his masculinity and always with the fear of being unveiled as trans. The tension that this creates in the every-day life of a transgender person is well explored, even if Brandon's transgender persona is ultimately undermined. Brandon is seen as continually flirting with danger by being a convincing and appealing male and actively refusing to be identified as a woman. However, as Julianne Pidduck (2001) points out, "Brandon becomes a dashing, sensitive outsider […] who, with his 'movie-star good looks,' enigmatic body, [and] a certain luminosity in the way his face is shot, promises to transcend the limitations of working-class masculinity" (2001, 98–100). Thus, Brandon is convincing as a male because, as Michele Aaron (2001, 93) argues, both the spectator and the female characters surrounding Brandon are seduced by his re-interpretation of masculinity. They are often knowingly complicit with that performance and this is seen, for example, in Lana's deliberate refusal to acknowledge the evidence of Brandon's anatomy. His interpretation of masculinity arouses suspicion and jealousy from the men he has befriended and results in a violent form of gender panic (Aaron 2001).

Thus, the film does dedicate a significant amount of its narrative to the dangerous aspects of the transgender experience and provides a space to explore the transgender gaze. Here, the fear of transgender identity that has been traditionally evoked in the audience is successfully shifted toward the horrific repercussions that are experienced by transgender individuals. Brandon's willingness to subject himself to masculine rites of passage and the daring way he approaches

---

5   Halberstam (1998, 25) argues that public bathrooms are often places where this is tested and can result in the most punitive repercussions.

intimacy with both men and women are often unnerving. He participates in bumper skiing, bar brawls, and seduces Lana with whom he becomes sexually intimate. Brandon constantly braves situations where he is dangerously close to being exposed. The moment which is far more punishing and, ultimately, leads to Brandon's harrowing rape and murder, occurs late in the film when Brandon has developed a romantic attachment to Lana and begins to take up a position as her boyfriend. Lana's friends and family have become suspicious and discover Brandon is trans, and they insist that both Brandon and Lana acknowledge this. When Lana denies their accusations, Brandon is dragged into the bathroom and stripped down to expose his genitals. This is another example of Brandon refusing the interpellation as a woman. At this point, there is a cut to a medium close-up of him looking up and out directly at the camera. The lighting becomes ethereal and the diegetic sound is removed. Brandon has what Halberstam (2001, 296) has described as an "out of body" experience. A cut to a reverse-shot shows Brandon fully dressed as one of the onlookers framed by a spotlight. He sees the scene of his disrobing from the perspective of the spectator and is then framed in a long shot with the silhouette of the other onlookers reiterating the position of the spectator. In this brief moment, the viewer and Brandon are cinematically aligned, and the audience becomes complicit in the violence perpetrated against the protagonist. This alignment also emphasizes the punitive way in which gender norms are policed in society and the distress that can be involved in articulating a transgender gaze.

This scene is Brandon's most salient example of his refusal to be identified as a woman, but there are several other moments in the film where he is seen resisting such interpellation, with less dire consequences. In a scene that re-enacts Althusser's (1972) hailing of a subject, Brandon is addressed by a policeman as "Miss Brandon." A medium shot shows the policeman approaching Brandon, who refuses to turn around and be "girled" (Butler 1993, 7). Earlier in the film, he is waiting in a courtroom, facing charges of fraud and car theft. Although he is sitting right before the judge, when he is summoned as "Teena," the name he was given at birth, he quietly walks away and goes completely unnoticed by the authorities. This is accentuated via a close-up showing the words "failure to appear" being stamped on the court docket. Even though the narrative positions Brandon as a woman and, therefore, a lesbian, the transgender gaze is well established in this film. This insightful portrayal is unique in the history of Hollywood cinema and the need to undermine this perspective demonstrates the trouble the film experiences in sustaining its progressive agenda.

While the critical discussion around *The Crying Game* ignores the integrity with which Dil treats her identity, the critical response to *Boys Don't Cry* exposes how the film narrative itself carries out this occlusion. There is a resistance to reading these characters as transgender and a tendency to position them as sexual inverts in a way that reinforces the perverse implantation. Nonetheless, these films place the characters in central roles and give them unprecedented attention within a commercial sphere. This has created a space in which Hollywood feels comfortable in making commercial investments in stories with transgender protagonists. However, this interest has come at the expense of reducing transgender identities to one very specific aspect, the interest in surgical intervention, and how this can reinforce conventional binary understandings of sex and gender. Hollywood filmmaking practices especially demonstrate an interest in promoting this perspective in the popular film *Transamerica*.

Transamerica

Transamerica is about trans woman Bree (Felicity Huffman) and her desire and struggle to undergo gender confirmation surgery. The story focuses on the importance of this surgery to Bree feeling authentic as a woman. Until this occurs, she is shown as a lonely person without a family or a love interest and as someone who feels incomplete. Before allowing her to have surgery, her therapist insists Bree must reconnect with the biological child she discovers she unknowingly had before she transitioned. Bree's son, Toby (Kevin Zegers), is a juvenile delinquent who has been jailed for soliciting and drug dealing while living in New York. In a bid to establish a connection with him, Bree and Toby take a road trip to California together. Bree conceals her transsexuality and the fact that she is Toby's biological parent, and this is a source of both humor and pathos. Toby is troubled when he discovers the truth, but the film has a reconciliatory ending where they come together as an unconventional family.

Bree feels she is incapable of "passing" as a woman while she still has a penis and finds this extremely upsetting. This is evident in numerous scenes, including one where she is interviewed by a psychiatrist assessing her readiness for her surgery. He asks, "How do you feel about your penis?" Bree grimaces as she responds, "It disgusts me." This is repeated in another scene when a girl in a diner turns around to ask Bree, "Are you a boy or a girl?" Immediately afterward, Bree is seen crying on the phone, talking to her therapist complaining that even an 8-year-old child was able to detect she was not a "real" woman. Once Bree has had the surgery, the narrative suggests her femininity takes on more authenticity. Bree's femininity in a post-surgery stage is more relaxed and less hyperbolic. For example, she is seen working as a waitress in a Mexican restaurant and no longer draws the attention of strangers in the way she does earlier in the film. This is reinforced through the idea that she can now occupy a role as a mother with her son Toby and become a family. Caster and Andrew note that "the final scene sees their tentative reconciliation in Bree's small living room, a domestic space for mother and son made radically queer, given that she was his biological father and he stars in gay porn" (2007, 135). The authors suggest that this queer re-imagining of the family is more inclusive and does not favor the heterosexual family in a way that necessarily excludes queer identities. However, the heterosexual model is clearly being replicated and deified in this closing sequence and conforms to an ideology of cisnormativity. D'Emilio (1993) argues that "while capitalism has knocked the material foundation away from family life, lesbians, gay men, and heterosexual feminists have become the scapegoats for the social instability of the system" (1993, 473). In this film, the angst, fear, and loathing traditionally evoked by negative representations of transsexuality are appeased because the queer family does not represent a threat. In fact, it is reaffirming the very structures it appeared to question at the outset.

The need to placate the social discomfort with people who exhibit alternative sexual identities is also evident in how the film portrays the experience of intimacy and romance. There is a hint of a romantic interest between Bree and a Native American man she meets during the trip to California, but this relationship is not developed. Physical contact between the two characters is avoided, even if it is left open as a distinct possibility. Traci B. Abbott (2013) argues that the transgender protagonists in films face the trans/romance dilemma: "Too often narrative expectation is subverted and romantic contact stifled because the filmmaker fears the audience will read the trans character's gender identity as inauthentic and the romance as transgressive" (2013, 32). Such angst means that sexual intimacy in stories about transgender people is yet to be explored in more detail in mainstream cinema. Portrayals of explicit lovemaking involving transgender characters is largely avoided and stories about their meaningful or long-term relationships are notably absent. This is no less the case with *The Danish Girl* which was a 2015 box office success.

The Danish Girl

This film is a dramatization of the story of Lili Elbe, played by Eddy Redmayne. Lili, who died in 1931, is known as the first trans woman to receive gender confirmation surgery. The film depicts Lili's life before and after she "came out" as a woman. Prior to that, she was known as an artist and a cisgender man by the name of Einar Wegener, who married fellow artist Gerda Gottlieb (Alicia Vikander). Lili's difficulty in coming to terms with her transsexuality dominates the narrative of the film. The film interprets the story in a way that makes the need for surgery the answer to what has been medically defined as "gender dysphoria." The formal diagnosis by the fifth edition of the *Diagnostic and Statistical Manual of Mental Disorders* (DSM-V) of the American Psychiatric Association defines the condition as the discomfort or distress caused by a discrepancy between a person's gender identity and the gender assigned at birth.

As a medical condition, the treatment involves gender confirmation surgery, among other things (Hadj-Moussa, Ohl, and Kuzon 2018). I argue that the film is especially interested in prioritizing not only the need for gender confirmation surgery but also in casting transsexuality as a mental disorder by suggesting that Lili simultaneously suffers from Dissociative Identity Disorder (DID). This condition is more commonly referred to as "multiple personality disorder" and, according to Sedehi and Kit, "Einar Wegener [Lili] underwent surgery not because he was transgender but because he suffered from dissociative identity disorder" (2017, 226). The authors find that those with this disorder have switching personalities which "control the patient's behavior and thoughts" and they discuss the ways in which the two personas exist independently of one another. Thus, from a psychoanalytic perspective, the loss of memory that both Einar and Lili experience in relation to the other persona is evidence of the personality and gender confusion.

While I consider this as an example of a response to the film which enacts a particularly pernicious form of instilling the perverse implantation, the characterization of Lili does fuel an association with mental illness. Lili encourages sympathy and understanding through a triumph narrative where she can assert herself, but this strategy incorporates an explicit pathologizing of transsexuality by positing her as the dominating personality that annihilates Einar. This reiterates the trope of a woman trapped in a man's body, often associated with trans women, a discourse which has frequently dominated screen representations of trans identity and reinforced the notion of the presence of a psychological disturbance. According to Andrés Armengol Sans, "The film reproduces a too much taken for granted liaison: transsexuality as a psychotic symptom" (2017, 83). While the psychosis does not entail murderous tendencies (as in *Psycho*), it does suggest the elimination of the masculine persona as an integral part of the experiences of trans women. In *Transamerica*, Bree's therapist insists that she should not use the third person to refer to the time when she went by her previous name, Stanley. This dialogue and Bree's initial reluctance to acknowledge Toby, both suggest that the experiences of transgender people do involve a tendency to deny their prior persona. Brandon in *Boys Don't Cry* also tries to eradicate the existence of Teena. However, contrary to *The Danish Girl*, this denial is often motivated by the need to evade criminal prosecution or violent reactions from others.

Transsexuality as psychosis is particularly reiterated via the narrative of the film by suggesting that Einar/Lili's desire to cross-dress results from a traumatic childhood experience. This is triggered when Gerda asks Einar to dress as a woman to pose for her paintings. Einar finds increasing satisfaction in cross-dressing and, as a couple who are also bohemian artists, they initially treat it as a playful way to test gender boundaries. However, Gerda becomes concerned when there are signs of an emerging persona and she is shocked to find that

Einar is gradually transforming into Lili.[6] Einar is increasingly comfortable in women's clothes and underwear and is attracted to men. In the phase of the film when Lili is emerging, she is portrayed as being offended by the presence of her penis, much like *Transamerica*'s Bree. Einar reveals that Lili has a sexual liaison with a man and also recounts a childhood episode where Einar kissed his friend, Hans, and was caught by his father, who violently responded to what he registered as homosexual tendencies. As he recounts the story, it becomes evident that Einar perceives this episode as the inner Lili expressing herself. These events are depicted as traumas, reawakened by the cross-dressing. But they also operate to emphasize the emergence of Lili as the authentic persona. For example, when Lili is alone kissing Henrik (Ben Whishaw), she is disturbed when he calls her "Einar." Henrik's use of both names suggests that he is aware Lili is trans and that this is not an obstacle to their sexual intimacy. However, Lili is no longer aroused, and she runs away, denying the former masculine identity. Einar's insistence on the fact there is a woman trapped in his body is also emphasized when Einar seeks psychiatric help. The explanation of homosexuality is continually dismissed and depicted as ridiculous. However, while the film is careful to avoid the association of homosexuality and mental illness, it does so at the expense of suggesting that Lili is a kind of alter ego, a personality that wishes to take control of Einar's body. This inevitably confirms the extra-diegetic diagnosis of DID and the existence of a pathology, reiterating the mechanism of Foucault's perverse implantation.

Later in the film, Einar reunites with Hans. In this scene, Einar confesses a desire to kill himself but is prevented by the realization that this would also kill Lili. Here, the idea of the split personality is given further credence. Earlier in the film, Gerda also encourages this dissociation when attending social functions by introducing Lili as her cousin. Einar and Lili frequently deny the existence of the other and they both experience memory loss in relation to the other persona. This leads to the notion that Lili can only exist at the expense of Einar, and that surgery is the only way to eliminate Einar and make way for Lili as an "authentic" woman. Thus, the desire for surgery is exploited to indulge and prioritize the diagnosis of gender dysphoria, and this serves to fuel the perverse implantation.

---

6   The author of this chapter uses the name that Lili had (before she publicly identified herself as a woman) in order to talk about her transitioning process. Therefore, the masculine name "Einar" is used only for the purposes of referring to the alleged personality disorder that was attributed to Lili. In no way does it constitute an attempt to misgender neither the fictional character nor the real-life artist. *Ed.*

CONCLUSION

The four films included in this discussion feature a transgender character and three of the four films focus on or address transitioning through gender confirmation surgery. This transitioning story is, however, often characterized by the pathologizing of this journey and demonstrates that increased visibility of transgender identity on screen does not necessarily result in more diverse or inclusive stories. Jay Stewart (2016) suggests that producing films with transgender protagonists is an unenviable task: "Representing trans lives in films or elsewhere is a nightmare task for anyone. [...] But this film [*The Danish Girl*] made by cis (non-trans) people and performed mostly by cis people [...] will be mostly watched by cis people" (2016, 163). Such a task also carries significant negative historical baggage given the trajectory of the representation of gay and transgender characters in commercial cinema. Moreover, Stewart's observation draws attention to the fact that stories created and performed by transgender individuals provide greater understandings of the enormous range and highly individual nature of transgender experiences. Such films predominantly operate in the independent sphere and are targeted to a transgender audience. There is a large body of films telling these stories, which include titles such as *The Queen* (1968), *Paris Is Burning* (1990), *Hedwig and the Angry Inch* (2001), *Wild Side* (2004), *Pay It No Mind: Marsha P. Johnson* (2012), *Drunktown's Finest* (2014), and *Tangerine* (2015). These stories address a variety of aspects of the experiences of trans people, including the challenge of not being visibly transgender, vulnerability to violence, social marginalization, and being subjected to ridicule and rejection. However, they also frequently explore or relish the fluidity and ambiguity of gender and the very different sexual identities and orientations they may entail.

Stuart Richards argues that "queer narrative is a stigma, which [...] strategic marketing campaigns must overcome to appeal to a mass audience" (2016, 28). Homosexual romance in commercial films is often surreptitiously disguised in the marketing collateral, indicating that there is still anxiety around explicit representations of queer romantic or sexual desire. Transgender romance particularly suffers from this stigma and remains to be fully explored. Intimacy between a transgender person and their lover is frequently recast as a homosexual attraction, as seen in *The Crying Game* and *Boys Don't Cry*. Suggestions of romances with trans people are rarely followed through unless they are co-opted for shock value, as seen in *The Crying Game*. Abbott (2013) notes that the small screen is more daring than film in its representation of trans romance via characters such as Carmelita (played by trans actress Candis Cayne) in prime-time television show *Dirty Sexy Money* (2007–2009). Here, romance and intimacy are represented as "respectful, passionate, and emotionally supportive" (Abbott 2013, 39). Television is a sphere which has made greater strides in its approach to transgender representation. While invisibility remains an issue, Capuzza and Spencer (2017) demonstrate that scripted series focus much less on transitioning narratives and portray transgender characters as more integrated in relation to cisgender characters.

Overall, through my analysis, I argue that, in cinema, there are still significant limitations to the advancement of the progressive agenda ostensibly promoted by the four films. Their transgender protagonists and characters are taken more seriously if they are seeking or have completed gender confirmation surgery. Stories that focus on transitioning tend to emphasize a desire to adhere to conventional gender norms rather than subverting them. In some instances, traditional gender norms are represented as the ideal they are striving to achieve, thus reinforcing essentialist notions of gender and an ideology of cisnormativity. This is conveyed not only through their narrative structure and characterization but also in the *mise-en-scène*. Except for Dil, the characters are depicted as believing that gender confirmation surgery will make them feel more authentic, although this can lead to the destruction of such individuals. In fact, the death of both Brandon Teena and Lili Elbe reiterates the impossibility of their transgender experience. Commercial filmmakers who are interested in engaging with characters who strive to exit conventional social and psychological positions of gender face the challenge of including representations that are more varied and complex. There is also a notable and continued resistance to employ transgender performers. Moreover, the commercial sphere clearly struggles to create sensitive characterizations where gender ambiguity can be affirmed or celebrated rather than obscured or undermined.

REFERENCES

Aaron, Michele. 2001. "Pass/Fail." *Screen* 42, no. 1: 92–6.
Abbott, Traci B. 2013. "The Trans/Romance Dilemma in *Transamerica* and Other Films." *The Journal of American Culture* 36, no. 1: 32–41.
Althusser, Louis. 1972. "Ideology and Ideological State Apparatuses." In *Lenin and Philosophy and Other Essays*. New York: Monthly Review Press.
Armengol Sans, Andrés. 2017. "'This is Truly Me': A Lacanian Reading of *The Danish Girl* (2015)." *Journal of Comparative Literature and Aesthetics* 40, no. 1: 83–94.
Bell-Metereau, Rebecca. 1993. *Hollywood Androgyny*. New York: Columbia University Press.
Boys Don't Cry. 1999. Directed by Kimberly Peirce. Fox.
Butler, Judith. 1990. *Gender Trouble*. New York: Routledge.
———. 1993. *Bodies that Matter*. New York: Routledge.
Caloiaro, Andrea. 2015. "'The Best Game in the World': Masculinity, Militarism, and the Geopolitical Boundaries of Sport in *The Crying Game*." *Aethlon: The Journal of Sport Literature* 33, no. 1: 13–30.

Capuzza, Jamie C. and Leland G. Spencer. 2017. "Regressing, Progressing, or Transgressing on the Small Screen? Transgender Characters on U.S. Scripted Television Series." *Communication Quarterly* 65, no. 2, 214–30.

Caster, Peter and Allison Andrew. 2007. "Transgender Nation: Crossing Borders and Queering Space in *Transamerica*." *English Language Notes* 45, no. 2: 133–9.

Cavalcante, Andre. 2017. "Breaking into Transgender Life: Transgender Audiences' Experiences with 'First of Its Kind' Visibility in Popular Media." *Communication, Culture and Critique* 10, no. 3: 538–55.

Chumo, Peter. 1995. "*The Crying Game*, Hitchcockian Romance, and the Quest for Identity." *Literature Film Quarterly* 23, no. 4: 247–53.

Coll-Planas, Gerard and Miquel Missé. 2015. "Identity in Dispute: Conflicts Surrounding the Construction of Transsexuality." *Revista de Sociología* 100, no. 1: 35–52.

Cormack, Aisling B. 2014. "Toward a 'Post-Troubles' Cinema?: The Troubled Intersection of Political Violence and Gender in Neil Jordan's *The Crying Game* and *Breakfast on Pluto*." *Éire-Ireland* 49, no. 1–2: 164–92.

D'Emilio, John. 1993. "Capitalism and Gay Identity." In *The Lesbian and Gay Studies Reader*, edited by Henry Abelove, Michele Aina Barale, and David M. Halperin, 467–76. London: Routledge.

DuttaAhmed, Shantanu. 1998. "'I Thought You Knew!': Performing the Penis, the Phallus, and Otherness in Neil Jordan's *The Crying Game*." *Film Criticism* 23, no. 3: 61–73.

Espineira, Karine. 2016. "Transgender and Transsexual People's Sexuality in the Media." *Parallax* 22, no. 3: 323–9.

Foucault, Michel. 1976. "The Perverse Implantation." In *The History of Sexuality Vol. 1: The Will to Knowledge*, 36–49. London: Penguin.

Grist, Leighton. 2003. "'It's Only a Piece of Meat': Gender Ambiguity, Sexuality, and Politics in *The Crying Game* and *M. Butterfly*." *Cinema Journal* 42, no. 4: 3–28.

Hadj-Moussa Miriam, Dana A. Ohl, and William M. Kuzon, Jr. 2018. "Evaluation and Treatment of Gender Dysphoria to Prepare for Gender Confirmation Surgery." *Sexual Medicine Reviews* 6, no. 4: 607–17.

Halberstam, Jack. 1998. *Female Masculinity*. Durham: Duke University Press.

———. 2001. "The Transgender Gaze in *Boys Don't Cry*." *Screen* 42, no. 3: 294–8.

Handler, Kristin. 1994. "Sexing *The Crying Game*: Difference, Identity, Ethics." *Film Quarterly* 47, no. 3: 31–42.

Hanson, Helen. 1999. "The Figure in Question: The Transvestite Character as a Narrative Strategy in *The Crying Game*." In *The Body's Perilous Pleasures: Dangerous Desires and Contemporary Culture*, edited by Michele Aaron, 49–66. Edinburgh: Edinburgh University Press.

Lester, Paul M. 2015. "Visual Communication from Abomination to Indifference: A Visual Analysis of Transgender Stereotypes in the Media." In *Transgender Communication Studies: Histories, Trends, and Trajectories*, edited by Leland G. Spence and Jamie C. Capuzza, 131–55. Lanham, MD: Lexington Books.

Lugowski, David. 1993. "Genre Conventions and Visual Style in *The Crying Game*." *Cinéaste* 20, no. 1: 31–35.

Miller, Lucy J. 2017. "Fear and the Cisgender Audience: Transgender Representation and Audience Identification in *Sleepaway Camp*." *Spectator* 37, no. 2: 40–47.

Pidduck, Julianne. 2001. "Risk and Queer Spectatorship." *Screen* 42, no. 1: 97–102.

Rich, B. Ruby. 2000. "Queer and Present Danger." *Sight and Sound* 10, no. 3: 22–25.
Richards, Stuart. 2016. "Overcoming the Stigma: The Queer Denial of Indiewood." *Journal of Film and Video* 68, no. 1: 19–30.
Russo, Vito. 1987. *The Celluloid Closet: Homosexuality in the Movies*. New York: Harper and Row.
Sedehi, Kamelia T. and Tay Lai Kit. 2017. "Dissociating Realities and Trans-Forming Self in David Ebershoff's *The Danish Girl*." *Indonesian EFL Journal* 3, no. 2: 225–30.
Stewart, Jay. 2016. "*The Danish Girl* (Film Review)." *Journal of Family Planning and Reproductive Health Care* 42: 163.
Swan, Rachel. 2001. "*Boys Don't Cry*." *Film Quarterly* 54, no. 3: 47–52.
Tasker, Yvonne. 1993. *Spectacular Bodies: Gender, Genre, and the Action Cinema*. New York: Routledge.
———. 1994. "Pussy Galore: Lesbian Images and Lesbian Desire in the Popular Cinema." In *The Good, The Bad and The Gorgeous: Popular Culture's Romance with Lesbianism*, edited by Diane Hamer and Belinda Budge, 172–83. London: Pandora.
The Crying Game. 1992. Directed by Neil Jordan. Miramax Films.
The Danish Girl. 2015. Directed by Tom Hooper. Universal Studios.
Transamerica. 2005. Directed by Duncan Tucker. Belladona Productions.
Willox, Annabelle. 2003. "Branding Teena: (Mis)Representations in the Media." *Sexualities* 6, no. 3–4: 407–25.

PART II
FROM IRRELEVANCE TO STARDOM, OR VICE VERSA

CHAPTER FOUR

Beyond Tipping Points, Trauma, and Trailblazing: *Adventure Time* and the Transordinary

BY EMMA A. JANE[1]

INTRODUCTION

The American celebrity Laverne Cox sits at the vanguard of what has been dubbed "the transgender zeitgeist" (Yardley 2017). Her photogenic activism, alongside her portrayal of Sophia Burset in the Netflix women's prison drama *Orange Is the New Black*, has led to her achieving a growing number of pop-cultural firsts. For instance, her Wikipedia page notes that she is the first openly transgender person to receive a Primetime Emmy Award nomination for acting, to win a Daytime Emmy as an executive producer, to play a transgender series regular on broadcast television, to have a wax figure of herself at Madame Tussauds Museum, and to appear on the covers of *Cosmopolitan* and *Time* magazines, the latter occurring in the edition in which the magazine famously heralded the arrival of a "Transgender Tipping Point" (Steinmetz and Gray 2014).

While Cox's talents, achievements, and advocacy for the larger trans community are admirable, these media framings are all rooted in her exceptionalism. She is remarkable, a trailblazer, quite literally the face of popular culture's turn

---

1 Emma A. Jane (formerly published as Emma Tom), Ph.D. Senior Lecturer at UNSW Sydney, Australia. Email: emma.jane@unsw.edu.au

to trans. Such coverage is an improvement on standard transphobic fare that invites cisgender audiences to laugh about yet another "normal" man "tricked" into a sexual encounter with what is framed as a contemptible female pretender. Yet, while these sorts of framings are negative, does it automatically follow that the best, or perhaps even the only, corrective is via over-effusive positive discourse such as that associated with the aforementioned media framings of Cox? A central objective of this chapter is to investigate, complicate, and offer new perspectives about what "positive" (or "progressive" or "useful") discourse might look like when it comes to representations of transgender characters and trans-related themes on television.

This chapter begins by identifying and interrogating two trans tropes that have become increasingly dominant in contemporary media: (1) expressly sympathetic portrayals of trans subjects as tragic, and (2) emphatically enthusiastic coverage of trans individuals as celebrities and trailblazers. While these might seem like progressive framings, my case is that attempting to counter overwhelmingly negative representations with only blazingly positive alternatives risks fortifying unhelpful binaries. Such discourse also tends to frame gender as being a person's only or defining characteristic and fails to capture many aspects, or arguably most aspects, of the diversity of lived transgender experiences. The children's cartoon *Adventure Time* (2010–2018), which is about a tight knit group of friends negotiating life on Earth nearly 1,000 years after a nuclear holocaust, is thus offered to illustrate an alternative approach. The show features several gender fluid, agender, multiply gendered, ambiguously gendered, and transgender characters. However, in contrast to the trans-related content in programs such as *Transparent* and *Orange Is the New Black*, the gender of the characters in *Adventure Time* is rarely the catalyst for plotlines or the subject of comment by others. Instead, it is depicted as one of several other characteristics of the world that is not especially consequential or worthy of special focus or comment.

This chapter goes on to explore the paradoxical way media representations of gender diversity as ordinary or unimportant may have the potential to be as liberatory as (or, for some viewers, even more liberatory than) those texts paying a great deal of attention to gender diversity, even if such attention is positive in the sense of being sympathetic or celebratory. This observation underpins the concluding argument in favor of increasing media representations capturing three, interrelated aspects of the "ordinary" in relation to transgender issues: the depiction of gender diversity as "normal" (in the normative sense in terms of as being regarded positive, desirable, and proper), the depiction of trans characters engaged in the quotidian events of everyday life, and the depiction of trans characters whose gender is framed intratextually as irrelevant.

METHODS, DEFINITIONS, AND AUTHOR'S STANDPOINT

Data for this study has been drawn from my rolling series of research projects dedicated to studying the representation of themes relating to gender, sex, and sexuality in popular media. The methodological approach is grounded in textual analysis and involves investigating and making a case for "likely interpretations" (McKee 2003, 1) rather than engaging in audience research. For this chapter, all 10 seasons and 283 episodes of *Adventure Time* were viewed to qualitatively code those characters, scenes, and plot developments that could be read as subverting normative and binary stereotypes relating to gender and sex. Key episodes were then returned to in order to engage in close readings. While not all the coded or closely examined episodes are referred to explicitly in this chapter, the nuance of my findings from analyzing all episodes in the series inform the entire chapter. My reasons for analyzing all 283 episodes of *Adventure Time* is that I initially watched the complete 10 series with my then 8-year-old daughter for recreational purposes. Then, having become intrigued with the program's highly unusual treatment of gender-related and other issues, I watched the entire series again from start to finish, taking notes and using quality coding. I have since published two other articles based on this research: one on the non-normative representation of female characters (Jane 2015) and another on the program's treatment of apocalyptic themes (Jane 2018). This chapter is the first which addresses trans-related themes.

A relatively large number of journalistic articles, blog posts, and other internet sources are referenced in this chapter for three key reasons: (1) they assist in increasing the trans voices contained in this research, since the majority of popular media texts selected for citation are written by or contain interviews with people who identify as transgender,[2] (2) because they offer insights into current norms in entertainment production from trans industry insiders that would not otherwise be available, and (3) because the publication turnaround for popular media texts is much faster than that in academic domains and, therefore, these sources assist in making this chapter more current than it would be if only scholarly sources were cited. Additionally, in many instances, these citations of popular media texts are offered to illustrate the transgender-related media framings under discussion: that is, they are part of the objects under analysis.

In this research, literature from gender, queer, and transgender studies supplemented by Stuart Hall's (1997, 2000) and Richard Dyer's (2002) work on representation are used as the primary theoretical lenses. Given that much of Hall's work concerns representation and race, it is important to clarify that it is not the

---

2   This is not to suggest that such approaches offer anything like the depth and texture available from scholarly methods such as qualitative interviews, ethnography, and so on.

intention of this chapter to suggest that regimes of representation around race (including the historical and systemic contexts these regimes reflect and constitute) map onto those associated with transgender and queer themes and experiences, not least because this would contribute to the obscuring or erasing of distinct issues faced by Black trans folks and Black queer people. I acknowledge the multitude of critical differences between the symbolic and material issues associated with gender and those associated with race. Rather, this chapter's references to Hall's work simply comports with the tradition of using various theoretical and conceptual frameworks in qualitative research to clarify epistemological disposition, identify the logic behind methodological choices, provide a guide or framework for the study, and potentially lay the groundwork for an epistemological inversion by which the original objects and subjects under investigation can be used as a lens to view the theoretical model itself.

The terms "transgender" and "queer" have been richly theorized and robustly debated both inside and outside of academia, particularly with regard to which people and what practices these terms encapsulate (Butler interviewed in Ahmed 2016; Stryker 2006; Valentine 2007). While I agree such debates are important, this terminology is only briefly addressed here in order to permit a focus on issues separate from those relating to the terminological definitions and the complex and intricate issues raised in the literature on such topics. In this chapter, the highly elastic term "queer" is deployed as an umbrella term for any non-normative sexuality and gender preference, along with an acknowledgment of queer theorists' use of the term to explicate the relational, contingent, and structurally and discursively created status of what is understood to be natural and normal.

Following Joanne Meyerowitz (2004), "transgender" and the less formal "trans" are used to refer to "various forms and degrees of cross-gender practices and identifications" (2004, 10), as well as Halberstam's definition as "expansive forms of difference, [where] trans* stands at odds with the history of gender variance, which has been collapsed into concise definitions, sure medical pronouncements, and fierce exclusions" (2018, 5). This also comports with Halberstam's determination to hold open the meaning of terms, rather than attempting to "deliver certainty through the act of naming" (2018, 3), and to make conceptual, cultural, political, and practical space for trans individuals to be "the authors of their own categorizations" (2018, 4). This chapter's generalizing terms such as "the transgender community" or "transgender people" are employed self-consciously for shorthand convenience and should not be taken to imply that these or any other communities are homogenous or fixed. It recognizes that the coherence ascribed to cultural and subcultural communities, as well as any associated activism, has an important imaginary facet and that such groupings involve an ongoing practice of becoming as well as being (Hall 2000, 706).

As with the terms "transgender" and "queer," there is a multiplicity of conceptualizations and analyses of what is meant by the "ordinary" and the "every-day" (Bennett 2005; de Certeau 1984; Featherstone 1991, 1995; Highmore 2002; Inglis 2005; Lefebvre 1991). There is a substantial canon of theoretical work which, among much else, recognizes the heterogeneity of individuals' inner and outer lives. This chapter follows David Inglis' figuring of the terms "ordinary" and "every-day" as simply referring to the "stuff from which our everyday lives are made" (2005, 1). Despite this chapter's furnishing of a fantastical cartoon in the form of *Adventure Time* as a case study, its prime concern is with "those quieter, less heroic, and less politically conspicuous" aspects of daily living, to borrow from the ethnographer Andre Cavalcante's (2018, 8) work on media and transgender belonging in everyday life; that assemblage of phenomena that is taken for granted, which, despite seemingly banal and of little consequence, is arguably both diagnostic and constitutive of the wider social and cultural order.

Finally, on the subject of positionality, I write from the standpoint of a queer, white, feminist, cisgender woman, and trans ally, strongly committed to promoting equity and social justice for the trans community, as well as gender equity and social justice more generally. In no way do I claim to speak on behalf of the broader queer and trans communities: the problematics posed by this chapter are not meant to be prescriptive but are offered simply for consideration.

TRANS TYPECASTING

A threat, a spectacle, an object of derision, or invisible. These, traditionally, have been the four main categories of transgender representation (or non-representation) on film and television (Cavalcante 2018; GLAAD 2012; Keegan 2013; Serano 2016). Now, citizens of many Western cultures are in a state of cultural transition from a time when trans media representations were rare and usually wildly derogatory, to an era involving an increase in both the quantity and quality of texts and images. For instance, in its analysis and forecast of LGBTQ characters on broadcast networks, cable networks, and streaming services in the 2018–2019 television season, GLAAD – a U.S. media monitoring the organization – identified 26 regular and recurring transgender and gender diverse characters on scripted broadcast, cable, and streaming programs, nine more than the 17 characters of the season before (2018). This includes 17 trans women, five trans men, and four non-binary characters (2018, 28). Yet, as Keegan (2013) argues, the "proliferation of signs" associated with the increasing number of transgender bodies and lives available for consumption in Western media should not be read as indicative of transgender equality in either a material or representational sense.

Observing that several years ago the simple fact of having a trans person on the screen might have seemed cool, edgy, and even progressive, trans writer Meredith Talusan (2016) nominates eight tired and unoriginal tropes in millennial media she argues should be retired: (1) the trans person as a crisis for cisgender people, (2) the gratuitous trans nude shot, (3) the token trans actor with a bit part, especially when the lead is a cisgender man, (4) the trans person whose sole goal in life is to be loved by a cisgender person, (5) the mentally unstable trans woman, (6) the hot girl who turns out to be trans to the disgust of cisgender men, (7) the straight cisgender men who dress up as women just for laughs, and (8) the huge imbalance in representations of trans women as opposed to trans men. Other representational clichés identified by trans members of the entertainment industry such as actors, critics, and talent managers, include an over-focus on surgery, transition, and coming out stories, and the tendency to cast trans women in sassy sidekick roles, like "the best friend that also has to enter a room and be like 'I'm a tranny'" (Beltran cited in D'Sa 2017). Evidence that entertainment media producers are still in the business of perpetuating trans stereotypes can also be found in the number of trans performers who report missing out on trans roles because casting directors and producers have told them that they don't look trans enough (D'Sa 2017; Levinson 2016; Tejada 2017). Having sketched general trends in contemporary trans-related media representations, the next section tightens focus and looks in more detail at two particular trans-related regimes of representation or "tropes": those involving tragedy and those involving trailblazing and celebrity.

EVERYTHING IS AWFUL, "EVERYTHING IS AWESOME"

The tragic trope and the celebrity or trailblazer trope have been chosen for analysis because: (1) they have emerged as prominent themes in contemporary media culture, (2) without a critical lens, they could easily be categorized as unambiguously "trans-friendly" (that is, while they seem designed to mobilize affective viewer responses such as sympathy and admiration, as opposed to contempt and ridicule, they are still rigid, simplistic, and binary-oriented), and (3) because they provide a strong contrast with the types of representations that can be found in *Adventure Time* and that are highlighted in the next section.

Tragedy and Trauma

The tragic trans trope involves representations of transgender individuals who suffer from mental health problems, self-harm, commit or attempt to commit suicide, or are bullied, bashed, sexually assaulted, or even murdered (Cavalcante 2018; Halberstam 2005; Keegan 2013). The potential problems associated with media representations of transgender people enduring various types of suffering and tragedy are not necessarily that these framings do not accurately represent many people's lived realities. Indeed, such depictions comport with research findings showing high rates of discrimination and violence against trans folks, as well as high rates of self-harm and attempted suicide by trans individuals (Lees 2017; Seaman 2016; Strauss et al. 2017; Weale 2017). That said, the tragic trans trope has been widely critiqued on account of what are perceived to be the cynical motivations of media producers who are usually cisgender and who are criticized for exploiting trauma experienced by trans people, and who endorse, either deliberately or inadvertently, the contentious "wrong body" trope.[3]

Superstars, Trailblazers, and Other Winners

Coverage about trans individuals as celebrities and trailblazers is reminiscent of the "Everything Is Awesome" song from *The Lego Movie* (2014), which insists citizens plaster rictus beams over anything resembling a personal or social problem, and contrasts with the "everything is awful" resonance of the tragic trans trope. That said, these tropes are frequently deployed together in that the achievements of a famous trans pioneer are often framed as being particularly worthy of celebration because of the tragic ordeals they had to overcome along the way. For example, the *Time* "tipping point" edition details Cox's attempt to get rid of her "impure" thoughts by "downing a bottle of pills" as a sixth-grader in its story, applauding her for subsequently becoming a "sought-after celebrity" and "unlikely icon" (Steinmetz and Gray 2014). Further, while gushy accounts of Cox's red carpet successes are certainly a thematic improvement on narratives depicting trans people as sexual predators, psycho killers, crass punch lines, or murder victims, they are arguably no more nuanced.

Cox (2015) publicly acknowledges that many aspects of her existence are not representative of the wider experience of transgender persons. Yet, consider the subtext of her response to a 6-year-old who attended a trans event in San Francisco, after they publicly asked Cox a question about being teased at school. Cox's reply, which reportedly received a rapturous audience response, was: "You're beautiful. You're perfect just the way you are. I was bullied too, and I was called all kinds of names, and now I'm a big TV star" (Steinmetz and Gray 2014). Without detracting from the warmth of Cox's response, the "success is the best revenge"

---

3 The "wrong body" trope refers to the idea that trans people feel "trapped" in the bodies they were born into. This trope has been critiqued as being simplistic, reductive, pathologizing, essentialist, and not representative of many trans people's experiences of their bodies, as well as shoring up the sorts of binary framings of gender that push surgery and other medical interventions. For discussion, please see: Keegan 2013; Kristy 2015; Talusan 2016.

subtext of the remark is dubious in its implication that the best way to respond to structural oppression is to beat the structural oppressors at their own game: more fame, more firsts, and more fortune. In addition to placing the onus on the trans person to intervene in the bullying and negativity by becoming an object of envy, it is a strategy that can only ever work for a fortunate few. As Premila D'Sa (2017) observes on the topic of transgender media visibility, while most people can now name a transgender actor, it is usually always Cox.

In the early periods of a social justice movement aimed at supporting and improving the prospects of a highly marginalized group, an initially useful strategy would almost certainly include affirmative action of various stripes. As part of such strategies, manifestly positive and perhaps conspicuously pedagogical or educational texts and images might be offered as a correction to years of neglect and patently negative texts full of vilification and misinformation. Nonetheless, even the most well-intentioned of such approaches arguably defeats the purpose if it inadvertently fortifies the negative side of the good/bad binary. Cogent here is Hall's work on representing difference and his consideration of the limits of positive representational practices in an effective politics of representation (1997, 225–6). Hall's suggestive argument is that, while presenting positive images does have the advantage of "righting the balance" because they invert the binary opposition, privilege the subordinate term, and sometimes read the negative as positive, the binaries remain in place and meanings continue to be framed by these binaries (1997, 272–4).

In summary, both the tragic trans trope and the celebratory trans trope regimes of representation are open to criticism for excluding important aspects of trans experiences. The former does not comport with the trans performer and writer Ora Uzel's call for representations of transgender characters "as people who survive and people who thrive" (2014), while the latter doesn't reflect the lives of those average trans people. So how might media representations of trans and gender diverse people be expanded on the other side of *Time*'s trans tipping point? Cox has called for depictions of trans folk who "don't necessarily align with cisnormative beauty standards" (2015). Yet, for transgender media representations to truly be more representative of the lived realities of trans individuals, it may not be sufficient to simply include a diversity of aesthetics or even a multiplicity of genders. In addition, it might also be useful to see a focus on the transgender *ordinary* as opposed to the strong, contemporary focus on the transgender *extraordinary*, in forms such as tragedy, fame, or singularity, all of which miss the humor, the banality, and sometimes even the non-eventful irrelevance that can be part of being trans (or at least part of being trans, part of the time).

It might seem counterintuitive that rendering someone's trans-ness irrelevant could be a positive move, which is why it is critical to draw a distinction between "irrelevant" and "invisible." In the context of this chapter, "invisible" can be understood as referring to both a complete absence of representation in some contexts, such as a scarcity of trans leads in romantic comedies; and also a lack of certain kinds of representations, such as a dearth of trans characters whose defining characteristic is something other than their trans-ness (for example, the fact that they are seahorse experts, collect Rubik's cubes, once made the TikTok leaderboard, etcetera—that is, hobbies or characteristics that are completely unrelated to being trans). The notion of "structuring absences" is helpful for understanding both these types of trans invisibilities. As Richard Dyer (2002) explains, a structuring absence does not refer to a thing which is simply not in the text, or which the critic thinks ought to be in the text. He describes it as "an issue, or even a set of facts or an argument, that a text cannot ignore, but which it deliberately skirts round or otherwise avoids, thus creating the biggest 'holes' in the text, fatally, revealingly misshaping the organic whole" (2002, 83). Also, cogent here is the argument that being excluded from the culture of representation amounts to "symbolic annihilation" (Gross cited in Himberg 2017, 10). Thus, in the context of this chapter, "invisible" refers to trans themes being conspicuously absent, ignored, or deliberately excised from representation, while "irrelevance" refers to the recognition that there are more important or interesting things to highlight about a person than their gender. Or, relatedly, that gender is just one of many identities a person may have and choose to foreground or background at any given moment. An unusual exemplar of the type of approach under discussion will be offered in the form of the cartoon *Adventure Time*.

ADVENTURE TIME'S UNDERSTATED GENDER OUTLAWS

Created by the animator Pendleton Ward, *Adventure Time* began airing as a series on Cartoon Network in the United States from 2010. Eight years, 10 series, and nearly 300 episodes later, the multi-award-winning show concluded in 2018. *Adventure Time* has been one of Cartoon Network's most popular programs, drawing—in the United States alone—between two to three million viewers per week during its rating heyday (circa 2011 to 2013) (Feeney 2013), while also attracting a diverse, international fan base. Set on a post-apocalyptic Earth roughly 1,000 years into the future, *Adventure Time*'s Land of Ooo is inhabited by a hallucinogenic variety of mutant species whose communities, kingdoms, and various interdimensional planes ooze and sprout from a scarred and devastated landscape. The series follows the adventures of a tightly-knit group of friends informally led by a teenaged boy called Finn (ostensibly the world's last surviving human), and his adopted brother Jake (a magic dog with shapeshifting powers). Other central characters of note include: BMO, pronounced "bee-mow," a sentient videogame console who lives with Finn and Jake in their treehouse fort;

Princess Bubblegum, a daffy genius and the ruler of the Candy Kingdom; Marceline the Vampire Queen, an electric bass-playing half-demon, half-human loner who used to date Princess Bubblegum; and The Ice King, an ostensibly evil wizard who lives in an ice palace in a quasi-marriage with a penguin called Gunter.

At first blush, the plot of the average *Adventure Time* episode seems relatively straightforward: a champion or champions (usually Finn and his friends) complete quests, face-off with villains, rescue or assist vulnerable beings in distress, and deal with various other kingdom-threatening disasters. Yet, while there is nothing out of the ordinary about these tropes in the abstract, *Adventure Time*'s approach to fleshing out the detail is idiosyncratic. For instance: one of Jake's quests involves fulfilling a lifelong ambition to experience what it feels like to be a brick in a brick shack when the shack falls down; one of the villains is a deer that rampages through the Candy Kingdom using its sticky orange saliva to imprison citizens in its underground lair; the vulnerable beings in need of rescue include a sleuth of raver bears on the verge of being turned into feces because they are partying in a monster's stomach; and one of the kingdom-threatening disasters is an immortal candy sphinx with mind-control powers cooked up by Princess Bubblegum from a recipe which included one of her baby teeth as well as some algebra dusted off a blackboard.

These types of storylines have prompted viewers and reviewers to effuse, and also sometimes to scratch their heads in bewilderment. A small but growing number of scholars, myself included (Flowerday 2014; Jane 2015, 2018; Olson and Reinhard 2017), have also turned their attention to the cartoon, focusing primarily on its transgender and queer thematic content. While a small handful of commentators in scholarly and media contexts have noted the show's trans themes (Dunn 2016; Flowerday 2014; Four rusted horses 2012; Kappel 2013; Olson and Reinhard 2017; peachipanda 2014), this focus has mostly only been in passing. However, this is not surprising given that *Adventure Time* is hardly a program about trans issues in the way that *Transparent* is a program about trans issues. For instance, the word "transgender" is never mentioned and there is only one character who can relatively easily be read as trans. Yet, it is precisely its understated approach that arguably makes *Adventure Time*'s transgender representations so powerful in that what it underplays is not so much the existence of gender diversity (there is plenty) but the noteworthiness of gender diversity (it is rarely remarked upon at all).

The most obvious character to discuss in terms of *Adventure Time*'s transgender inclusions is Princess Cookie, an ostensibly male chocolate chip cookie who desperately wants to live as a female princess. Facing belittling stigma and suffering what has been read as "extreme gender dysphoria" (peachipanda 2014), in the episode "Princess Cookie" (season 4, episode 13), the titular character holds hostages in a candy store before attempting suicide by jumping off a cliff and ending up straitjacketed in a psychiatric institution. The sympathies of *Adventure Time*'s makers seem to lie firmly with Princess Cookie, and the episode's grim presentation of the potential consequences of bullying, oppressive gender regimes, mental illness, and institutionalization may be a useful and potentially educational addition to a cartoon primarily aimed at children. That said, the episode is still subject to the limitations discussed above in relation to the tragic trans trope. As such, the Princess Cookie character and episode will be placed to one side in favor of the characters of BMO and Gunter, arguably more interesting from a transgender studies perspective.

BMO, the sentient games console who lives with Finn and Jake in their treehouse, identifies as both female and male, is referred to by other characters using both male and female pronouns as well as by both feminine and masculine pet names, and is voiced by a woman. True to the series' overall ethos of "social androgyny" (Jane 2015, 234), BMO enjoys activities stereotypically coded as masculine, such as skateboarding, solo adventuring, and inviting groups of "bikini babes" over for dance parties. But BMO also engages in activities stereotypically coded as feminine, such as cooking, cleaning, and ensuring their chosen family members Finn and Jake take their baths. In one episode, BMO sings a wishful song about being pregnant while wearing a cup containing an egg strapped to their midriff and referring to their "perfect body," while, in another, they are depicted wearing a spotty, pink, bra-style bandeau and admitting, "I was too embarrassed to get a bra fitting. I know they're professionals, but it's just too intimate" (season 8, episode 7).

Also interesting—and endearingly queer—is that BMO's romantic attachments vary in terms of gender and species. For instance, in one episode BMO falls in love with and agrees to marry a masculine-sounding air bubble after the couple spend some time parenting a lost baby called either Ricky or Sparkle (it's a long and weird story), while, in another, BMO refers to a previous romance with a scarlet lipstick-wearing chicken called Lorraine. In these respects, the characterization of BMO comports with Susan Stryker's case that transgender phenomena interrogate and extend received wisdom, including those in queer studies and gay and lesbian communities, about the multiplicity of ways "bodies, identities, and desires can be interwoven" (2006, 8), as well as Jane McCredie's observation stemming from her survey of sex-related science that humans exist not in binaries but in "a dizzying array" of possibilities (2011, 11–12).

Ultimately, however, sex and gender are irrelevant, both intratextually and extratextually, for BMO and for the many beings who adore them. The intertextual insignificance of BMO's gender can, therefore, be seen as having compelling extratextual significance, in that the makers of *Adventure Time* reinforce the notion that gender lies on a non-binary continuum and that, while gender might be part of a person, it is not all a person is. From a meta-perspective, the character of BMO also issues a strong invitation to viewers to take a sort of grounded theory approach to gender, showing that, at least for some, gender is fluid, self-determined, performed, and an enjoyable work in progress. *Adventure Time*'s framing of gender and identity as aqueous and opt-in- and opt-out-able, rather than fixed and inflicted, may not feel as spacious and liberating to those trans viewers who, as Judith Butler puts it, "do not want to be romanticized as existing 'beyond all categories'" but instead require "a clear gender category within a binary frame" in order to "make life livable" (Ahmed 2016, 490). This, however, simply highlights the way the multiplicity of trans experiences invites diversity in representation.

In contrast with BMO, Gunter the penguin does not play with gender so much as it is unknown to other characters and viewers if Gunter has one sex and gender, a number of sexes and genders, or a lack of either sex or gender. Once again, however, the most interesting thing about this information gap is how uninteresting it is to everyone else. Gunter is generally referred to using male pronouns and their signature cry of "wenk!" is voiced by a male actor. Nevertheless, the Ice King often refers to Gunter affectionately using feminized pet names such as "girl" and "sweetie," and they are known to wear feminized clothing and accessories, including wigs and skirts. In the episode "The Chamber of Frozen Blades" (2011), Gunter is revealed to be pregnant and, after experiencing "the horrifying beauty of birth," produces an egg out of which hatches a glowing pink kitten. One character expresses a short burst of surprise at the possibility that Gunter's sex is female prompting the Ice King to glance momentarily at his soulmate's nether regions. This interest, however, quickly wanes and life goes on, with no one, not even Gunter, considering it relevant to discuss again.

BMO and Gunter are exemplars of *Adventure Time*'s anti-essentialist sensibility, in that sex, gender, and identity are routinely depicted as volatile, complex, poly, indeterminate, and having a status of "whatever whatevs," to use one of Finn's expressions. When it comes to enumerating the significant forms of gendered personhood, the cartoon has no problem "counting past two," as Stryker puts it (2006, 8), in those instances where counting is possible at all. Furthermore, BMO and Gunter sit within a far broader disruption of gender stereotypes in the cartoon in terms of characters' personalities, appearances, social roles, interpersonal relationships, and identities. Given that I have discussed this at length in previous work (Jane 2015), this chapter sketches just a few examples of how the series normalizes and celebrates gender variance, nonconformance, and subversion. These occur via its inclusion of:

- Four episodes in which the genders of the binary characters are swapped, without initially attracting attention to this explicitly.

- Multiple themes of metamorphoses, reinvention, and transition in which characters have adventures and misadventures which radically alter their appearances, statuses, genders, sexes, and identities (most of their fellow citizens in the Land of Ooo quickly adjust).
- Ostensibly male characters engaged in maternal activities, including conceiving and giving birth. Perhaps the most salient example is in episode 177 (season 6, episode 20), in which it is revealed that Jake was born from his father's skull after his father was inseminated by a shape-shifting, male alien.
- A framing of people's usual roles and identities as performed rather than innate and natural (for example, in one episode, Finn and Jake self-consciously attempt to perform as human and dog, respectively). This is reminiscent of activist efforts to pique consideration of the fact that, despite its routine exnomination, "cis" is still an identity that may involve a degree of performativity (though it is difficult to imagine seeing a character coming out as cisgender on primetime television any time soon).
- An avoidance of "othering" and an ethics of care and diversity which involves not just patronizingly "tolerating" the eccentric and "enfreaked" (Stryker 2017, xii), but warmly embracing and "grinding" in "phat party-clubs"[4] with them.
- Non-stereotypical gender aesthetics and social androgyny. For example, when a man who calls himself the "King of Ooo" successfully runs against Princess Bubblegum in a ballot, he begins referring to himself as "the one true princess of Ooo" and "the Princess King of Ooo," while wearing Princess Bubblegum's frilly pink clothes and a long pink wig and joyfully shouting, "Tell Bubblegum I wear her nightgown! Tell everyone!" (season 7, episode 2).
- Various queer romances and connections, including hero crushes and homoeroticism.
- A focus on the love and support offered by found and chosen families as opposed to biological families and families of origin. This might resonate with trans viewers given studies showing that nearly half of transgender and gender-nonconforming individuals experience a moderate or high amount of rejection when coming out to their families of origin, with the likelihood of suicide attempts or substance abuse correlating with rates of family rejection (Seaman 2016). I am not suggesting the family project be abandoned entirely. It is, arguably, both useful and validating to depict alternative sources of family-style love and support.

---

4 This is the locution used in season 2, episode 21.

This section provided brief examples of some of the various ways *Adventure Time*'s imaginative reinvention rather than a simple inversion of gender stereotypes exemplifies the sort of approach that might avoid the pitfalls of the positive/negative representational strategy described by Hall (1997, 272–4). Although *Adventure Time*'s treatment of gender does not seem intended as a serious treatise, neither is it played for cruel, exploitative laughs. Instead, gender is played for pleasure, the pleasure of having the freedom to adopt gendered roles, states, and signifiers without having to fear the sorts of brutal category policing that tends to occur in the real world when people and things turn up in the wrong category, or in no category at all. Such representations are useful for avoiding tragic trans narratives because the sorts of people who might be maligned and mistreated as gender outlaws by gender defenders[5] (Bornstein 1994, 74) in real-life contexts are free to go about their gender-bending, blending, and affirming in peace. In the Land of Ooo, the cultural order is rarely threatened by the unstable, the hybrid, or the uncategorizable because making sense of and peace with instability, difference, and sweet weirdness is the order of the day.

THE TRANSORDINARY

In this section, the textual analysis of *Adventure Time* is used as the basis for a more general discussion about the value of media representations that capture three potentially interrelated aspects of "ordinary" as it relates to trans issues. Namely: (1) the depiction of gender diversity as ordinary and normal, in the normative sense; that is, being depicted as a state that is socially sanctioned and desirable, (2) the depiction of trans individuals whose trans-ness is paid some attention but who are depicted doing relatively banal, trans-related activities[6] rather than having people's transgender status constantly positioned at the epicenter of various types of high drama or attention, and (3) the depiction of gender diversity as visible in a range of forms but as mostly or entirely irrelevant, such as in the British television series *Hit and Miss* whose contract killer protagonist goes at least part of the way toward constituting a trans character whose trans-ness is not the sole driver of plot progression. Given that the first of these points is mostly self-explanatory, only points (2) and (3) are to be explicated in further detail.

---

5   Kate Bornstein defines a gender defender as "someone who actively, or by knowing inaction, defends the status quo of the existing gender system, and thus perpetuates the violence of male privilege and all its social extensions" (1994, 74).

6   For a nonfictional example, see Olivia Jaramillo's (2017) account of an average day in her life as a trans woman serving in the U.S. Air Force.

Here it is cogent to refer to Cavalcante's (2018) and Viviane K. Namaste's (2000) objection to the fact that the mundane, quiet, and domestic aspects of trans experiences are frequently overlooked or dismissed not only by media producers but also by researchers and theorists. *Pace* those who argue that trans-ness and queerness is or ought to be always or predominantly coupled with radical politics (Warner 2000; Duggan 2002; Halberstam 2011), Cavalcante observes that even the "queerest of the queer" gay men, lesbians, bisexuals, and trans individuals go food shopping, make dinner, and sometimes do "normal stuff" (2018, 19). Namaste, meanwhile, writes fiercely about transgender being more than performance or a theory that explains how gender works:

> Our lives and our bodies are [...] much less glamorous than all that. They are forged in details of everyday life [...] constituted in the mundane and uneventful. [...] Although banal, these events merit consideration: anything less produces a knowledge of little practical relevance to our lives. (Namaste 2000, 1–2)

While noting Namaste's reservations about the tendency for scholars to over-theorize trans issues, it is still worth making the point that a focus on the transgender ordinary instead of, or at least in addition to, the transgender extraordinary in media representations makes good sense theoretically in that it might be one way of dismantling the "spectacle of otherness" (Hall 1997) that tends to generate both fetishistic fixation and damaging vilification.[7] The contemporary shift to representing trans subjects as fascinating and exotic (and this brings to mind Cox and Jenner on the covers of *Time* and *Vanity Fair*) has not put an end to hate and vituperation. Indeed, if we subscribe to Hall's purview, we should entertain the possibility that the former framings of positively-valenced trans extraordinariness might be advertently fortifying the latter. It is sobering, for instance, that in the years since *Time*'s tipping point declaration, Meg-John Barker (2017) has identified not a brave, new, post-gender world, but a transgender moral panic. It would be useful, too, to conduct further research inquiries into whether every day or casual representations of trans individuals might provide a useful counter to everyday or casual transphobia (Dexaeris 2015).

Another strong argument in favor of including more of the transordinary in media is that there is good evidence that these are the sorts of images many transgender media consumers wish to see, or at least to see more of. Cavalcante's interviewees identify "transgender everydayness [as] an object of desire" (2018, 24–5) and report looking to media texts as they manage, navigate, and overcome the challenges and risks associated with routine daily tasks, such as running errands or using public restrooms. Yet:

---

7 Charles Goehring (Chapter 2, this book) goes over examples of trans fetishism on scripted primetime television series. *Ed.*

> It is exactly the every-day that participants felt was woefully missing from media representations of transgender. [...] Over and again they expressed a desire to see people not defined by their transgender identity, but rather as people who, as they said, "happen to be" transgender. (Cavalcante 2018, 22, 24)

My case is that it is this quality—of just happening to be transgender—that could be captured via a regime of representation focused on the interrelated aspects of the transordinary as described in this chapter.

CONCLUSION

Attempting to settle on a formula for transgender media representations that achieves the Goldilocks' standard of being neither too focused, nor not focused enough is a difficult or nearly impossible enterprise. Misrepresentation (and complaints about misrepresentation) is understood to be a general condition of all representation (McKee 2005). That is, it would be impossible to settle on one representation of trans that is "just right," such that all or most transgender folks applaud it as striking exactly the right balance between accuracy and intrusion, sympathy and paternalism, progressiveness and prescriptiveness, seriousness and humor, and so on. As is evident in debates around homonormativity and transnormativity, even a seemingly innocuous representation, such as a scene in which a trans person stays home to cook a meal for their partner, risks accusations of objectionable apoliticality (Cavalcante 2018; Duggan 2002; Vipond 2015; Warner 2000). In the politics of trans representation, as in the larger politics of queer counter-publics, there will likely always be tension between "the pull of queerness and ordinariness, sameness and difference, closeness and distance, stability and instability, and outsiderness and insiderness" (Cavalcante 2018, 22–3). Also, the ordinary and the irrelevant are, by their nature, embedded and difficult to manifest, to see, and to appraise. Yet, the difficulty of ever finding one perfect and perfectly positive representation of trans need not distract us from continuing to experiment with and expand the repertoire of trans images circulating in popular culture in the hope of reaching the point where, as Uzel puts it, "we think no more of a transgender character being in a storyline than we might think of a black person on *Star Trek* or a short person in *Star Wars*" (2014).

The trans community deserves a multiplicity of representations, some of which focus exclusively on telling uniquely trans stories. This chapter, however, has argued in favor of the benefits to be gained, especially at this particular moment in time, from approaches rooted in what I have called the "transordinary" as exemplified by the representations of gender in *Adventure Time*. Some might find it hard to imagine a character in a mainstream television series discovering, in the middle of season two, that their life companion is not the gender they thought they were and responding with a barely interested "Fuh" (as per the Ice King's final word on Gunter's sex and gender status) before getting back to whatever they were doing beforehand. Yet, consider Osgood Fielding III's famous reply of "nobody's perfect" when his *fiancée* Daphne reveals that they are actually Fielding's *fiancé* Jerry in the final scene of *Some Like It Hot* (1959). Alongside transgender stories about trailblazing, triumph, and tragedy, there would likely be benefits if there were more transgender stories in which gender is triaged as being of absolutely no consequence when it comes to characters' decisions about who should share their lives and their treehouse forts.

REFERENCES

Adventure Time. 2010. Created by Pendleton Ward. Cartoon Network Studios, 2010–2018.
Ahmed, Sara. 2016. "Interview with Judith Butler." *Sexualities* 19, no. 4: 482–92.
Barker, Meg-John. 2017. "A Trans Review of 2017: The Year of Transgender Moral Panic." *Conversation*, December 28, 2017. https://theconversation.com/a-trans-review-of-2017-the-year-of-transgender-moral-panic-89272
Bennett, Andy. 2005. *Culture and Everyday Life*. Thousand Oaks: SAGE.
Bornstein, Kate. 1994. *Gender Outlaw: On Men, Women and the Rest of Us*. London: Routledge.
Cavalcante, Andre. 2018. *Struggling for Ordinary: Media and Transgender Belonging in Everyday Life*. New York: New York University Press.
Cox, Laverne. 2015. "Official Laverne Cox Tumblr." *Tumblr*, June 2, 2015. http://lavernecox.tumblr.com/post/120503412651/on-may-29-2014-the-issue-of-timemagazine
D'Sa, Premila. 2017. "What Trans People Think About Trans Representation in Film and TV." *Vice*, November 13, 2017. https://www.vice.com/en_au/article/ne3498/what-trans-people-think-about-trans-representation-in-film-and-tv
De Certeau, Michel. 1984. *The Practice of Everyday Life*. Berkeley, CA: University of California Press.
Dexaeris, Stefani. 2015. "Casual Transphobia in My Media?" *Huffington Post*, November 7, 2015. https://www.huffingtonpost.com/delia-melody/casual-transphobia-in-my-_b_8462272.html
Duggan, Lisa. 2002. "The New Homonormativity: The Sexual Politics of Neoliberalism." In *Materializing Democracy: Toward a Revitalized Cultural Politics*, edited by Russ Castronovo and Dana D. Nelson, 175–94. Durham: Duke University Press.
Dunn, Eli. 2016. "*Steven Universe*, Fusion Magic, and the Queer Cartoon Carnivalesque." *Gender Forum: An Internet Journal for Gender Studies* 56: 44–57.
Dyer, Richard. 2002. *The Matter of Images: Essays on Representation*, 2nd edition. London and New York: Routledge.
Featherstone, Mike. 1991. *Consumer Culture and Postmodernism*. London: SAGE.
———. 1995. *Undoing Culture: Globalization, Postmodernism and Identity*. London: SAGE.
Feeney, Nolan. 2013. "The Weird World of *Adventure Time* Comes Full Circle." *Time*, March 29, 2013. http://entertainment.time.com/2013/03/29/the-weird-world-of-adventure-time-comes-full-circle/
Flowerday, Kaelyn. 2014. "Learning to Read (Gender): Children's Animation and the New Heterosexism." *Anthós* 6, no. 1: 73–91.

Four rusted horses. 2012. "Forum: Princess Cookie?" *Adventure Time with Finn and Jake Wiki.* http://adventuretime.wikia.com/wiki/Forum:Princess_Cookie%3F

GLAAD. 2012. "Victims or Villains: Examining Ten Years of Transgender Images on Television." https://www.glaad.org/publications/victims-or-villains-examining-ten-years-transgender-images-television

———. 2018. "Where We Are On TV: 2018–2019." https://glaad.org/files/WWAT/WWAT_GLAAD_2018-2019.pdf

Halberstam, Jack. 2005. *In a Queer Time and Place: Transgender Bodies, Subcultural Lives.* New York: New York University Press.

———. 2011. *The Queer Art of Failure.* Durham: Duke University Press.

———. 2018. *Trans*: A Quick and Quirky Account of Gender Variability.* Oakland: University of California Press.

Hall, Stuart. 1997. "The Spectacle of the 'Other.'" In *Representation: Cultural Representations and Signifying Practices*, edited by Stuart Hall, 223–90. Thousand Oaks: SAGE.

———. 2000. "Cultural Identity and Cinematic Representation." In *Film and Theory: An Anthology*, edited by Robert Stam and Toby Miller, 704–14. Malden, MA: Blackwell Publishing.

Highmore, Ben, ed. 2002. *The Everyday Life Reader.* New York: Routledge.

Himberg, Julia. 2017. *The New Gay for Pay: The Sexual Politics of American Television Production.* Austin, Texas: University of Texas Press.

Inglis, David. 2005. *Culture and Everyday Life.* New York: Routledge.

Jane, Emma. A. 2015. "'Gunter's a Woman?!'—Doing and Undoing Gender in *Adventure Time*." *Journal of Children and Media* 9, no. 2: 231–47.

———. 2018. "It's Not the End of the World: Post-Apocalyptic Flourishing in Cartoon Network's *Adventure Time*." In *Mimetic Theory and Film*, edited by Paolo Diego Bubbio and Chris Fleming. New York: Bloomsbury.

Jaramillo, Olivia. 2017. "Ordinary Life." *Transgender Universe*, July 11, 2017. http://archive.transgenderuniverse.com/2017/07/11/ordinary-life/

Kappel, Heather. 2013. "Princess Cookie." *Adventure Time Analyzed*, May 6, 2013. http://adventuretimeanalyzed.tumblr.com/post/49801538639/princess-cookie

Keegan, Cael M. 2013. "Moving Bodies: Sympathetic Migrations in Transgender Narrativity." *Genders* 57. https://www.colorado.edu/gendersarchive1998-2013/2013/06/01/moving-bodies-sympathetic-migrations-transgender-narrativity

Kristy, Ethan. 2015. "Why Be Happy When You Could be Normal? Deconstructing the Transnormative." *ethankristy.com*, September 30, 2015. http://www.ethankristy.com/essay-trans-normative/

Lees, Paris. 2017. "Trans People Already Face a Hostile World. Now the Media Is Making It Worse." *The Guardian*, November 18, 2017. https://www.theguardian.com/global/commentisfree/2017/nov/17/trans-people-children-suicide-bullying-rightwing-media

Lefebvre, Henri. 1991. *The Critique of Everyday Life, Volume 1.* Translated by John Moore. London: Verso.

Levinson, Dana A. 2016. "You Don't Look Trans Enough." *Huffington Post*. September 18, 2016. https://www.huffingtonpost.com/entry/you-dont-look-trans-enough_us_57df1bfde4b0d5920b5b2f1d

McCredie, Jane. 2011. *Making Girls and Boys: Inside the Science of Sex.* Sydney, NSW: University of New South Wales Press.

McKee, Alan. 2003. *Textual Analysis.* Cambridge, MA: Cambridge University Press.

———. 2005. *The Public Sphere*. Cambridge, MA: Cambridge University Press.

Meyerowitz, Joanne. 2004. *How Sex Changed: A History of Transsexuality in the United States*, 2nd edition. Harvard: Harvard University Press.

Namaste, Vivian K. 2000. *Invisible Lives: The Erasure of Transsexual and Transgendered People*. Chicago: University of Chicago Press.

Olson, Christopher J. and Carrielynn D. Reinhard. 2017. "A Computer Boy or a Computer Girl? *Adventure Time*, BMO, and Gender Fluidity." In *Heroes, Heroines, and Everything In Between: Challenging Gender and Sexuality Stereotypes in Children's Entertainment Media*, edited by Carrielynn D. Reinhard and Christopher J. Olson, 177–94. London: Lexington Books.

peachipanda. 2014. "Princess Cookie; Themes of Gender Dysphoria and the Trope of the Tragic Trans Character: Queer Content in *Adventure Time*." *Medium*, May 13, 2014. https://medium.com/@peachiipanda/princess-cookie-themes-of-gender-dysphoria-and-the-trope-of-the-tragic-trans-character-58c5b46a837e

Seaman, Andrew M. 2016. "For Trans People, Family Rejection Tied to Suicide Attempts, Substance Abuse." *Reuters*, May 28, 2016, https://www.reuters.com/article/us-health-transgender-suicide-rejection/for-trans-people-family-rejection-tied-to-suicide-attempts-substance-abuse-idUSKCN0YI22T

Serano, Julia. 2016. *Whipping Girl: A Transsexual Woman on Sexism and the Scapegoating of Femininity*, 2nd edition. Berkeley: Seal Press.

Steinmetz, Katy and Eliza Gray. 2014. "America's Transition." *Time* 183, no. 22, 38–46.

Strauss, Penelope, Angus Cook, Ashleigh Lin, and Sam Winter. 2017. "Almost Half of Trans Young People Try to End Their Lives. How Can We Reduce This Alarming Statistic?" *The Conversation*, September 1, 2017. https://theconversation.com/almost-half-of-trans-young-people-try-to-end-their-lives-how-can-we-reduce-this-alarming-statistic-83221

Stryker, Susan. 2006. "(De)Subjugated Knowledges: An Introduction to Transgender Studies." In *The Transgender Studies Reader*, edited by Susan Stryker and Stephen Whittle, 1–18. New York: Routledge.

———. 2017. *Transgender History: The Roots of Today's Revolution*, revised edition. New York: Seal Press.

Talusan, Meredith. 2016. "8 Trans Tropes We Need to Retire In 2016." *BuzzFeed*, January 11, 2016. https://www.buzzfeed.com/meredithtalusan/tired-trans-tropes-we-need-to-retire-in-2016

Talusan, Meredith, Jacob Tobia, Tiq Milan, and Nico Fonseca. 2016. "Telling Trans Stories beyond 'Born in the Wrong Body.'" *BuzzFeed*, May 15, 2016. https://www.buzzfeed.com/meredithtalusan/telling-trans-stories-beyond-born-in-the-wrong-body?utm_term=.ahD2rEZVr#.auEd4ZnK4

Tejada, Chloe. 2017. "New Ryan Murphy Show Will Have Largest Cast of Transgender Actors Ever." *Huffington Post*, October 26, 2017. http://www.huffingtonpost.ca/2017/10/26/pose-transgender-actors_a_23256770/

Uzel, Ora. 2014. "Tragic Tropes: Transgender Representation in Contemporary Culture." *Geek Melange*, March 7, 2014. http://www.geekmelange.com/2014/03/tragic-tropes-transgender-representation/

Valentine, David. 2007. *Imagining Transgender: An Ethnography of a Category*. Durham, NC: Duke University Press.

Vipond, Evan. 2015. "Resisting Transnormativity: Challenging the Medicalization and Regulation of Trans Bodies." *Theory in Action* 8, no. 2: 21–44.

Warner, Michael. 2000. *The Trouble with Normal: Sex, Politics, and the Ethics of Queer Life*, 2nd edition. Cambridge, MA: Harvard University Press.

Weale, Sally. 2017. "Almost Half of Trans Pupils in the U.K. Have Attempted Suicide, Survey Finds." *The Guardian*, June 27, 2017. https://www.theguardian.com/education/2017/jun/27/half-of-trans-pupils-in-the-uk-tried-to-take-their-own-lives-survey-finds

Yardley, Miranda. 2017. "Transgender, Transtrender, Identity and Validity." *Medium*, August 21, 2017. https://medium.com/@mirandayardley/transgender-transtrender-identity-and-validity-2a7e5f4f8fff

CHAPTER FIVE

Performing as a Trans Reality Star: Chaz Bono and Isis King

BY ERIKA M. THOMAS[1]

INTRODUCTION

The proliferation in the visibility of transgender people in public culture can be described, in Susan Stryker's words, as a "wild profusion of gendered subject positions, spawned by the ruptures of 'woman' and 'man' like an archipelago of identities rising from the sea" (1998, 148). However, these recent and emerging depictions require a cautious analysis. Media and rhetoric scholar John Sloop (2004) warns against the wholesale embracement of all LGBTQ representations. He is cautious of the representations that seemingly highlight and encourage the "de-literalizing aspect of gender ambiguity [...] at the expense of critiquing the very persistent ways in which cultural expectations and mechanisms continue to discipline each of us" (2004, 12). Following Sloop's insights, my research interrogates the roles and casting of two transgender individuals in reality television shows to expose the ways their portrayals utilize scripts and performances to reinforce normative understandings of gender and constrain the subversive potential of trans identities. I conduct a textual analysis of the discourse and framing of performances of transgender contestants in *America's Next Top Model* (*ANTM*) and *Dancing with the Stars* (*DWTS*). I closely study *ANTM*'s season 11 (2008),

---

[1] Erika M. Thomas, Ph.D. Associate Professor, Department of Human Communication Studies, California State University, Fullerton. Email: erthomas@fullerton.edu

which features transgender model Isis King, and season 13 of DWTS (2011), where author and trans activist Chaz Bono participates.

I apply the performative concepts of "faking," "making," and "breaking" (Bell 1999; Conquergood 1998) to trace how the shows depict trans individuals. "Making it" refers to portrayals or perceptions of an individual meeting the social expectations of gender identity, while "breaking it" is about exposing the (de)constructions of gender on the screens, and "faking it" is portraying performances of gender as imitations. I first examine how trans identities "make" and "break," revealing the framings in the shows that are progressive. Next, I look at how the portrayals are illuminated as "fake," tracing the shows' discourse that reaffirms trans individuals as childlike, as in transition, and incomplete contestants unable to succeed in the competitions due to insufficient gender performances. Though there is some potential to "break" gendered assumptions and common representations, the discourse, and narrative of "faking it" direct the storylines of *ANTM* and *DWTS*, undermining trans identities and feeding the cultural notion that gender performance is secondary to essentialist definitions of identity. I conclude by examining the implications of trans inclusion and how the framing of performances can both advance and impede social understanding of trans communities.

THEORETICAL FRAMEWORK

The visibility and various portrayals of identities are crucial to LGBTQ politics (Joyrich 2009, 17). Though some of these portrayals are viewed positively for relaying knowledge about subjectivities, others are criticized for their lack of representational "correctness" (Battles and Hilton-Morrow 2002; Callahan 2009; Manning 2015). It is for this reason that critics must analyze current representations. Following the definition of Adams (2015), here I use "trans" as the most inclusive nomenclature for individuals whose gender is different from the one assigned at birth. Trans representations are now expanding and they are particularly recognizable through public personalities, icons, or characters found in mainstream scripted and unscripted films, television shows, and news programming (Booth 2015; Capuzza and Spencer 2017; Halberstam 2010; Lovelock 2017; Thomas 2017). For example, Lovelock (2017) argues that roles in unscripted and scripted television shows or talk shows have helped propel trans individuals into the limelight. Personalities and celebrities, such as Jazz Jennings, Caitlyn Jenner, Laverne Cox, and Chaz Bono have become relatively well-known figures and household names. Documentaries, reality television shows, and specific texts also address the trans community, and they are credited today as successful examples of representational politics in mainstream media (Booth 2015; McIntyre 2017; Morse 2017; Poole 2017).

In many instances, there are positive representational qualities found in contemporary shows that reflect progression and encourage the acceptance of trans individuals, or that portray complex or genderqueer characters, even though the futurity of trans television has yet been achieved (Capuzza and Spencer 2017; Poole 2017; Siebler 2012; Villarejo 2016). In reality television shows, trans people have also contributed to "supportive representations of certain queer subjectivities" by navigating around the stereotypical performative expectations and the normative framings through tactics like humor and queer expression (Morse 2017, 88). Despite examples of progress, regressive and problematic trends are still locatable in programming, such as underrepresentation, trivialization, silencing, and politicizing, or relying on non-normative storylines or narratives void of diversity (Capuzza and Spencer 2017; Drushel 2017, 20).

The inclusion of trans people in reality television can rupture predictable or limiting frames and traditional discourses or tropes. However, programs often include trans people as long as they remain recognizable and "safe," as bodies in transition, following binary gender norms, and adhering to heteronormativity. Lovelock (2017) argues that for people, like Jazz Jennings and Caitlyn Jenner, their celebrity status articulates codes of sameness in feminine, white, and economically privileged qualifiers, ultimately erasing the visibility of diverse trans subjectivity. Siebler (2012) traces a dominant approach to transgender people as transitioning, therefore maintaining a distinction between sex, gender, and sexuality. Mocarski et al. (2013) examine Chaz Bono's performances and argue that they reinforce hegemonic masculinity and heteronormativity. Booth (2015) studies the tendency of the documentary genre to compromise a subject's gender identity by depicting transition-related surgeries and framing them as a rite of passage and a confirmation of their identity. In short, audience comfort is prioritized at the detriment of varied expressions of trans subjectivities. Given the media's reliance on particular generic characteristics, scripts, and audiences' expectations, portrayals rarely present trans subjectivities without dominant or traditional binary framings, which can "reify strict gender binaries and discipline transgender identities" (Spencer 2015, xv).

Television is an influential channel for relaying messages and ideas that ultimately construct and structure everyday life. Lembo (2007, 464–5) argues that individuals who encounter the medium will evoke a type of televisual knowledge, a behavior influenced by television viewing to facilitate meaning-making and to understand the world. The various investigations referenced above reveal televised representations can inform the public.

Unscripted or reality television shows are a significant component of both national and international television programming, and their format embraces complex frames of hybridity, celebrated stars, and every-day people. Today, reality programming is a "stronghold" in the mass media and a television genre focusing on the everyday, generating representations focused on the ordinary, authentic, and less predictable experience (Andrejevic 2004, 9; Bauwel and Carpentier 2010, 3). Thus, the genre of reality television problematizes and simultaneously constructs representations involving qualities of what is "real" while giving insights into the types of messages and visual representations that are consumable by modern audiences. Furthermore, reality television uniquely establishes and/or relies on a certain level of digital interactivity with its audience given its use of voting by live audiences or at-home viewers, online community discussions, or other interactive strategies and approaches. Therefore, the genre has "a relationship with the politics of audience response" (Holmes 2004b, 149), in some cases, providing empowerment and authority to viewers and inviting audience participation in ways that are far more interactive in audience feedback and response than other television genres. Reality television's elements of audience engagement and its structuring of participatory culture therefore challenges the assumption that reality television only appeals to viewers considered "passive," foolish or simple voyeurs. Holmes (2004a) argues that the blurring of viewer interactivity with the textual subject serves as a justification to engage in audience reception studies alongside textual analyses that examine how "relations between the viewer and text are narrativized on screen" (2004a, 226). Thus, the relevance of audience interactivity can provide indications of approval or resistance toward the representations and portrayals on unscripted television programs.

Given the varied theoretical considerations involved in reality television and its significance, McIntyre argues that this genre's handling of trans representation is particularly influential:

> Reality TV shows that foreground transgender people and themes are important cultural texts in their treatment of gender queerness. Shows that incorporate transgender individuals among a range of cisgender participation bring to light broader social attitudes towards transgender [people] in the given cultural context as well as the positive political potential of this genre. (McIntyre 2017, 90)

The reality qualifier, though not entirely free of fabrications, constructed intentions, deliberate performances, and conflicting reactions from viewers, still carries the impression that this medium actively includes the participation of the general public, casting a selection of particular candidates while also engaging with ordinary members of the population and inviting polysemic readings. McIntyre concludes that the participation, visibility, and representative approaches to trans people are particularly persuasive and can impact "the public's lack of understanding or acceptance of this population, potentially fomenting transphobia and discrimination" (2017, 215).

PERFORMANCE THEORY AND METHODOLOGICAL APPROACH

An examination of reality television's portrayals of performances through performance theory may seem circular or obvious. However, similar to Bell's study (1999), I find that the medium of reality television is "at once 'real' and 'faked,' […] framed as an event by video cameras and then reframed for consuming audiences" (Bell 1999, 174). Storylines are viewed as real, or slightly more real, occurring in supposed every-day locations, and they are viewed as improvised rather than scripted programs, and, yet, most audiences accept the semi-scripted environments, the performative choices of participants, and the intentional cutting, framing, and story-telling by producers and directors. Morse (2017) confirms this generally accepted understanding, arguing that "RTV [reality television] is based on the premise that audiences are watching 'reality,' not mediated performances. However, RTV makes demands on its participants that require carefully calibrated performances" (2017, 170).

Coincidentally, the calibrated and even unintended gender expression of people has been understood as performance, in turn exposing the sex-gender system for what it is, the rigid and regular production or appearance of substance and ontology of gender. Butler (1990) theorizes that sex-gender is always materialized through regulatory norms, whether referential or performative, and operates as citations on the body. However, the sex-gender system can also be subverted. In the case of trans identities, Stryker (2006) illustrates the applicability of Butler's theory stating that:

> A woman, performatively speaking, is one who says she is—and who then does what woman means. The biologically sexed body guarantees nothing; it is necessarily there, a ground for the act of speaking, but it has no deterministic relationship to performative gender. (Stryker 2006, 10)

Butler's theory of performativity (1993) explains the fluidity of gender and reveals the materialization and subversion of sex-gender reification.

Performance theories can be useful to theorize about gender. Conquergood (1998, 31) explains that the definitions of "performance" ranged from *mimesis* (performance as faking) to *poiesis* (performance as making), and finally to *kinesis*, a political form of performance as breaking and remaking. In other words, this concept was first understood as mere imitation, then it was understood as a construction, and, finally, it was seen as a form of dynamism that allows individuals to deconstruct dominant views and discourses. Conquergood critiques approaches of performance that are responsible for "stabilizing the *status quo* and norms and expectations" (1998, 32). According to the author, a performance can transgress by engaging in political struggles and rupturing the static meanings, norms, and traditions. Therefore, performance should not equate with texts and invention, but, instead, it should represent construction and intervention. Bell (1999) adds that the tension between faking, making, and breaking "is both constant and simultaneous," but they also "hold the possibility of doing all at once," revealing the perilous parameters of approaches (Bell 1999, 176). Bell argues that acts become questions of utility seeking to determine what performance does, because they are reflexive, revealing the cultural struggles at stake through the process.

In the next sections, I employ a rhetorical, textual analysis, broadly describing or interpreting the characteristics in the televised text to illustrate how prime time reality television represents trans individuals. Although the reality television genre presents unique opportunities to examine empirical studies of audience response in relation to representations, this analysis follows the approach suggested by Holmes (2004a) to examine the ways that programs ideologically construct performances and discourses around trans participants. Presentations of the findings derive from my identification of representative and performative categories according to the patterns and associations communicated via the text. I analyze the contestants' performances and, more specifically, how the rhetoric surrounding the performances in *ANTM* and *DWTS* are used to frame contestants' performances as "making" it, "breaking" it, or "faking" it. The analysis traces the ways that these representations reveal the performative nature of gender but also the way the portrayals affirm the gender binary and traditional cisgender expectations.

"MAKING" IT AND "BREAKING" IT?

This section examines how the shows frame and emphasize contestants' performances as making it and, therefore, the portrayal is generally confirming and positive. The dancing of Bono on *DWTS* and modeling and King on *ANTM* are used to show them as "making" it, showing them as they wish to be seen, embracing their gender, and including them in the competitions accordingly. Both reality shows contain moments that support the contestants and contribute to revealing the performative origin of the sex-gender binary system as a construction, which exposes its cultural reliance on the essentialist myth that there are only two sexes and two genders. In these instances, as Bell (1999, 176) explains, "Cultural performances can illuminate precarious boundaries," exposing the very values, patterns, and structures that constitute binary identities and leaving them open to scrutiny and critique. However, while the performances of King and Bono, their actions, and the discourse around them reveal progressive ideals and representations, their visibility is not necessarily queer or non-binary and it reifies a gender binary, one grounded in notions of hegemonic femininity and masculinity (Siebler 2012).

On the other hand, the castings of Bono and King operate to broaden social acceptance of trans identities and their advancement, given the history of problematic mediated approaches of trans individuals, including pronoun misuse or the various trivializations or dismissals of trans experiences. Throughout the series and in most of the episodes, King's and Bono's identities were accepted, commended, and mostly respected by many of the contestants, hosts, and judges. The casting Bono and King and their general treatment confirm their genders. Their genders are even emphasized and intensified throughout the competition, and the representations of both Bono and King are revealed as appropriately masculine or feminine. Bono's casting becomes more than mere performances of dance, just as King's acts are more than just a performance of modeling.

Chaz Bono

Surrounding Bono's casting in *DWTS*, media hype was initially controversial (Effron and Dolak 2011). The season 13 debut strategically placed Bono as the last performance, likely encouraging full viewing. Judge Carrie Ann Inaba further incites provocation by referencing Bono's participation, acknowledging that "people have been waiting all night to see you, Chaz." Despite the climatic build-up surrounding his first performance and the controversy created by casting Bono on the show, the hosts do not introduce Bono as trans. Instead, he is announced as an "author and activist." Bono is then given a testimonial or voiceover soundbite to clarify his identity, which is one of the only explicit references to him as transgender. He says, "I'm Chaz Bono and I'm the first transgender star on *DWTS*, which means that I was born with a female body, but I have transitioned and I am now a male." Bono's description acknowledges the transition as past tense and his maleness. The strategy in this discursive approach makes his identity non-negotiable. The program never draws any other explicit attention to Bono as trans, nor does it present him as trying to be something he is not. Bono is assigned a female dance partner, Lacey Schwimmer, and he is taught the dancing moves assigned to men. In short, "*DWTS* does not frame him in an overtly negative way" (Mocarski et al. 2013, 253). Further, his gender is never directly challenged by any judge, host, contestant, or his dance partner.

Gendered aspects of the dance performances are consistent with Bono's identity. For example, the selections of songs and his reaction to them reflect support for him. "Laugh at me" is described by Bono as a song about "being a different kind of man." The selection represents his male identity, recognizing the differences that exist in expressions of masculinity, while also asserting an indifference toward a world that may try to reject him as authentic. Similarly, in another episode that requires the contestants to pick a song from a film, Bono argues that he likes the movie *Rocky* because it is "related to being an underdog." He adds, "I loved Rocky and I wanted to be just like him." Lacey Schwimmer furthers the analogy stating, "It kind of relates to you and *your journey* on this show" [emphasis added]. While it is not clear why Bono can be considered an underdog, his identity as "transgender" can contribute to the skepticism from viewers and his initial dismissal as a legitimate contender in the competition. Bono later uses the song "Love is all around," which says, "You're gonna make it after all." Even though Mocarski et al. (2013) contend that the song's collective memory is that of *The Mary Taylor Moore Show*, noting that the association can neuter Bono's masculinity, the song's message is optimistic, supportive, and is made gender-neutral by editing the lyrics and removing the word "girl." Bono's performance is also signaled as a "brand new beat," as referenced by the song "Dancing in the Street" and the song's selection.

Bono's wardrobe, actions, and moves are masculine artifacts and performances. He is only ever shown in masculine attire: dress shirts, ties, retro suits or other masculine styles from a particular period, and masculine-styled active wear. In one number, he is shown combing his hair like T-Bird from *Grease*. After Bono's performance, Judge Len Goodman declares, "I admire your grit and determination." Goodman's choice of words includes adjectives that highlight traditionally masculine qualities. In the Rumba routine, Bono performs in a sleeveless leisure suit, which exposes another masculine marker: tattoos on his biceps and arms. In the Samba number, his performance is reminiscent of John Travolta's character in *Saturday Night Fever*. At the start of the number, he flirts with Schwimmer and takes off his suit jacket, disrobing in a masculine fashion. When he plays the role of a boxer, the judges reinforce his masculinity in their description of his perseverance, addressing stereotypical masculine qualities such as fighting and having strength. Judge Bruno Tonioli adds, "In the true spirit of Rocky, [...] you keep fighting and you keep getting stronger." Bono's final appearance is inspired by the masculine and mysterious phantom from *Phantom of the Opera*. In general, all the artifacts, songs, clothing, and performative traits construct and reify "Bono as hegemonically masculine" (Mocarski et al. 2013, 257).

Because Bono's performances represent and enact masculine cultural expectations and traits, they have the added effect of "breaking" the roles that Western culture attributes to assigned-at-birth sex-gender characteristics. In this sense, I contend that Bono's perseverance and state of mind about his dancing capabilities contribute to a positive representation. In the episode where Bono meets his dance partner's father, Buddy Schwimmer, a world-renowned swing dancer, Bono says, "I can totally relate to Buddy. He's a big guy and if he can do all the stuff that he does, then I can certainly do it better than I'm doing it." While this claim implies the shared physical similarities between Bono and Schwimmer, it also signals that Bono realizes he can enact the same dancing moves, exposing the constructive and performative assumptions behind his gender. Bono's abilities are backed up by the judges as he continues in the competition despite many low placings. After his performance in week five, Inaba tells Bono, "Obviously, your confidence is still blossoming." This implies that he appears more secure in the particular dancing role, thus "making" it like a man. This is reinforced again when he makes it to week six. Bono explains that he is "really happy to make it to the second half of the show. I really want to show people that I'm still in the game and deserve to be here." Initially, Bono has succeeded by meeting a key milestone constructed by the program. At the same time, this same set-up ultimately contributes to an overarching framing that, upon Bono's elimination, shows that both his talent and identity cannot "make it," an analysis that will be discussed later on.

Isis King

ANTM's season 11 sends mixed messages about the show's first trans contestant. At times, King is treated fairly, equally, and even commended on her talent as a model. However, at other times, problematic tropes and framings can influence viewers' understandings of her performance. Unlike *DWTS*, *ANTM* acknowledges King as someone who is "different" from the other participants, but it does so in a way that affirms why King deserves to be there. Although it ultimately outs King as trans, it also sets her up to describe her past on her own terms. Referring to King's brief appearance in the previous season, host Tyra Banks says, "There's a reason you're here because you know how to give me *couture*." At that moment, King changes her facial expression and poses for the camera. Banks tells King, "It blew me away, and I tell my staff, I'm like, 'this girl is absolutely amazing.'" She then asks, "What's different about that girl?" King responds:

> I was born physically male, but mentally, everything else, I was born female. Some people might say that I'm "transgender." Some people might say "transsexual" [rolls her eyes]. Personally, I prefer "born in the wrong body," meaning I was born physically male on the outside, but everything else about me was female.

In addition to using the proper gender labels for King, Banks admits she did not know or doubt King's womanhood. Banks uses "*couture*" and King's talent as justifications for her casting. Tyra Banks proves that King is "making it," complimenting her modeling style. On the other hand, her set-up has now revealed King as a trans contestant, which brings a sense of spectacle to her performance, and familiar tropes are expressed. First, King explains she was "born in the wrong body." Second, King is asked about her body, specifically whether it is pre- or post-op,[2] placing her in a precarious position as "still in transition," an established

---

2 These are common expressions to signal if a transgender person has had a gender confirmation surgery. *Ed.*

strategy in the mass media (Booth 2015; Siebler 2012). Despite these problematic patterns, King is given a platform for testimonials to provide a defense of her authenticity and to account for herself.

Similar to Bono, King's gender is not explicitly challenged by Banks or the judges. There are many dialogues that affirm her identity as a woman, using King's pronouns. Banks only ever identifies King as a woman or girl, using the same language she would use for any other contestant. Banks introduces King as "one of the girls," calls King "a lovely girl," references all the contestants (including King) as "ladies," and begins her elimination monologue by stating how many "beautiful girls stand before me." Although King is eliminated from the competition, her identity is still confirmed. Furthermore, viewers can observe that King is treated in a supportive way by other participants, including some of the contestants and the show's permanently-casted and guest judges. Although contestant Kacey singles out King as someone she does not consider a threat, she does not disparage her by misgendering her. Instead, she states, "I'm not going to let no girl take my spot. Like, all those girls—go home. I got this." Participant McKey refers to King as "a pretty cool chick," and Sheena, despite calling attention to King for "who she is," also acts unconcerned about King's trans identity and respects her willingness to compete. She claims, "For Isis, to be so brave and so secure with who she is and being able not to let anything bother her. It is very commendable." Now that King's difference is known and often the subject of conversation, some cast members are defending her rather than dwelling on her body, identity, or the constructed tensions generated by her choice to model.

More relevant than simply gendering Isis properly is the fact that King's performance as a model is marked as successful. The commentary, especially from the judges, operates as a form of gatekeeping and directs the audience to see each person's actions as positive or negative. Thus, the show's evaluation of performances, especially in the case of trans contestants, contributes to the confirmation of their gender. Often, the commentary does expose how the gender of the trans contestant is viewed as more performative than the stable identity of cisgender contestants. This is evident in the first episode, where Banks looks at King's first photographs and praises how beautiful her eyes are. Jay Manuel adds, "Isis truly is trying to be a woman and there are certain prejudices out there that concern me. Do I think Isis can be a high-fashion model and turn heads? For sure." Banks immediately agrees. Even though this commentary establishes a framing of King as "trying" to be something, it immediately confirms that King has the talent, ability, and look to become a fashion model. After that sequence, King is the twelfth woman to be selected to continue in the competition over 19 other semi-finalists who did not make the cut.

Throughout the season, some positive comments about King work to equalize and commend her, though problematic statements or tropes still operate as reminders of King's trans identity. Here, I argue that the framings of King's performances are mostly progressive despite some implications that she is "faking" her feminine acts. For instance, after working with King on her first photoshoot session, photographer Nigel Barker claims that King "is actually the only one that really knew her stuff. But, that being said, there's something about Isis that was very unusual." In this comment, Barker gives King one of the highest compliments compared to the other contestants, yet he leaves open a sense of mystery that is eventually revealed in the deliberation process. After evaluating King's photographs from such session, the judges critique her performance:

J. Alexander:	Isis put "Isis" on the cake.
Porizkova:	This girl is a model.
Barker:	She looks fantastic.
J. Alexander:	And there's also something special about Isis. She was born male.
Nigel:	Whoa.
Porizkova:	[nods head] Wow.
Barker:	Whoa. Well, I think with the transgender issue, it's very easy to caricature someone like Isis. But when I spoke to her the other day, she knew her light, she knew what to do, and she was smart. She's got real emotion and feeling, and I think it's because she lived.

Once again, King's identity is marked, an element that is both unnecessary and irrelevant to the subject at hand. However, the comments also operate to reveal that King is "making it," in fact, more so than the other cisgender contestants, who were critical of King's modeling performance upon discovering she was trans. Additionally, the judges indicate that she is so good that they are unaware that she is trans. Further, the dialogue is also significant because it implies that King has even more to offer. The judges portray her ability as inherently connected to her trans experience. Her emotion and feeling are signified as "real" and fueled by the resilience of her life experiences as a trans woman. King's picture is selected as the second-best among the fourteen contestants, which operates to denounce the simple claim that King does not belong because "she was born male." King is hailed as a female model. The judges say she "absolutely nails it" and they describe the photo as beautiful. In the end, King receives some compliments on her modeling; both the theme of the photograph and her story are read as beautiful once again.

In the second, third, and fourth episodes, viewers witness King's insecurities, especially in regard to bathing suit photoshoots. Although the swimsuit challenge still impedes King's confidence, King is often reassured that she has "made it."

Despite a critique of having a sleepy eye and limiting her poses, Porizkova says, "I think the pose is actually very becoming. I think you look wonderful. The bikini looks good." In another scene, in a conversation at the contestants' house, King admits that women are intimidated by her. McKey replies with a question, "Because you do 'girl' better than most girls?" McKey's question, seeking King's affirmation, is both rhetorical and a compliment to King's modeling ability. When King is shown practicing her runway walk, a contestant's voice (possibly McKey's) is heard saying, "And you're one of us, Isis." Though King is eliminated at the end of that episode, such affirmation confirms both her talent as a model and her belonging in the competition.

"FAKING" IT: CHILDLIKE AND TRANSITIONING

While both shows frame the performances with some positivity, they also have significant problems. Often, *DWTS* and *ANTM* portray Bono and King as trying to be something they are not. There are two primary ways that the shows reveal Bono and King as "faking" it, thus undermining their identity. The first is the way they are often described or treated like children, an association that is a trope for trans individuals. Not only is it discriminatory, but the approach makes both Bono and King easier to disregard as competition. Secondly, their dismissals from the competitions contain ideas that may lead to attribute their elimination to their trans identities.

Chaz Bono

Although details of Bono's physical transition are avoided on the program, there are other ways that Bono is treated differently than the other male contestants, as he is often infantilized and treated as a child. Despite the representations of hegemonic masculinity hyped by Bono's performances, the commentary around and directed toward Bono's performances contradicts the traditional treatment of men. After his first dance, Judge Inaba celebrates his acting and yells, "Chazzie boy, you can dance!" Judge Goodman also addresses Chaz as most would address a young boy and says, "Chaz, let me tell you something. First of all, my young soldier, that was the best dance that I've seen you do." Goodman acts as if Bono is a young boy pretending to be a grown man. Even Bono's dance partner Lacey Schwimmer has a playful moment during the theatrical montage they shoot before his *Rocky*-themed performance. She says to him, "All right, champ, you got one more challenge." The use of the word "champ" from *Rocky* is not nearly as empowering or hegemonic as it is in the original context, especially when the soundbite is paired with images of Richard Simmons, who is invited as a humorous and motivating guest trainer in Bono's training routine. Bono comes off as childlike, as Schwimmer talks to him in the same tone that a teacher or parent would use when addressing a kid. Even when Schwimmer's father is invited to assist Bono's performance, Lacey tells Chaz, "I'm going to bring someone in to help you feel like a cool dude." Her choice of words implies that Bono is experiencing low self-esteem or insecurities. Though having a mentor and role model is not traditionally emasculating, the fact that Schwimmer states that the guest will help him feel like a "cool dude" suggests that Bono is still looking for guidance on mastering gender performances.

Finally, judge Tonioli provides the most commentary and pop culture analogies to emasculate Bono. After Bono's first performance, Tonioli says, "Cheeky, but so cute and cuddly. I had no idea you were so cuddly and cute." After another performance, he tells Chaz, "There is a likeability about you. It's like watching a little Ewok dance with Princess Leia. It is cute and it is lovely." Despite Bono's masculine performance, Bono is compared to a teddy bear. Tonioli also calls Bono "darling" multiple times. Tonioli adds that his performance "was a different phantom, wasn't it, darling? It was like watching a cute little penguin trying to be a big menacing bird of prey." Tonioli emasculates the role of the Phantom by marking it as different and draws attention to Bono's acting in the role of the Phantom and its ultimate failure. The childlike treatment is reinforced by the attention received when singer Cher, Bono's mother, participates as an audience member watching her son. Mocarski et al. (2013) explain that Bono is seen "as primarily a son, and therefore juvenile and unsexed. […] The absence of his fiancé, in this reading, means that Bono does not fit the typical gender roles of a man to make the man/woman dyad possible" (2013, 255). Bono even points out to the hosts that another family member is there to support him. While family members are often showcased as audience members and Cher, in particular, increases media hype given her celebrity status, it is not common for a male performer's mother to receive this much attention, especially while other family members, including significant others, are ignored.

Isis King

Siebler (2012, 86) argues that surgery and hormones are the "coming of age" rituals in mediated portrayals of queer or trans youth. Similar to Bono, the discourse on *ANTM* contributes to portraying King as insufficient and childlike, with a few scenes and lines that emphasize the similarities of transitioning to growing up or developing as if she was a juvenile female, but not yet a woman. In one scene that reinforces this trope, King says that "transitioning is kind of like going through puberty all over again. […] I started out as a kid and now I'm developing." McKey replies, "You're like a butterfly." Though McKey's comment implies that King has achieved her end goal, since the butterfly is the final stage of metamorphosis, the conversation is focused on King in a state of transition.

In contrast, Banks provides criticism that makes King look insufficient while reinforcing the trope that King, as a trans woman, is like a girl. Although Banks was previously shown to support and compliment Isis, she directly compares King to a child and thereby makes her critique sound like a reprimand. She states, "Isis, you look like 'elementary school.' You really have to be edgier." Contestants Clark and Joslyn are shown laughing at King. This scene depicts King as failing to "pass." Banks continues, "You have to, like, think more 'model' and not just [like] a 'normal girl.'" In the next scene, King is fixing her hair. The suspense builds throughout the judges' commentary and it becomes unclear whether King can go home for this transgression.

However, Bank's critique in these scenes is not about King's modeling performance in a particular challenge. Instead, King is being chided for not looking enough like a model in everyday settings. Thus, Banks' lesson to the contestants is that a high-fashion model must look after her appearance and attire at all times. Though King's dress code can be read as more casual on that particular occasion, a double standard is exposed. King is still feminine, as she wears a skirt and a shaped cami. Banks is not as harsh on the other contestants, though they do not look particularly preen and glamorous in this particular setting. In spite of that, King is not eliminated. At the end of that episode, Banks tells Isis that her beauty still "needs to be aspirational and relatable" and that the judges "don't want to see a junior high, high school girl." The specific criticism of King's looks as if she was from elementary or junior high school reminds viewers of girls who are trying to look older but failing. In this instance, King's *naiveté* in dress and physical appearance implies that she is "faking" her femininity. Though King moves on after learning the lesson and remains in the competition, it is an example of what can happen when someone fails to meet societal expectations of gender and transition without a flaw.

"FAKING" IT: DISMISSALS OF THEIR GENDER IDENTITIES AS GROUNDS FOR DISMISSAL

Both *DWTS* and *ANTM* show that Bono and King are insufficient in the competitions, but they also reveal shortcomings in their societally expected gender characteristics that further justify their elimination from the reality television shows.

Chaz Bono

First, a recurring critique made primarily by the judges in *DWTS* focuses on Bono's character or personality. His role or performance is continually marked as insufficient and is often the reason that he ranks low each week. After his *Phantom of the Opera* performance (episode 6), Tonioli claims, "Some roles fit certain characters and some roles don't, and to me, this character didn't fit you." Bono is eventually critiqued for his technique, but other issues tend to take precedence, such as his ability to be a particular character. Prior to his elimination, Goodman tells him, "You know, in the tango, the hold should be tighter, there should be a little bit more aggression. [...] But, it was a good job; it was a tough dance for you. It didn't suit your personality, but well done." The specific choice of the word "aggression," though certainly characteristic of the tango, is commonly recognized as a masculine cultural attribute. Thus, Bono's insufficient performance that "didn't suit his personality" is both a reflection on his dancing skills but also on his manhood.

The judges' focus on his personality and role provides a critique of Bono's performance of masculinity more than his actual dancing. In her feedback, Judge Inaba says:

> You know, I tend to agree with Bruno [Tonioli] a little bit, but at the same time, I felt like, you know, each person has their own journey on this show. It's about how can you maximize what you have and what your assets are, and how well you do with what you've been given in life. And I think that in this dance, this was the most aggressive I've seen you. I felt like you were definitely stomping into your thing. [...] We gotta push you just a little further.

Once again, Inaba's comments are not highly technical nor criticism of precise dance techniques. Although she contradicts previous comments by crediting Bono for acting the "most aggressive," the tension created with Goodman's comments show the level of aggression expressed by Bono is still insufficient. The rest of the discourse is ambiguous and raises subtle questions about Bono's identity. She indicates that Bono's aggression is improving but a work-in-progress by claiming that this was "the most aggressive I've seen you" as he was "stomping into your thing." There is an essentialist paradox in Inaba's ideas. On one hand, Bono, like any gendered identity, is performing those "assets" as he should be seen, but, on the other hand, Inaba's word choice can raise doubts that Bono is capable of "maximizing" the identity because of his sex assigned at birth. Since the audience knows Bono is trans, sex-gender characteristics are simultaneously implicitly referenced and conflated as the source creating challenges. Even his dance partner, Lacey Schwimmer, contributes to the reading that Bono is not ready for more advanced performances. She gives him credit by saying that "you've been filling it [the performance] up with your personality." However, she warns him, "Everything has to be pretty legit." Again, the comment is ambiguous and it is unclear what actions require "legitimacy." Since the dominant message is that he fails to fall in line with his character, the media representations imply a failure on the part of Bono's identity: that he cannot attain manhood.

Isis King

In addition to the characteristics traced in the framings of Bono, *ANTM* fuels a similar subtext, especially when King is eliminated from the competition. Before King's final episode, there are explicit moments when King is called out as failing as a woman and as a female model. First, *ANTM* includes cases of pronoun misuse when referencing or discussing King. She does not directly encounter the misuse, but some contestants misgender her or reference her as male or as manly. More than any other contestant, King is made a target for critique by some competitors. Although some of the contestants are supportive, as shown earlier, others frame Isis as a competitor that is not model material due to her identity. In the first episode, Kacey describes King's looks as "a little manly." Upon learning King is transgender, Kacey asks her, "Girl, ain't this supposed to be a girl competition? How did you get through the door?" Kacey's comment suggests that King does not qualify as a "girl" and should not be in this competition. Clark also tells her fellow contestants that King "said that she used to be a man." Clark misgenders Isis again, stating, "If I have to get along with Isis, I will, but then, again, if it comes between me and my goal, I'll stomp that man right out of the competition." Clark uses additional degrading discourse calling King a "he-she." ShaRaun also calls King "a man" stating, "This is the funniest thing that's in my head, her, trying to be sexy. Reality is [that] she's a man." ShaRaun claims that King cannot perform sexiness. Though the pictures that come from the shoot are good and commended, the footage shows King moving awkwardly to find a pose. It appears that some contestants, judges, and coaches define King according to the sex-gender she was assigned at birth.

King is periodically rejected as a competitor. Contestants dismiss her ability to win without providing a warrant for their claims. Kacey states, "I don't see Isis as competition. I'm being completely honest. I mean, I'm not discriminating against her, but, sorry, honey, no." Clark adds, "I just don't see Isis being booked because of the way her body is now, it's still very manly, like the hands, the feet, and the waist." ShaRaun further dismisses King saying, "Isis is over the top. America's next top model is not gonna be a drag queen. I'm sorry. It's not." The comment also implies that the program would never allow trans contestants or "drag queens" to win the competition. Viewers are led to believe that King will not succeed due to being trans.

Second, King's body and other aspects of her transition are cited as elements impacting the quality of her performance in the competitive photoshoots. The requirements that some of the challenges posed are deemed to be more challenging for King due to her body and physiological changes. In episode 2, King is shown giving herself a shot of hormones. She explains that these injections have a physiological impact that leaves her feeling nauseous. She adds, "I'm just going to make sure to keep my face as long as I [can] stay focused. That's all that really matters." Judges argue that King's posing is good but that her face is not and that King is forgetting to focus on it. In judge deliberations, Barker compliments the picture but then jumps to an unexpected conclusion: "You know, it looks good. It's well-framed. That being said, I think Isis in person is just falling apart." The phrase "falling apart" is ambiguous enough that audience members may assume that King is struggling to keep herself together emotionally or physically. Barker does not provide any further explanation. During the judges' feedback session, the contestants arrive wearing casual and relaxed attire, yet King is scolded for her look, as described earlier. Banks sets up the challenge reveal, hoping the photo "is better than you look in person today." Even though the program focuses on the contestants' modeling, King seems to be held to a higher standard, even when she is not shooting photos. When the judges see King looking less feminine and less "beautiful," they use this as a reason to consider dismissing her.

The end of episode 2 establishes a line that will prove difficult for King to walk. Before revealing that King is safe for another week, Banks says:

> Isis, you started almost at the top of the pack last week and slid so far down with your pictures. And one thing that I noticed is when you walked in here, you did not look like a model at all. And what happens is, when the judges see something that is so different, they wonder, are your good pictures just a fluke? Isis, maybe, it's not a fluke. Isis, you know I love you, girl. And, every time, it's always something different, and I completely understand.

In addition to explaining the beauty standard that King will be held to, the commentary shows the importance of King's performance of self-monitoring outside of the shoots. Banks questions whether King's success is a mere chance, yet she claims to understand her completely. This line can provide viewers with an unstated assumption that trans identity is somehow difficult to manage.

King's underperformance is associated with her trans identity and the fact that she has not had gender-affirming surgery. This is evident in episode 3, when King admits feeling uncomfortable and nervous about the photoshoot in her swimsuit, saying that wearing a bathing suit places a lot of pressure on her. King moves on in the competition because she looks "absolutely gorgeous." But the next week, in episode 4, King is required to wear a bikini bottom again, even though the photoshoot centers on her eyes peering out over the water and not the modeling of her entire body. In these scenes, Isis is likely prompted by an interviewer in the confessional setting to reveal the act of "faking" through preparation for the shoot. She claims to be nervous because "there's some things that I have to do extra that the other girls don't have to. I have on like three pairs of undergarments, just in case the tape did peel off because of the water." Although the footage of the cameras was meant to focus on her face, one of the cameras shows King's entire body from under the water, but no other contestant is filmed from this angle. Likewise, this was apparent in the previous swimsuit session, where the cameras focused on King's body from behind and on the lower half of her body.

During the deliberation process, King's photograph is called out as one of the worst ones. Barker tells King, "You got so wrapped up with your swimsuit and various other elements. [...] You made too much of a big deal about it, even for yourself, 'cause you let it hamper your performance." King's body and her own insecurities are revealed as the causes that undermined her performance as a model. Thus, the show implies that she is "faking" her womanhood, which in turn contributes to her failure as a model. King's elimination also contains vague commentary when attempting to justify why she is eliminated. The judges state that she is failing to stand out, a claim that establishes a quandary for a trans contestant, especially one who was also warned against being too different. Standing out has its challenges since King's trans subjectivity reflects a desire to conform to the societal expectations, roles, and qualities of a female model, as shown in this exchange:

> **Porizkova:** She tries so hard to blend in with everybody else. She's becoming forgettable. She's not extraordinary in any way.
> **Banks:** I think she's scared to stand out. I think you're right.
> **Porizkova:** She's scared to stand out, and in her position, she has to stand out. She has to stand out, or there's nothing there.

Following a trend, there is not an explanation of why King must stand out. While this expectation may be placed on all the models, it is not applied or explained to the other contestants. There seems to be a unique demand for King to meet expectations of femininity and high beauty standards while simultaneously highlighting some other differences.

In the end, King's conventional behaviors are the source of her demise. Banks says, "One of our judges said that you're just coasting into nothingness because you're afraid to stand out. But if you want to be a model, you can, and you're already an inspiration for the gay, lesbian, transgender, bisexual community." Banks' commentary implies that King's gender performances are now too mundane to stand out from her trans identity. While King's visibility and participation are cited as inspirational to the larger LGBTQ community, it marks King as a trans person who is insufficient as a model.

CONCLUSIONS

This research examines the portrayals of performances of two trans participants in unscripted television shows and analyzes the ways that reality television shows frame trans individuals, their bodies, acts, and identities. Ultimately, *ANTM* and *DWTS* provide some visibility and legitimacy to trans identities. They progressively permit contestants to present themselves and their identities on their own terms. Generally speaking, the representations are more sophisticated than initial tropes and representations commonly found on TV programs about trans individuals at that time. Yet, in line with Sloop's (2004) critique, this chapter reveals these portrayals fail at queering or troubling gender. Instead, the performances uphold hegemonic masculinity and femininity, reinforcing gender binaries and disciplining trans identities to affirm normality. Siebler (2012, 83) argues that "transgender people are reduced to very un-queer definitions of masculinity and femininity, maleness, and femaleness." As such, *DWTS* and *ANTM* reaffirm the same approach by casting Bono and King, proving that "regressive models of sexuality, sex, and gender feel far less 'queer' than they purport to be" (Siebler 2012, 84). Thus, the appearances of Bono and King carry the conditions of possibility for change and rethinking of gender binaries, but they still operate to stabilize traditional definitions and dichotomous approaches to gender.

However, even though they reinforce the gender binary, trans individuals in *DWTS* and *ANTM* seem not trusted or fully accepted at least by other participants in the show. The research shows the subtle ways the programs establish a false privileging of cisgender performances and they construct trans contestants as if they were in a state of transition or undermining their identity's affirmations, portraying an inevitable failure in the competitions. These reality television shows make evident the struggles that exist for the articulation of a contingent, queer subject. Even when identities are confirmed through portrayals of performances, they risk being subtly challenged and minimized through discursive framings produced for a mainstream audience. Although this research does not study audience reception and cannot determine how these portrayals are actually read or interpreted by the audience, I conduct an initial examination of the discursive and textual approach toward portrayals of trans performances to determine the dominant framings that can impact viewers' understandings of the contestants. In these programs, King and Bono make strides in controlling their recognition, but viewers witness a clash between the subjects and the institutions of power. Judges and other participants stand-in for social expectations, redirecting and critiquing the lack in the contestants' performances and exposing the limits of their trans subjectivities. The consequence is that, like other problematic representations, these portrayals harm trans intelligibility. Even though King and Bono are modeling hegemonic gender roles, the nature of the competitions and the programs still constructs their identities as incomplete, insufficient, or as an ongoing work in progress. As Mocarski and others (2013, 253) argue, trans individuals "are still feared by more pure followers of the binary and are subject to ridicule [even though] they adhere to the gender binary." The final message in their eliminations is that these individuals, though allowed to compete, cannot win because of the insufficiencies in meeting the social expectations that they need to overcome.

I have shown that representations contain advancements and problems, but, most importantly, this study of the unscripted shows' strategies illustrate the ways that discourse around bodies and performances can "fake," "make," and "break" meaning and interpretation of gender. Thus, trans visibility remains an important first step in the deconstruction of current, constricting gender norms, especially if it reveals diverse, non-normative identities. Butler (2004) reminds us that LGBTQ people "make us not only question what is real and what 'must' be, but they also show us how the norms that govern contemporary notions of reality can be questioned and how new modes of reality can be instituted" (2004, 29). The performances of Bono and King, as portrayed in the competitions, expose the performative nature of gender norms and serve as evidence that gender acts are reiterations of cultural expectations. If "performance is ultimately about transformation, and cultural performances […] are always threatened by the potential for radical and reflexive ways of performing anew" (Bell 1999, 190), then it follows that trans performative acts of self-expression reveal the construction and performative nature of gender. Expressions of trans identity are conditions of possibility for future invention, as long as the "breaking" of gender norms are not coopted and reframed by others.

REFERENCES

Adams, Mary A. 2015. "Traversing the Transcape: A Brief Historical Etymology of Trans* Terminology." In *Transgender Communication Studies: Histories, Trends, and Trajectories*, edited by Leland G. Spencer and Jamie C. Capuzza, 173–85. Lanham: Lexington Books.

America's Next Top Model. 2008. Season 11. Directed by Tony Croll, Amy Elkins, Claudia Frank, and Bob Schermerhorn. The CW, September–November 2008.

Andrejevic, Mark. 2004. *Reality TV: The Work of Being Watched*. Lanham: Rowman & Littlefield Publishers.

Battles, Kathleen and Wendy Hilton-Morrow. 2002. "Gay Characters in Conventional Spaces: *Will and Grace* and the Situation Comedy Genre." *Critical Studies in Media Communication* 19, no. 1: 87–105.

Bell, Elizabeth. 1999. "Weddings and Pornography: The Cultural Performance of Sex." *Text and Performance Quarterly* 19, no. 3: 173–95.

Booth, E. Tristan. 2015. "The Provisional Acknowledgment of Identity Claims in Televised Documentary." In *Transgender Communication Studies: Histories, Trends, and Trajectories*, edited by Leland G. Spencer and Jamie C. Capuzza, 111–26. Lanham: Lexington Books.

Butler, Judith. 1990. *Gender Trouble. Feminism and the Subversion of Identity*. New York: Routledge.

———. 1993. *Bodies That Matter: On the Discursive Limits of "Sex."* New York: Routledge.

———. 2004. *Undoing Gender*. New York: Routledge.

Callahan, Gerald N. 2009. *Between XX and XY: Intersexuality and the Myth of Two Sexes*. Chicago: Chicago Review Press.

Capuzza, Jamie C. and Leland G. Spencer. 2017. "Regressing, Progressing, or Transgressing on the Small Screen? Transgender Characters on U.S. Scripted Television Series." *Communication Quarterly* 65, no. 2: 214–30.

Conquergood, Dwight. 1998. "Beyond the Text: Toward a Performative Cultural Politics." In *The Future of Performance Studies: Visions and Revisions*, edited by Sheron J. Dailey, 25–36. Washington DC: National Communication Association.

Dancing with the Stars. 2011. Season 13. Directed by Alex Rudzinski. ABC, September–November 2011.

Drushel, Bruce E. 2017. "A State of the Union: LGBTQ Representation and the Concept of Community." In *Locating Queerness in the Media: A New Look*, edited by Jane Campbell and Theresa Carilli, 11–22. Lanham: Lexington Books.

Effron, Lauren and Kevin Dolak. 2011. "*Dancing with the Stars* Premiere: Chaz Bono Cha-Chas into Millions of Homes." *ABC News*, September 19, 2011. https://abcnews.go.com/Entertainment/dancing-stars-premiere-chaz-bono-nancy-grace-dwts/story?id=14555326

Halberstam, Jack. 2010. "The Pregnant Man." *The Velvet Light Trap* 65: 77–8.

Holmes, Su. 2004a. "'But This Time You Choose!': Approaching the 'Interactive' Audience in Reality TV." *International Journal of Cultural Studies* 7, no. 2: 213–31.

Holmes, Su. 2004b. "'Reality Goes Pop!': Reality TV, Popular Music, and Narratives of Stardom in *Pop Idol*." *Television and New Media* 5, no. 2: 147–72.

Joyrich, Lynne. 2009. "Epistemology of the Console." In *Queer TV: Theories, Histories, Politics*, edited by Glynn Davis and Gary Needham, 15–47. New York: Routledge.

Lembo, Ron. 2007. "Components of a Viewing Culture." In *Television: The Critical View*, edited by Horace Newcomb, 455–70. New York: Oxford University Press.

Lovelock, Michael. 2017. "'I Am … ': Caitlyn Jenner, Jazz Jennings, and the Cultural Politics of Transgender Celebrity." *Feminist Media Studies* 17, no. 5: 737–54.

Manning, Jimmie. 2015. "The Rhetorical Function of Laugh Tracks in Situation Comedies: Examining Queer Shame in *Will and Grace* and *Roseanne*." *Relevant Rhetoric: A New Journal of Rhetorical Studies* 6: 1–16.

McIntyre, Joanna. 2017. "Transgender Idol: Queer Subjectivities and Australian Reality TV." *European Journal of Cultural Studies* 201, no. 1: 87–103.

Mocarski, Richard, Sim Butler, Betsy Emmons, and Rachael Smallwood. 2013. "'A Different Kind of Man': Mediated Transgendered Subjectivity, Chaz Bono on *Dancing with the Stars*." *Journal of Communication Inquiry* 37, no. 3: 249–64.

Morse, Nicole. 2017. "A Double-Take on Reality Television: Laverne Cox's Political and Pedagogical Gestural Humor." *Feminist Media Studies* 17, no. 2: 168–80.

Poole, Ralph J. 2017. "Towards a Queer Futurity: New Trans Television." *European Journal of American Studies* 12, no. 2: 1–23.

Siebler, Kay. 2012. "Transgender Transitions: Sex/Gender Binaries in the Digital Age." *Journal of Gay and Lesbian Mental Health* 16, no. 1: 74–99.

Sloop, John. 2004. *Disciplining Gender: Rhetorics of Sex Identity in Contemporary U.S. Culture*. Boston: University of Massachusetts Press.

Spencer, Leland. 2015. "Centering Transgender Studies and Gender Identity in Communication Scholarship." In *Transgender Communication Studies: Histories, Trends, and Trajectories*, edited by Leland G. Spencer and Jamie C. Capuzza, ix–xxii. Lanham: Lexington Books.

Stryker, Susan. 1998. "The Transgender Issue: An Introduction." *GLQ: A Journal of Lesbian and Gay Studies* 4, no. 2, 145–58.

———. 2006. "(De)Subjugated Knowledges: An Introduction to Transgender Studies." In *The Transgender Studies Reader*, edited by Susan Stryker and Stephen Whittle, 1–17. New York: Routledge.

Thomas, Erika. 2017. "Transitioning Stories about Transitioning Genders: Tracing Generic Forms and Their Implications in Trans Autobiographies." In *Locating Queerness in the Media: A New Look*, edited by Jane Campbell and Theresa Carilli, 109–22. Lanham: Lexington Books.

Van Bauwel, Sofie and Nico Carpentier. 2010. *Trans-Reality Television: The Transgression of Reality Genre, Politics, and Audience*. Lanham: Lexington Books.

Villarejo, Amy. 2016. "Jewish, Queer-ish, Trans, and Completely Revolutionary: Jill Soloway's *Transparent* and the New Television." *Film Quarterly* 69 no. 4: 10–22.

PART III

TRANS NARRATIVES AND THEIR SPECTATORS

CHAPTER SIX

Trans, White, and Privileged: The Public Framing of Caitlyn Jenner on Twitter

BY NATHIAN SHAE RODRIGUEZ, JENNIFER HUEMMER, AND MARY E. BROOKS[1]

INTRODUCTION

This study examines how the public viewed and, ultimately, framed Caitlyn Jenner's mediated transition on Twitter after the *20/20* interview with Diane Sawyer on April 24, 2015, until July 2015, with the debut of Jenner's reality show *I Am Cait* (2015–2016). The interview marks the beginning of Caitlyn Jenner's mediated transition, and the three following months were full of key mediated moments, each reaping high audience viewership. The Diane Sawyer interview set a rating record with 17 million viewers, the Kardashian family interview on May 17 pulled in 4.2 million viewers, and 8 million spectators watched her acceptance at the Arthur Ashe Courage Award at the ESPYS on July 15. *I Am Cait* premiered on July 26 to 2.73 million viewers, and with four airings of the show across the night, a total of 6.2 million viewers watched the first episode (O'Connell 2015). If Jenner's mediated transition is to be established as both confession

---

[1] Nathian Shae Rodriguez, Ph.D. Associate Professor of Digital Media, San Diego State University. Email: nsrodriguez@sdsu.edu
Jennifer Huemmer, Ph.D. Assistant Professor of Strategic Communication, Ithaca College. Email: jhuemmer@ithaca.edu
Mary E. Brooks, Ph.D. Assistant Professor of Media Communication, West Texas A&M University. Email: mbrooks@wtamu.edu

and education that must be acknowledged and recorded by the audience in the United States, it is necessary to examine how her transition is constructed in the minds of the spectators.

"BRUCE JENNER: THE INTERVIEW"

Diane Sawyer stands with her hands in the pockets of her black pants suit. One screen reads "Bruce Jenner: The Interview, a Diane Sawyer Special." Above the title is a shadowed picture of Jenner and Sawyer facing each other. Their profiles are dark against the bright blue glow of the screens in the back. "Good evening," Sawyer says while addressing the audience directly. "We're so glad you're with us for the Bruce Jenner interview" (2015). The camera begins to pan closer to Sawyer as she says, "I don't know about you, but we've observed there's a kind of generational divide that can be charted by how you recognize his name."[2] The camera continues to move closer to her, revealing an image of Bruce Jenner on the large screen behind her. He sits relaxed on a couch with one arm stretched out wide. His hair hangs long framing his face and a slight smile forms at the corners of his mouth. Diane Sawyer continues as she speaks to the camera:

> For a lot of people, he's the dad on that big reality show [*Keeping up with the Kardashians*]. For others, we remember the superstar athlete who triumphed at the Olympics in 1976. But for the next two hours, Bruce Jenner is going to tell you something else about his life and we think it's a story that can only be told by someone who lived it. ("Bruce Jenner: The Interview" 2015)

This introduction to the interview highlights the culturally established masculine roles for which Jenner has received world fame, namely as a powerhouse Olympian and a famous father figure on the reality television show *Keeping up with the Kardashians*. The introduction also indicates that the Bruce Jenner we are about to encounter has an "other" quality that must be confessed publicly and is separate from the masculine roles mentioned above. For months, tabloids speculated about the "truth" of Jenner's gender and hinted at "Bruce's Secret Double Life" (Us Weekly 2014). All speculation was put to rest within the first six minutes of the interview as Sawyer tilted her head to look at Jenner as she asked, "Are you a woman?" Jenner paused and furrowed his eyebrows. "Um," he hesitated. "Yes, for all intents and purposes, I am a woman" (2015).

---

2   Diane Sawyer stated that "Bruce Jenner said at this moment for this interview we should use the familiar him or he," although Jenner's name is Caitlyn. As the scope of this paper only encompasses Jenner's representation of herself during this event, we reference Jenner within the boundaries of the discussion of this interview as "he" and as "Bruce," rather than "she" or "Caitlyn."

The next two hours of the interview are presented to the audience as Jenner's confession of a true authentic self. LaFountain explains, "The basic premise of the confession is the notion that the individual can be helped by authorities/experts to tell the truth, and by being shown how to tell it, he or she learns the truth about the self" (1989, 132). The themes of truth and self-realization permeate Jenner's confession. This is like Dow's (2001) analysis of Ellen DeGeneres' declarations of authenticity and realization of "true self" when confessing that she was gay in the 1990s. As Dow argues, it can seem liberating or powerful that the mainstream media is acknowledging the voice of members of the LGBTQ community, but what is important is to examine how and what elements of this production are used to liberate or repress. As lesbian and gay rights become more mainstream, arguably, with the inclusion of more dimensional representations of lesbian and gay characters on television, transgender people become the new site of deviance (Valentine 2003). Though still deficient, media have slowly begun to include representations of transgender people and highlight transgender actors and actresses on popular television shows, such as Laverne Cox. The media environment seems primed (much as it was when DeGeneres came out) to acknowledge the voice of a transgender confession while simultaneously creating the boundaries and rules around which the U.S. audience makes sense of the transgender community.

Jenner's Foucauldian confession then positions Sawyer as the expert who listens to and guides the confession while simultaneously narrating throughout the course of the show. The role to "police" the implications of Jenner's confession is, however, ultimately placed in the hands of the audience. The construction of power is then established by the determination that this platform, this audience, and this circumstance are appropriate for Jenner's discussion about sex and gender. Thus, according to Foucault, "these discourses on sex did not multiply apart from or against power, but in the very space and as the means of its exercise" (1978, 32).

Foucault argues that during the eighteenth century "there emerged a political, economic, and technical incitement to talk about sex. And not so much in the form of a general theory of sexuality as in the form of analysis, stocktaking, classification, and specification, of quantitative or causal studies" (1978, 23–24). The purpose of the confession was not to understand sexuality in any great depth but to know when, where, and among whom sex occurred to regulate the act of sex and the spaces where it occurred. This is highlighted by the fact that at many points in the interview Diane Sawyer attempts to ask Jenner to explain, analyze, and classify not only her gender, but also her sexuality. Much of this discussion is built around the premise that these types of classifications and clarifications are necessary for the education of the U.S. spectatorship. Beneath the thin guise of "education," the role of the audience becomes explicit as the population that must be both provided education and answers. LaFountain further emphasizes the role of the audience stating, "For the whole truth does not reside in the confessor but rather is 'incomplete, blind to itself' and only reaches completion in the one who assimilates and records it" (1989, 132).

LITERATURE REVIEW

Media studies have examined transgender representations in film and discourses surrounding popular film (Cavalcante 2013), but little has been said about how the media produces real-life stories of transgender people. Caitlyn Jenner's story is unique not only because she was already a famous celebrity, but because her initial television interview was viewed by 17 million people (Kissell 2015), thus solidifying this interview's role as the pivotal media production moment of Caitlyn Jenner's transition. In line with the argument that "queer studies now more than ever need to refocus its critical attention on public debates about the meaning of democracy and freedom, citizenship and immigration, family and community, and the alien and the human" (Eng, Halberstam, and Muñoz 2005, 2), this article intends not only to ask how the media constructs knowledge about trans people through discourse about Caitlyn Jenner, but also how Caitlyn's various intersections of gender, race, age, and socioeconomic status are used to make a case for or against her acceptance in the minds of the audience.

Representations in the Media

Hollywood's fascination with transgender representations visibly increased during the late half of the twentieth century (Cavalcante 2013). In an examination of portrayals of transgender people on screen, Phillips (2006) identifies that cross-dressing was frequently utilized in comedic films such as *Mrs. Doubtfire* and *Tootsie* as a means to an end rather than as an acceptable way of being. He also recognizes the role of transgender people in horror films where transsexuality is explored while simultaneously othering transsexuals as a source of fear and mental instability. Cavalcante argues that representations of transgender people in films emphasize tragedy and victimization in the narratives of transgender people (2013).

The representation of transgender bodies as scripted characters in a film may differ dramatically from the media portrayal of "real" transgender bodies. For example, Sloop's analysis of the media portrayal of Brandon Teena uncovered an emphasis on Teena's female body versus Brandon's masculine performance as well as a focus on Brandon's sexual prowess (2000). In the book *Sex Change, Social Change: Reflections on Identity, Institutions, and Imperialism*, Viviane Namaste (2011) takes critiques of media representations of transgender people a step further by arguing that transgender individuals do not even have the access to have their voices heard by the media. It is important that Caitlyn Jenner, a famous wealthy celebrity, gained access to the media. Acknowledging the intersectional positionality that allowed her to gain that access is necessary to deconstructing how she is represented.

Definitions of Transgender

Stryker defines transgender individuals as "people who move away from the gender they were assigned at birth, people who cross over (trans-) the boundaries constructed by their culture to define and contain that gender" (2008, 1). This definition emphasizes the temporality of time and place rather than conceptualizing the term as an immutable and prescriptive label. While much of queer theory has turned to the transgender body as some form of transgression or ideal queerness, Jack Halberstam questions the presumed transgressive function of transgender identity in postmodernity as "a fulfillment of postmodern promises of gender flexibility" (2005, 18). He suggests that transgender people often aim to live within the normative boundaries of society rather than working to attempt to reshape the boundaries entirely.

Sloop's analysis of mainstream discourse about Brandon Teena, the transgender man who influenced the film *Boys Don't Cry*, argues that although transgender identities have the potential to disrupt gender binaries, dominant Western discourse still works to "stabilize sex and reiterate sexual norms, rather than to encourage/explore gender fluidity" (2000, 168). Similarly, Cavalcante (2013) notes that when the media produce potentially subversive texts such as *Transamerica*, a film about a transgender woman, the secondary texts or "paratexts," surrounding the media production, like posters and press releases, are used to defuse inflammatory audience reactions by demonstrating that the media production primarily reflects the dominant Western social norms and just happens to include a transgender person or character. These studies emphasize the importance of examining significant cultural texts regarding transgender people to understand what is being said in the text and what the text does. Furthermore, are these cultural representations, particularly in the media, depicting transgender people as monolithic or intersectional?

Beyond Sexuality and Gender

Intersectionality is a theory that was first introduced in the late 1980s by lawyer and academic Kimberlé Crenshaw to describe violent actions against Black women. In her seminal piece about intersectionality, Crenshaw (1989) posits that intersectionality happens when Black women are marginalized and discriminated against on multiple levels. This multi-level discrimination is defined as "the combined effects of practices which discriminate on the basis of race, and on the basis of sex" (Crenshaw 1989, 149). Thus, Black women are often battling racism and sexism together.

Since the theory's inception, other scholars have contributed to its evolution by applying it to various disciplines including law (Dale 2018), pedagogy (Goldberg and Allen 2018), and advertising (Tan et al. 2019). Additional applications of intersectionality include examining it from a wide variety of perspectives including from a religious viewpoint of being a Muslim living in a highly populated Christian environment in the South in the United States (Shams 2015), from a human rights legal context focused on persons with disabilities including disabled women, disabled children and disabled persons of color (de Beco 2020), and within the field of health and youth sports (Dagkas 2016).

Due to its prevalence in feminist thinking and literature, the journal *Sex Roles* has twice used its publication as a special issue related to intersectionality and how the theory has evolved and been adapted to include examining gender, race, and ethnicity alongside social status and sexual orientation (Shields 2008; Parent, DeBlaere, and Moradi 2013). In several interviews, Crenshaw has discussed how intersectionality has become a catch-all concept that is often misinterpreted, but at its core it is "a lens, a prism, for seeing the way in which various forms of inequality often operate together and exacerbate each other" (Steinmetz 2020). In an interview at Columbia Law School, where Crenshaw is a professor, she states:

> Intersectionality is a lens through which you can see where power comes and collides, where it interlocks and intersects. It's not simply that there's a race problem here, a gender problem here, and a class or LBGTQ problem there. Many times that framework erases what happens to people who are subject to all of these things. (Interview to Crenshaw by Columbia Law School 2017)

Eng, Halberstam, and Muñoz (2005) put forth a rallying cry for queer theorists to include a more holistic approach to queer theory that examines not only sexuality but gender, socioeconomic status, nationality, and religion. An examination of citizenship as a site for negotiating both normalcy and equality is particularly relevant when considering representations of the transgender population (West 2014). Cautioning against queer theorists' tendencies to reject citizenship as normalizing and therefore unproductive, West suggests that theorists conduct a reparative reading to understand how transgender individuals perform citizenship through a series of acts to "exercise agency in these interactions and make the worlds around them more inhabitable by queering public cultures" (2014, 29).

Ferguson further discusses the implications of heteronormativity and race in the construction of standardized national citizenship. In the article "Race-ing Homonormativity" (2005), Ferguson argues that, in modern Western culture, same-sex intimacy has already been institutionalized as a "new category of normativity" (2005, 59). To achieve this normativity, the differences of sexuality were relegated to the private sector, while the gay and lesbian movement emphasized other commonalities of U.S. citizenship, namely those of whiteness and middle-class values. Ferguson claims sexual differences must be regulated to afford the appearance of cohesive citizenship and that this regulation often manifests through racial bias (2005, 61). Valentine (2003) agrees that sexuality became gender-normative by marking trans people as gender deviant since they are considered a public concern. As transgender individuals are highlighted more frequently in the media, it becomes increasingly difficult to relegate all transgender people to the category of "other." He adds that in the twenty-first century, we are afforded the opportunity to record the assimilation of transgender individuals into the institutionalization of U.S. citizenship. As such, it is crucial to examine the processes that occur as the transgender community is "regulated" and institutionalized.

Framing Theory

The concept of framing, which is the process of message construction, is the theoretical framework applied to this study. Framing, in media, is concerned with how media structures stories, people, issues, or events that in turn affect the public's views on what is being framed and how those frames influence the receivers' understanding of the message (Shah et al. 2009). At its core, framing is meant to "select some aspects of a perceived reality and make them more salient in a communicating text, in such a way as to promote a particular problem definition, causal interpretation, moral evaluation, and/or treatment recommendation for the item described" (Entman 1993, 52). Through the positioning, manipulation, and replication of words and images, framing allows fragments of information to become significant and noteworthy to media consumers. What is omitted from or in the background of frames is just as important, although texts and visuals are more salient when they are framed prominently or repetitively, the absence of certain frames can be just as prominent (Entman 1993).

Another element of framing is how images and texts shape a person's reality. Gamson and others (1992) write that media messages, both visual and verbal, have the power to indoctrinate certain morals and beliefs that allow society to interpret the world regardless of the media producer's objective. Chong and Druckman posit that the weight people place on various elements or dimensions of a particular topic is based on several factors that are specific to an individual, their particular attitudes, and their "frame in thought" (2007, 105). Additionally, Gamson and Modigliani (1989) write that people's worldviews contribute to meaning-making. The authors also refer to framing elements as "interpretive packages" (1989, 2) that billow and plummet in importance, frequently changing to adapt to novel developments.

The evolution of framing in politics, journalism, and by those working in the news industry, has been a primary theme for scholars. Much of this research has changed from examining framing from the traditional news source means, including newspapers, magazines, and television, to social media-based platforms, primarily through Twitter (Burch, Frederick, and Pegoraro 2015; Kreiss 2016; Parmelee and Bichard 2013; Wasike 2013). For example, Wasike (2013) found that television and print news social media editors differ on the story frames they post to Twitter, the number of issue-framed stories posted, and the personalization level of their tweets.

Scholars are expanding the application of framing theory in order to understand gender, including gender stereotype frames of Hillary Clinton and Sarah Palin in the 2008 political campaign (Carlin and Winfrey 2009), the framing of Katie Couric as the first female to anchor the CBS Evening News alone (Gibson 2009), and how women Olympic athletes are framed in media (Kian, Bernstein, and McGuire 2013). The study of the framing of LGBTQ issues in the media has also been on the rise, specifically looking at the frames of how college football standout, Michael Sam, and former National Basketball Association player, Jason Collins, came out (Billings et al. 2015; Cassidy 2016; Kian, Anderson, and Shipka 2015). Billings and others (2015) compared the themes of newspaper articles to the themes of tweets posted about Collins for seven days after he came out in *Sports Illustrated*. In both the traditional and social media outlets, the overarching themes were framed in primarily positive tones. However, the themes of the newspaper articles were more structured in their writing than that of the tweets. This is not unusual given that social media has been described as "participatory and collaborative" (Kaplan and Haenlein 2010, 61) where seemingly anyone with or without journalistic credentials can contribute to newsworthy issues.

Research on transgender issues has also developed in recent years, perhaps because of the increase in media coverage, political stances, and entertainment options that permeates society (Morrison 2016). Scholars have written about the portrayal of transgender people in the media (Espineira 2016; McInroy and Craig 2015), the violence against those identifying as trans (Lombardi et al. 2002; Lubitow et al. 2017), issues related to the intersectionality of transgender and racial identities (Singh 2013), and the tension that has arisen over transgender bathroom rights (Watkins and Moreno 2017; Williams 2017).

Specific to Caitlyn Jenner, scholars have analyzed the historic Diane Sawyer interview from various angles. Li (2017) examined how news stories from national newspapers and broadcast networks that concentrated on transgender issues were reported before and after the Sawyer interview. News report discourse changed to reflect more non-binary terminology as well as an increase in showcasing persons who identify as agender. Furthermore, Li found that the intersectionality of race, class, and sexuality as it applies to transgender persons was also an element of news reporting that increased after the interview. Miller and Behm-Morawitz (2017) analyzed real-time Twitter chats happening during the Sawyer broadcast. The top tweets, retweets, and themes identified during the interview were primarily supportive and positive. They also found that opinion leaders, including Oprah Winfrey, Laverne Cox, Lance Bass, and Jennifer Lopez, were all instrumental in using Twitter as a platform for providing Caitlyn Jenner with accolades and approval for coming out. One gap in the research literature is how the intersection of race, ethnicity, age, sexuality, and class of a transgender individual is perceived by society throughout the coming out process. The current chapter aims to address this gap by examining representations of Caitlyn Jenner while considering how she evolved from an Olympic hero to a reality show patriarch to, now, a possible face of activism for transgender rights.

METHOD

How has the public viewed Caitlyn Jenner throughout her mediated coming out process and, specifically, what public discourse surrounds her sexuality, race, ethnicity, socioeconomic status, age, and celebrity status? To answer this research question, a textual analysis was employed on tweets containing the phrase "Caitlyn Jenner" and the hashtag #CaitlynJenner, which was the common identifier that connected all of the events in the three month mediated coming out transition of Caitlyn Jenner (see Figure 6.1). The timeframe began on April 24, 2015, the date of the Sawyer interview where Bruce announced his transition to Caitlyn; and ended on July 26, 2015, with the premiere of *I Am Cait*. The timeframe also included other key moments such as the Kardashian family interview on May

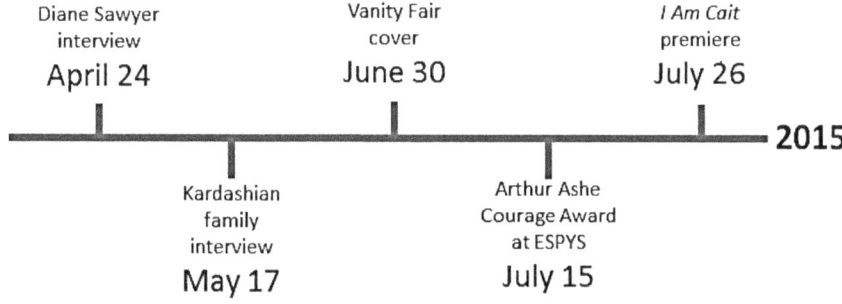

Figure 6.1: Events Related to Jenner's Coming Out
Source: Authors

17, Caitlyn's cover of *Vanity Fair* on June 30, and her acceptance of the Arthur Ashe Courage Award at the ESPYS on July 15. A random sample of 200 tweets was taken from each of the five dates, a one-week timeframe for each date, three days before and three days after. This yielded a purposive sample of 1,000 tweets. The tweets were entirely in English and were limited to 160 characters.

Tweets were then coded and analyzed according to the approach taken by DeCuir-Gunby, Marshall, and McCulloch (2011), who stress the importance of data-driven codes in research. Raw information in the tweets was reduced into smaller units by lumping together data with similar levels of meaning. Themes within the subsamples were identified. Another round of analysis was conducted to determine if the resulting themes needed to be expanded or if themes could be combined into a loftier theme. The resulting themes were then compared with the theoretical framework. Overall, four main themes organically evolved: (1) white and male privilege, (2) fame, celebrity, and wealth, (3) political ideologies, gender, and age, and (4) trans representation and education.

ANALYSIS

White and Male Privilege

Peggy McIntosh (1997) defines white privilege as an unearned, unacknowledged entitlement that an individual receives in everyday life simply because their skin is white. Tweets that demonstrate this privilege in our sample are "Jenner Is The Epitome Is [sic] White Privilege. She's Being Glorified For The Same Shit Black Transgenders Are Being Slaughtered For" and "Caitlyn Jenner is [the] epitome of white privilege, if something doesn't affect her she doesn't care about it."[3]

White privilege has been a systemic problem as racism rooted in history (McIntosh 1997). Tweets directly placed the blame for white privilege in the hands of pop culture and the media, "#hypocritical #WhiteAmerica only talks about #TransGender when its [sic] #WhitePeople #MainStreamMedia #WhitePrivilege #CAITLYNJENNER #Media #LGBT."

The male privilege was another privilege highlighted in the tweets. Individuals wrote "Male privilege is reaping the rewards of manhood for decades until it earns you enough to purchase womanhood from a surgeon. #CaitlynJenner," and "#CaitlynJenner would not be at all famous had he been born a woman. The fact that we're even talking about him at all is male privilege." The tweets reinforce the contested position that all transwomen benefit from male privilege and are not seen as "real" women (Fischer 2017).

---

3 These are unedited reproductions of the original tweets. *Ed.*

In some instances, the intersection of white privilege and male privilege was found to be the focal point of the tweets, "Her perceived beauty is a result of the white male privilege leading to the economic privilege from which she benefitted #CaitlynJenner." However, others pointed out that this intersection wasn't always the best way to compare Jenner to other transwomen, "Using Caitlyn Jenner to say all trans women benefit frm [sic] male privilege is like using Beyoncé to say all black women benefit frm [sic] being black."

Another small subset of tweeters vehemently denied any sort of privilege in relation to Jenner: "Besides, saying 'Caitlyn Jenner has white male privilege' is ridiculous. She is now a woman, she lost both her male AND her cis privileges"; "Male privilege must not amount to much if Bruce Jenner is willing to give it up so easily #feminism #meninist #CaitlynJenner"; and "WHY are people making Caitlyn Jenner about white privilege? That makes NO SENSE."

Fame, Celebrity, and Wealth

Jenner's star status as a former Olympian, coupled with her relationship to the Kardashians and Jenner sisters, was the focus for many of the tweets. Users wrote: "#CaitlynJenner has celebrity status, a high profile, a platform and wealth to help her transition unlike most transgenders"; "I don't think Caitlyn Jenner being 'Woman of the Year' has to do with white privilege. It's just her name, fame, and status"; and "I'm excited as hell for #CaitlynJenner but pls [sic] remember her wealth opens doors many other trans women have been trying to open for decades."

The amount of money Jenner has accumulated because of her fame and celebrity status was also highlighted in the tweets. "Yes Caitlyn I'm sure it is 4u. Wealth + privilege have shielded u from reality of being trans in US," "Please note how Bruce Jenner's Whiteness and Wealth has allowed for a more seamless and accepted transition into #CaitlynJenner," and "caitlyn jenner represents a privilege that many trans folk will never have. the wealth to look the way she wants." These tweets imply that Jenner's access to money and other forms of wealth afforded her access to resources that other trans women have been denied.

In a similar fashion to the other themes, there was an intersection of identities manifested in some of the texts. Fame, celebrity, wealth, and race were highlighted in tweets such as "If Caitlyn Jenner's journey proves one thing, it is this: Race & wealth impact and shape gender. White folks can't ignore this anymore"; "@Caitlyn_Jenner has money and white privilege that has allowed her to grace the cover of @vanityfair," and "Caitlyn Jenner winning the Arthur Ashe Courage Award is white male privilege at its finest #Espys." Although the tweets address the intersection of identities, they also suggest that those identities are influenced by one another. For example, wealth is a result of race and fame, and fame is the result of race and wealth. Identities are not mutually exclusive, nor do they merely intersect; rather, they are constitutive of one another (Hames-García 2011).

Political Ideologies, Gender, and Age

Many of the tweets pointed out a dichotomy of political ideologies. Conservative individuals tweeted "Just heard some idiot liberal talk about how Caitlyn Jenner is strong b/c she's giving up her male privilege. Umm.. smart take? Not!" and "In the contest to deny reality, liberals just allowed white male privilege to trump white female privilege. #RachelDolezal #CaitlynJenner." Conversely, liberal individuals tweeted "@Caitlyn_Jenner idk why people are surprised your [sic] republican. U were the definition of white privilege = a white male so of course ur rep" and "@BZBwoy Waiting to see @Caitlyn_Jenner address her welcome by #Conservatives & #GOP #Politicians now she has less #WhitePrivilege as a woman to them."

There were many other instances of tweets that highlighted misogyny and objectification: "Damn Caitlyn Jenner I see you with your beautiful tig ol' bitties! Boing!!! #Caitlyn #sexy #Canimotorboat #breastfeedme #suckleonyourteet," "I won't even front. If I was single I'd bone #CaitlynJenner. For pleasure & wealth," and "Caitlyn Jenner and Kim K are some sexy ass bitches." Like the online sexual harassment that cisgender women endure online, these tweets demonstrate the use of power dynamics and hegemonic masculine entitlement that serves to reify heteronormativity and patriarchy (Fischer 2017).

Not only were individuals quick to treat Jenner "like a woman" but there were also many tweets from the media sexualizing her. For example, tweets like "Caitlyn Jenner Rocks A Sexy Lace Jumpsuit" from *The Huffington Post*, "Check out Caitlyn Jenner's super sexy Christmas Eve outfit" from *People Magazine*, and "Sexy lady @Caitlyn_Jenner shows cleavage for screening of the film Tangerine" from *X17 Online*, showcase the use of fashion to portray Jenner as a sexual object.

Additionally, Caitlyn's age was the focus of many of the tweets, "#CaitlynJenner is old AF," "Old … PASS @Caitlyn_Jenner!!!"; "#CaitlynJenner #CallMeCaitlyn Bruce is 2 old for a sex change, he'll be an old hag. It's 2 late to be a pretty Transvestite, he's hideous!" and "#CaitlynJenner is proof, money won't buy you happiness. U've got 2 be really angry at yourself to have to change yourself into an old woman." These tweets highlight the negative ways in which older LGBTQ adults are treated both online and in non-digital spaces. They often experience higher rates of lifetime discrimination and verbal and physical abuse (Choi and Meyer 2016).

There were other tweets that praised Jenner in relation to her age. "As an older transwoman I appreciate @Caitlyn_Jenner," tweeted one user, showing the importance of representation in the media. Another person wrote, "I hope the #CaitlynJenner story increases acceptance of all LGBTQ people. You're never too old/young 2B the real you. Proud 2B #StraightAlly." This addresses the positive aspects of Jenner's age. Here, her age is used to showcase the acceptance of true self.

Some tweets focused on the intersection of age with other facets of Caitlyn's identity: "@CaitlynJenner forgets that she has lived 65 years as Bruce, in full possession of his #whiteprivilege #LGBTQ" and "Caitlyn Jenner still has the mindset of a man who's lived 60+ years of her life wallowing in male, white privilege." Jenner was also sexualized regarding her age in tweets such as "Who knew a 65 year old could be so attractive. #CallMeCaitlyn #CaitlynJenner @Caitlyn_Jenner," "For a transgender and 65 year old, #CaitlynJenner looks better than most girls out here!," and "#CaitlynJenner is kinda hot for being old."

Trans Representation and Education

The biggest contention among the tweets was that Jenner was not representative of the trans community at large. Individuals tweeted "@CaitlynJenner How can u be a role model/spokesperson for a disenfranchised group with ur straight white male privilege still intact?" and "Don't let Caitlyn Jenner's success erase the struggle of trans people who don't have white privilege and tons of money." The tweets highlight the fact that Jenner was not characteristic of the vast amount of trans women of color who are disproportionately affected by poverty and violence (James et al. 2016).

In fact, many users compared Jenner to other trans women of color who have been largely ignored by mainstream media. Some tweets that make this comparison include: "White privilege is Bruce Jenner transforming into Caitlyn Jenner and winning awards for it while Lavern Cox is completely ignored" and "#CaitlynJenner again? @janetmock @Lavernecox never had this PR rollout OR media love. #WhitePrivilege allows for #overthetopness #nerdland."

A small group of tweeters looked past the inequities and noted that Jenner's transition was still a step in the right direction for trans visibility. One of them tweeted, "Inspired by @Caitlyn_Jenner's speech. While it's true she still has white privilege as a trans woman, every drop of progress counts." Another individual tweeted, "yes caitlyn jenner has had it easier than most trans people bc of her wealth but it doesn't mean she can't be rewarded for it." The tweets demonstrate how Jenner uses her celebrity status to exercise agency and queer public cultures, bringing trans issues into the public's attention (West 2014).

Furthermore, some people pointed out that Jenner's mediated transition, albeit full of controversy, was a learning opportunity. Tweets such as "Love that they highlight that Caitlyn Jenner's experience as one of white privilege on her show" and "@Caitlyn_Jenner @IAmCait Every week is a wealth of knowledge. Thank you for sharing! #IAmCait" demonstrate that the audience was learning from the show. Where transgender people are a concerning issue to some (Valentine 2003), Jenner's lack of empathy and knowledge about the trans community was a way of disseminating much-needed lessons to the viewing audience at home.

CONCLUSION

The study used Twitter as a space to examine public discourse surrounding the mediated transition of Bruce Jenner to Caitlyn Jenner. The analysis utilized a random sample of tweets from Bruce Jenner's Diane Sawyer interview in April 2015 through the debut of Caitlyn Jenner's reality show in July 2015. Results revealed themes of white privilege, male privilege, fame, celebrity status, wealth, trans representation, political and gender ideologies, age, and education. In most instances, these identity markers were not mutually exclusive, nor did they merely intersect; rather, they were constitutive of one another (Hames-García 2011). The inclusion of tweets focused on multiple identities by the audience directly mirrors the increase of intersectional reporting post-Sawyer interview (Li 2017). Jenner's set of privileges not only affords her the current opportunities she has but also separates her from a majority of the trans community. Jenner's mediated representation neglects the lived experiences of trans women, specifically those of color, who are disproportionately affected by harassment, poverty, and violence (James et al. 2016).

There was notable contention on the acceptance of Jenner as a role model and as a representative for the trans community in the media. Most of the tweets were negative, in disagreement with the findings of Miller and Behm-Morawitz (2017), who found tweets surrounding the Sawyer interview were primarily positive and supportive. This could be due to the fact that the current study extended the sample timeframe to include Jenner's cover of *Vanity Fair* and her show *I Am Cait*. The increase in negative discourse demonstrates the audience's discontent with Jenner's performance of gender as it intersects with her race, fame, wealth, and age. As Crenshaw emphasizes, intersectionality highlights various forms of inequality, how they operate together and how they exacerbate each other (Steinmetz 2020). Although Jenner has power in regard to race and wealth, her gender identity as a trans woman diminishes this power. As her transition progresses in the media, Jenner is marginalized from normative society, while also being marginalized from the LGBTQ community, creating a paradox of power. Jenner's intersectionality highlights both the oppressions and opportunities tied to each of her identities.

Public discourse on Twitter provides mostly negative reactions to Jenner's transition, however, there were a few positive aspects that emerged in some of the audience's tweets. Jenner's highly publicized coming out can be considered a step forward for visibility of the trans community and awareness of distinctive trans issues. Specifically, the education of Jenner on her reality show *I Am Cait* was a space where audience members were able to learn alongside Jenner, highlighting the ability for Jenner to queer normative culture (West 2014).

Media has the power to cultivate attitudes, cognitions, and behaviors. For some, the trans community may not be an obtrusive population. Some public's only contact or point of reference regarding trans issues is television. If Jenner and the multiplicity of her identities are the only mediated representation they have, the public may construct their beliefs on transgender people based on her. As expressed in the analysis, most audience members framed Jenner as privileged, conservative, ignorant of trans issues, and as not representative of the trans community. The audience's tweets are, of course, influenced by their own individual circumstance and frame of thought (Chong and Druckman 2007). In turn, these framed tweets have the power to indoctrinate certain morals and beliefs about the society that aid in the interpretation and importance of issues, both positive and negative, concerning transgender individuals (Gamson and Modigliani 1989; Gamson et al. 1992).

Furthermore, the study demonstrates that gender roles are socially constructed. Jenner's mediated representations in traditional media, such as her interviews and reality shows, showcase how she performs gender. On the other hand, digital media is a space where individuals are afforded the power to respond to and police Jenner's performances. Thus, Twitter becomes the very space and means to exercise power (Foucault 1978). Some criticized Jenner's performance as well as her rhetoric, while others praised her. Others were quick to sexualize and objectify her. Lastly, a group of people used her age as a reference point to judge her gender. Jenner's truth is incomplete and does not reside in her as a confessor, but rather is shaped and reshaped by her audience who uses Twitter as a means of assimilation and public recording (LaFountain 1989).

The main limitation of the study is the inability to analyze the identities of those individuals who were tweeting. It would be beneficial, for example, to know the age, gender identity, political affiliation, and other relevant identity markers of each Twitter user to better understand how an individual's positionality influences their meaning-making processes as they evaluate and interact with content pertaining to Caitlyn Jenner and the larger transgender community. Of particular interest would be whether or not people who have prior knowledge of trans issues, or any interaction with trans individuals, engage with media differently than those who have not. Future research should look at how the identities of digital media users influence their interpretations of mediated depictions of transgender individuals. Nonetheless, this research provides a case study of how a transgender celebrity and the multiplicity of her identities are framed by her audience on Twitter.

For the audience, Caitlyn Jenner's mediated transition transcends confession. It is both education and representation, used to construct identity about oneself and the others. The study demonstrated how Caitlyn Jenner serves as a synecdoche for the trans community, how the media constructs knowledge about trans people through discourse about Caitlyn Jenner's intersectional representation. Transgender identities disrupt gender binaries, however dominant Western discourse, particularly in media, still works to stabilize sex and reiterate sexual norms (Sloop 2000, 168). To use Valentine's (2003) words, we as a society get to witness how transgender people and issues are "regulated" and institutionalized in modern media, in this instance using frames of white and male privilege, fame, celebrity status, wealth, political ideologies, gender, and age. Jenner's mediated transition, however, leaves out other intersectional representations of trans people.

"Intersectionality is a lens through which you can see where power comes and collides, where it interlocks and intersects," said Crenshaw in 2017. An individual's identity is more than self-identification, it is directly tied to the intersecting larger social structures and group memberships; each identity influencing and being influenced by another (Hames-García 2011). This multiplicity generates both oppression and opportunity for confessor and audience, and it is specifically salient for those who identify as transgender. Caitlyn Jenner and her brand arguably have the power. Other transgender people may not see themselves represented in her, nor in other mediated representations. They remain disempowered, disenfranchised, and intersectionally disadvantaged in the media.

REFERENCES

Billings, Andrew C., Leigh M. Moscowitz, Coral Rae, and Natalie Brown-Devlin. 2015. "The Art of Coming Out: Traditional and Social Media Frames Surrounding the NBA's Jason Collins." *Journalism and Mass Communication Quarterly* 92, no. 1: 142–60.

Burch, Lauren M., Evan L. Frederick, and Ann Pegoraro. 2015. "Kissing in the Carnage: An Examination of Framing on Twitter during the Vancouver Riots." *Journal of Broadcasting and Electronic Media* 59, no. 3: 399–415.

Carlin, Diana and Kelly L. Winfrey. 2009. "Have You Come a Long Way, Baby? Hillary Clinton, Sarah Palin, and Sexism in 2008 Campaign Coverage." *Communication Studies* 60, no. 4: 326–43.

Cassidy, William. 2016. "Inching Away from the Toy Department: Daily Newspaper Sports Coverage of Jason Collins' and Michael Sam's Coming Out." *Communication and Sport* 5, no. 5: 534–53.

Cavalcante, Andre. 2013. "Centering Transgender Identity via the Textual Periphery: *Transamerica* and the 'Double Work' of Paratexts." *Critical Studies in Media Communication* 30, no. 2: 85–101.

Choi, Soon Kyu and Ilan H. Meyer. 2016. *LGBT Aging: A Review of Research Findings, Needs, and Policy Implications*. Los Angeles, CA: The Williams Institute.

Chong, Dennis and James N. Druckman. 2007. "Framing Theory." *Annual Review of Political Science* 10, no. 1: 103–26.

Columbia Law School. 2017. "Kimberlé Crenshaw on Intersectionality, More Than Two Decades Later." June 8, 2017. https://www.law.columbia.edu/news/archive/kimberle-crenshaw-intersectionality-more-two-decades-later

Crenshaw, Kimberlé. 1989. "Demarginalizing the Intersection of Race and Sex: A Black Feminist Critique of Antidiscrimination Doctrine, Feminist Theory, and Antiracist Politics." *University of Chicago Legal Forum* 1, no. 8: 139–67.

Dagkas, Symeon. 2016. "Problematizing Social Justice in Health Pedagogy and Youth Sport." *Research Quarterly for Exercise and Sport* 87, no. 3: 221–9.

Dale, Amanda. 2018. "International Women's Human Rights and the Hope for Feminist Law: Intersectionality as Legal Framework." *Canadian Woman Studies* 33, no. 1–2: 37–50.

De Beco, Gauthier. 2020. "Intersectionality and Disability in International Human Rights Law." *The International Journal of Human Rights* 24, no. 5: 593–614.

DeCuir-Gunby, Jessica, Patricia L. Marshall, and Allison W. McCulloch. 2011. "Developing and Using a Codebook for the Analysis of Interview Data: An Example from a Professional Development Research Project." *Field Methods* 23, no. 2: 136–55.

Dow, Bonnie. 2001. "Ellen, Television, and the Politics of Gay and Lesbian Visibility." *Critical Studies in Media Communication* 18, no. 2: 123–40.

Eng, David L., Jack Halberstam, and José Esteban Muñoz. 2005. "What's Queer about Queer Studies Now?" *Social Texts* 84, no. 5: 1–17.

Entman, Robert. 1993. "Framing: Toward Clarification of a Fractured Paradigm." *Journal of Communication* 43, no. 4: 51–8.

Espineira, Karine. 2016. "Transgender and Transsexual People's Sexuality in the Media." *Parallax* 22, no. 3: 323–9.

Ferguson, Roderick A. 2005. "Race-ing Homonormativity: Citizenship, Sociology, and Gay Identity." In *Black Queer Studies: A Critical Anthology*, edited by E. Patrick Johnson and Mae G. Henderson, 52–67. Durham, NC: Duke University Press.

Fischer, Mia. 2017. "Trans Responses to Adichie: Challenging Cis Privilege in Popular Feminism." *Feminist Media Studies* 17, no. 5: 896–9.

Foucault, Michel. 1978. *History of Sexuality. Volume 1: An Introduction*. Translated by Robert Hurley. New York: Vintage Books.

Gamson, William A. and Andre Modigliani. 1989. "Media Discourse and Public Opinion on Nuclear Power: A Constructionist Approach." *American Journal of Sociology* 95, no. 1: 1–37.

Gamson, William A., David Croteau, William Hoynes, and Theodore Sasson. 1992. "Media Images and the Social Construction of Reality." *Annual Review of Sociology* 18: 373–93.

Gibson, Katie L. 2009. "Undermining Katie Couric: The Discipline Function of the Press." *Women and Language* 32, no. 1: 51–9.

Goldberg, Abbie E. and Katherine R. Allen. 2018. "Teaching Undergraduates about LGBTQ Identities, Families, and Intersectionality." *Family Relations* 67, no. 1: 176–91.

Halberstam, Jack. 2005. *In a Queer Time and Place: Transgender Bodies, Subcultural Lives*. New York: New York University Press.

Hames-García, Michael R. 2011. *Identity Complex: Making the Case for Multiplicity*. Minneapolis, MN: University of Minnesota Press.

I Am Cait. 2015. Produced by Caitlyn Jenner. E! Network, 2015–2016.

James, Sandy E., Jody L. Herman, Susan Rankin, Mara Keisling, Lisa Mottet, and Ma'ayan Anafi. 2016. *Executive Summary of the Report of the 2015 U.S. Transgender Survey*. Washington DC: National Center for Transgender Equality.

Kaplan, Andreas M. and Michael Haenlein. 2010. "Users of the World, Unite! The Challenges and Opportunities of Social Media." *Business Horizons* 53, no. 1: 59–68.

Kian, Edward, Alina Bernstein, and John S. McGuire. 2013. "A Major Boost for Gender Equality or More of the Same? The Television Coverage of Female Athletes at the 2012 London Olympic Games." *The Journal of Popular Television* 1, no. 1: 143–9.

Kian, Edward, Eric Anderson, and Danny Shipka. 2015. "'I Am Happy to Start the Conversation': Examining Sport Media Framing of Jason Collins' Coming Out and Playing in the NBA." *Sexualities* 18, no. 5–6: 618–40.

Kissel, Rick. 2015. "Bruce Jenner Interview Ratings: 17 Million Watch ABC Special." *Variety*, April 25, 2015. http://variety.com/2015/tv/news/bruce-jenner-interview-ratings-17-million-watch-abc-special-1201479968/

Kreiss, Daniel. 2016. "Seizing the Moment: The Presidential Campaigns' Use of Twitter during the 2012 Electoral Cycle." *New Media and Society* 18, no. 8: 1473–90.

LaFountain, Marc. 1989. "Foucault and Dr. Ruth." *Critical Studies in Mass Communication* 6, no. 2: 123–37.

Li, Minjie. 2017. "Intermedia Attribute Agenda Setting in the Context of Issue-Focused Media Events: Caitlyn Jenner and Transgender Reporting." *Journalism Practice* 12, no. 1: 56–75.

Lombardi, Emilia, Rikki Anne Wilchins, Dana Priesing, and Diana Malouf. 2002. "Gender Violence: Transgender Experiences with Violence and Discrimination." *Journal of Homosexuality* 42, no. 1: 89–101.

Lubitow, Amy, JaDee Carathers, Maura Kelly, and Miriam Abelson. 2017. "Transmobilities: Mobility, Harassment, and Violence Experienced by Transgender and Gender Nonconforming Public Transit Riders in Portland, Oregon." *Gender, Place and Culture* 24, no. 10: 1398–418.

McInroy, Lauren and Shelley L. Craig. 2015. "Transgender Representation in Offline and Online Media: LGBTQ Youth Perspectives." *Journal of Human Behavior in the Social Environment* 25, no. 6: 606–17.

McIntosh, Peggy. 1997. "White Privilege and Male Privilege: A Personal Account of Coming to See Correspondences through Work in Women's Studies." In *Critical White Studies: Looking behind the Mirror*, edited by Richard Delgado and Jean Stefancic, 291–9. Philadelphia, PA: Temple University Press.

Miller, Brandon and Elizabeth Behm-Morawitz. 2017. "Exploring Social Television, Opinion Leaders, and Twitter Audience Reactions to Diane Sawyer's Coming Out Interview with Caitlyn Jenner." *International Journal of Transgenderism* 18, no. 2: 140–53.

Morrison, Sara. 2016. "Covering the Transgender Community. How Newsrooms Are Moving beyond the 'Coming Out' Story to Report Crucial Transgender Issues." *Nieman Reports*, January 12, 2016. http://niemanreports.org/articles/covering-the-transgender-community/

Namaste, Viviane K. 2011. *Sex Change, Social Change: Reflections on Identity, Institutions, and Imperialism*. Toronto, ON: Canadian Scholars' Press.

O'Connell, Michael. 2015. "TV Ratings: Caitlyn Jenner's E! Show Draws 2.7 Million Viewers." *The Hollywood Reporter*, July 28, 2015. https://www.hollywoodreporter.com/live-feed/caitlyn-jenners-tv-ratings-i-811447

Pamelee, John H. and Shannon L. Bichard. 2013. *Politics and the Twitter Revolution: How Tweets Influence the Relationship between Political Leaders and the Public.* Lanham, MD: Lexington Books.

Parent, Mike C., Cirleen DeBlaere, and Bonnie Moradi. 2013. "Approaches to Research on Intersectionality: Perspectives on Gender, LGBT, and Racial/Ethnic Identities." *Sex Roles* 68: 639–45.

Phillips, John. 2006. *Transgender on Screen.* New York: Palgrave Macmillan.

Shah, Dhavan V., Douglas M. McLeod, Melissa R. Gotlieb, and NamJin Lee. 2009. "Framing and Agenda-Setting." In *The SAGE Handbook of Media Processes and Effects*, edited by Robin L. Nabi and Mary Beth Oliver, 83–98. Thousand Oaks, CA: SAGE.

Shams, Tahseen. 2015. "Bangladeshi Muslims in Mississippi: Impression Management Based on the Intersectionality of Religion, Ethnicity, and Gender." *Cultural Dynamics* 27, no. 3: 379–97.

Shields, Stephanie A. 2008. "Gender: An Intersectionality Perspective." *Sex Roles* 59: 301–11.

Singh, Anneliese A. 2013. "Transgender Youth of Color and Resilience: Negotiating Oppression and Finding Support." *Sex Roles* 68, no. 11–12: 690–702.

Sloop, John M. 2000. "Disciplining the Transgendered: Brandon Teena, Public Representation, and Normativity." *Western Journal of Communication* 64, no. 2: 165–89.

Steinmetz, Katy. 2020. "She Coined the Term 'Intersectionality' over 30 Years Ago. Here's What It Means to Her Today." *Time*, February 20, 2020. https://time.com/5786710/kimberle-crenshaw-intersectionality/

Stryker, Susan. 2008. *Transgender History.* Berkeley, CA: Seal Press.

Tan, Andy S., Elaine Hanby, Ashley Sanders-Jackson, Stella Lee, Kasisomayajula Viswanath, and Jennifer Potter. 2019. "Inequities in Tobacco Advertising Exposure among Young Adult Sexual, Racial and Ethnic Minorities: Examining Intersectionality of Sexual Orientation with Race and Ethnicity." *Tobacco Control*, December 19, 2019.

20/20. "Bruce Jenner: The Interview." ABC News, April 24, 2015.

Us Weekly. 2014. "Bruce's Secret Double Life." *American Media Inc.*, Issue 1032.

Valentine, David. 2003. "'I Went to Bed with My Own Kind Once': The Erasure of Desire in the Name of Identity." *Language and Communication* 23, no. 2, 123–38.

Wasike, Ben. 2013. "Framing News in 140 Characters: How Social Media Editors Frame the News and Interact with Audiences via Twitter." *Global Media Journal, Canadian Edition* 6, no. 1: 5–23.

Watkins, Paul and Edward Moreno. 2017. "Bathrooms without Borders: Transgender Students Argue Separate Is Not Equal." *The Clearing House: A Journal of Educational Strategies, Issues and Ideas* 90, no. 5–6: 166–71.

West, Isaac. 2014. *Transforming Citizenships: Transgender Articulations of the Law.* New York: New York University Press.

Williams, Melvin L. 2017. "'I Don't Belong in Here!' A Social Media Analysis of Digital Protest, Transgender Rights, and International Restroom Legislation." In *Social Media, Culture and Identity*, edited by Kehbuma Langmia and Tia C. M. Tyree, 27–48. Lanham, MD: Lexington Books.

CHAPTER SEVEN

Her Story, Educating a Mainstream Audience

BY KATERINA SYMES[1]

INTRODUCTION

In the opening scene of *Her Story* (2016), two friends are seated at a bar. They are Allie (Laura Zak), a white lesbian woman, and her friend Lisa (Caroline Whitney Smith). Allie shares her plan to write an article on trans women in the Los Angeles LGBTQ community for the fictional publication *Gay LA*, and, upon hearing this news, Lisa groans "Oh come on. Jerry Springer's been doing that for decades." Unwilling to be deterred by Lisa's lack of enthusiasm, Allie insists "No, no, no. Like, in *our* community. Like, who are they? Who are they dating? Where do they go to meet people?" and she gestures toward a nearby server, Violet (Jen Richards). Allie says: "What about that waitress?" Lisa ogles a different server, and, after incorrectly assuming that she is the woman Allie is referencing, Lisa scoffs "Are you out of your mind? That? That's all woman." Allie rolls her eyes at Lisa and nods again at Violet: "No, her, over there. How do I approach her? Like, what is a polite way to ask what someone is?" Lisa quips, "Seriously? Like, you've never seen a hot woman before and just been like this: 'Yo gay?'" Allie shakes her

---

1 Katerina Symes, Ph.D. candidate, Concordia University in Montreal, Canada. Instructor in Humanities at Vanier College. Email: katerinasymes@gmail.com

head, still uncertain: "I can usually tell. This is different." Lisa shrugs indifferently and replies: "So, worst case, you piss him off. And then there's one more pissed off tranny in the world. They're all pissed off anyway."

Lisa's misgendering of Violet reflects the discriminatory premise that trans women are not real women, and it reinforces the prevailing cultural assumption that gender is reducible to sex characteristics—that is, the absence or presence of specific physical body parts related to development and reproduction. But Allie's insistence that her article focus on trans women "in our community," as well as her correct use of the pronoun "her" to reference Violet, contrasts Lisa's position. Through this exchange, *Her Story* exemplifies a predilection for the pedagogical: the series' characters and narrative storytelling offer viewers multiple perspectives on trans issues. Although Lisa's problematic comments reveal the age-old tropes and approaches that reify stereotypes of trans people in the media, *Her Story*'s inclusion of this opening scene primarily addresses cisgender viewers. *Her Story* may center the lives of two transgender women, Violet (Jen Richards) and Paige (Angelica Ross), with the express purpose of intervening within a body of transgender media projects created and acted by cisgender people, but this chapter argues that the didactic function of the show's character proxy structure necessitates an address to multiple categories of viewership. Although *Her Story* may have been written by and for people who are queer and trans, the show must continue to make assumptions about who is watching and who needs educating about transgender issues.

Debuting in January 2016, the web series *Her Story* was co-written and co-executive produced by trans activist Jen Richards and Laura Zak, and directed by Navajo trans woman Sydney Freeland. The critically-acclaimed and Emmy-nominated program follows the dating and romantic experiences of a diverse group of queer and trans women. It depicts a range of characters with overlapping identities of gender (cisgender, transgender, masculine, feminine), sexuality (lesbian, queer), class (working, upper-middle-class), and race and ethnicity (Caucasian, Black American). As a series about queer and trans women, *Her Story* speaks to, for, and about an intersection of subjects and identities that are largely absent from television. This chapter examines how the combination of *Her Story*'s characters, representations, and storylines addresses multiple viewers. As I argue, this character proxy structure not only folds queer, trans, and larger audiences into the series' content but also serves a pedagogical function. *Her Story* educates cisgender viewers within and outside of the LGBTQ community who are unfamiliar with the complexity of trans life and, in doing so, it intervenes within an emerging body of transgender media projects that have largely been told by cisgender creators with trans roles played by cisgender actors.

HER STORY, DIGITAL TELEVISION, AND QUEER CROSSOVER PROGRAMS

There has been a recent proliferation of scripted digital television programs engaging with queer and trans content. These programs introduce queer and trans characters and themes to multiple audiences, and their circulation reflects the confluence of several factors: television's changing modes of production, distribution, and consumption; the popularity of and critical acclaim received by works centering queer and transgender content; and a public climate characterized by a growing need to have queer and trans people tell their own stories. *Her Story* is part of this emergent body of television programming, which I term "queer crossovers."

Situated at this historical juncture, *Her Story* offers different ways of knowing and representing queer and trans life. To think of the series' crossover potential acknowledges the effect of its circulations among different audiences. The term "crossover" is meant to emphasize *Her Story*'s cultural effects within and across programming genres and audiences, as it traverses and renegotiates the boundaries both between and within queer and heteronormative cultures. It is with some hesitation that I have chosen the term "queer" to describe this program. My intent is neither to subsume transgender under the queer umbrella, as has been done previously, nor to suggest that *Her Story* is intrinsically queer, whether through its inclusion of queer and trans characters and narrative themes, or in its aesthetic and formal qualities made possible by digital television. Instead, "queer" indicates how *Her Story* cannot be confined to a single entity. I draw from Sara Ahmed's (2004) understanding of the affective potential of queer, which she refers to as "queer feelings." In her words, queerness is:

> Not about assimilation or resistance, *but about inhabiting norms differently*. The inhabitance is generative or productive insofar as it does not end with the failure of norms to be secured, but with possibilities of living that do not "follow" those norms through. (Ahmed 2004, 155)

Thus, the traversing of queerness into dominant and mainstream culture is not meant to be uncomfortable or anxiety-inducing, but rather a perturbation of the heteronormativity of television. The cultural effects of *Her Story* reveal the norms and values that make queer *queer* in the first place.

As a queer crossover program, *Her Story* mediates in multiple directions: it is not the property of a single culture, whether queer or heteronormative. *Her Story* recognizes the encounter between queer and heteronormative cultures, while at the same time, it resists the idea that this exchange between different cultural organizations of knowledge is politically neutral. Instead of positioning heteronormative culture as the invisible ground against which these programs emerge, *Her Story* implies a dynamic relationship, one wherein references to the dominant and mainstream almost always refer to the straight, white, and cisgender culture as sites of power. *Her Story* demonstrates possibilities for exchange between non-dominant (which is to say, queer) cultures. In this vein, I consider *Her Story* as inherently compromising. Rather than equivocate between critiques of *Her Story*'s normative dimensions and its possibilities for queer and trans representation, I imagine what *Her Story* might do pedagogically, not only in its programming, but also around it, in its industry pressures and representational politics, and in its support and mentoring of queer and trans writers, actors, and producers.

Her Story is an expression on behalf of a group of people who share the same political commitment to represent most accurately the complexity of queer and trans life onscreen. Its writers and producers are either queer or trans, and their commitment to queer and trans politics extends beyond their work with the series. Jen Richards' list of accomplishments includes a website sharing positive transgender experiences called We Happy Trans, co-founding and co-directing The Trans 100, an annual list celebrating trans activists and influencers, and regular appearances on Caitlyn Jenner's reality television series *I Am Cait*. At the same time, Laura Zak co-created, co-wrote, produced, and starred in 2013 in the web series *Hashtag* made by Tello Films, a Chicago production company and new media platform that creates and supports queer women's filmmaking. *Her Story* is thus characterized by an explicit engagement with queer and trans content through its centering of queer and trans characters, the narrative exploration of queer and trans themes, and the employment of over 80% female and LGBTQ professionals. As a series produced by, for, and in consultation with queer and trans communities, *Her Story* makes a critical departure from other queer crossover works: the show speaks to the communities it represents and, simultaneously, it addresses a broader audience.

Her Story engages with a medium platform that allows for the continued creation of original stories: all 6 episodes are available online via YouTube for free, a decision made possible by the support the show received from the crowdfunding website Indiegogo. For executive producer Katherine Fisher, this campaign allowed the communities *Her Story* represented to be a part of the creative process (Bonney 2016), while, for Richards, it gave trans people who are unable to afford subscriptions to services like Netflix or Amazon Prime Video a rare opportunity to see themselves represented (Jusino 2015). Online platforms like YouTube are cheap, mobile, and accessible, and they provide alternatives to mainstream representations of gender and sexuality. As Zak notes, a web series gives creators "so much freedom, content-wise, because there isn't anyone other than the production company policing content" (Ennis 2015). *Her Story*'s commitment to online accessibility reflects the growing influence of digital communications technologies within transgender communities. According to Andre Cavalcante, "technology has become increasingly 'ready-to-hand' for transgender individuals: personalized computers with Internet access have increasingly become part of the everyday life of being transgender, and the affordances of online spaces" (Cavalcante 2016, 110). *Her Story* highlights how digital television can offer trans people increased opportunities for recognition and self-representation: through the creation, distribution, and sharing of transgender content, trans people are able to navigate the complexities of trans subjectivity within a world that excludes them (Cavalcante 2016). Online spaces and new media platforms position trans people as experts, "contesting the expertise over trans bodies claimed by medical professionals, educators, and parents" (Dame 2013, 46).

In the following sections, I examine a selection of press reviews and promotional materials accompanying *Her Story*'s debut. My discursive analysis examines the "work of representation" (Hall 1997; Rose 2008). I not only identify how the series responds to and intervenes within competing discourses of transgender representations on television, but also suggest that self-representation has become a cornerstone debate within transgender politics. Then, I conduct a close reading of the series to examine how *Her Story*'s representations, narratives, and operational aesthetics come together to create specific viewing positions for audiences. My textual analysis focuses specifically on how the series first introduces its trans characters to viewers. I argue that *Her Story* aims to address and educate cisgender viewers who are unfamiliar with trans issues, despite being a series created by and for trans and queer people. Here I use the term "pedagogy" in a broad sense to refer to the methods and visual, narrative, and aesthetic practices by which *Her Story* creates specific viewing positions for audiences to educate them about life as trans.

(SELF-) REPRESENTATION AND TRANSGENDER POLITICS

Her Story parallels a broader history of queer and transgender political and scholarly interests, particularly surrounding questions of visibility. Although related, these histories reflect different cultural moments, audiences, and industry attachments. Therefore, it is necessary to briefly outline and distinguish these trajectories. Within queer television studies, research has centered on textual analyses and hermeneutic readings of specific episodes or programs, and it has addressed the incorporation of gays, lesbians, and queers on screen. The 1990s is framed as a period of increased diversity: many long-running television programs included gay and lesbian characters and storylines, and new programs featured these characters as central to their series, such as *Ellen*, *Will and Grace*, *Queer as Folk*, and

The L Word. Although some scholars considered this increased visibility a sign of substantive progress, others have been more apprehensive of the incorporation of gay, lesbian, and queer people into dominant currents and televisual flows. These later critiques have generally focused on problematizing the presence or absence of gay, lesbian, and queer people on television, and they have identified how these characters are depicted either visually or narratively. Many of these analyses have examined at length how gay, lesbian, and queer characters are either heterosexualized or presented in "asexual contexts" (Raley and Lucas 2006, 25), particularly when compared to their heterosexual counterparts (Farr and Degroult 2008).

Although the question of visibility remains important to a politics of representation, other queer television scholars have critiqued the idea that television can be queered and subsequently diversified by the incorporation of gay, lesbian, and queer characters and themes. Melanie Kohnen (2016) identifies how queerness is framed through discourses of whiteness: the normative white gay and lesbian identities remain central to imagining queer subjectivities in Western culture, which renders some queer identities, practices, and knowledge visible while obscuring others. Amy Villarejo (2013) cautions against this conflation of queer visibility with LGTBQ emancipatory struggles and instead argues that queer life must be historicized in relation to the varied history of television itself. Her point is that the apparatus of television is a complex temporal and spatial system wherein "television's changing time and spaces organize and respond to also changing queer times and spaces" (2013, 7). In this vein, queer television studies have sought to move beyond this visibility/invisibility binary, offering more socially and historically situated medium-specific analyses.

The history of trans representations is both closely tied to queer televisual trajectories, yet they maintain a vexed relationship. Like queer television studies, transgender critical accounts have emphasized the absence of trans and gender diverse people (Booth 2015; Serano 2007). On the rare occasion they are represented, trans people are portrayed as victims, or stereotyped as villains, sex workers, and sexual deviants, which follow larger patterns of racialization. Such representations have been distancing and objectifying. They frame trans people as either freaks or curiosities (Namaste 2005). In implying a cisgender audience, they "establish a logic of 'us' (non-trans) looking at 'them' (trans)" (Horak 2014, 577). Although trans critiques share similar attachments to the question of visibility as queer television studies, many have noted how trans individuals have historically been stigmatized to make gay and lesbian sexuality appear more acceptable (Gamson 1998, 2001; Ng 2015).

As Joshua Gamson argues:

> A new, postcloset kind of normalization pattern is at work here: the acceptability of lesbian and gay families, and of lesbian and gay people into their birth families, is predicated on their *not* exhibiting [...] the "freakish" gender of transgendered people. (2001, 83)

For Gamson, gay, lesbian, and queer sexualities are normalized against trans identities, which remain secondary and are subsequently marginalized. For Capuzza and Spencer (2017), this strategic industrial practice has contributed to the marginalization of trans bodies and practices.

Given the recent success of equality campaigns in the United States and Canada to help gay, lesbian, and queer people access marriage, the military, employment, and economic security, trans politics is discursively positioned as "America's next civil rights frontier" (Steinmetz 2014). In the last several years, there has been an increase in trans visibility in both scripted and reality television series, alongside public attention paid to transgender issues: the imprisonment of CeCe Macdonald, the success and rising celebrities of Janet Mock and Laverne Cox with the latter on 2014's cover of *Time*, the highly publicized transitioning procedures of Caitlyn Jenner and sisters Lana and Lilly Wachowski, the release of the first transgender doll by The Tonner Doll Company in 2017, and the appearance of the first openly transgender playmate on *Playboy* magazine. What might be characterized as a "transgender turn" thus provides context for television's increased engagement with trans lives.

Rendering trans people visible within public discourse is a shift in both the political and televisual landscape, but many scholars have noted a subsequent regulation of transgender identities and expression. These critiques underscore how programming is shaped by a gender binary discourse and they focus on how cisgender normativity is either challenged or upheld. According to Kay Siebler (2012), transgender characters are often depicted within transition or coming out narratives. These storylines emphasize how a trans character's experience of gender transition impacts the cisgender people around them and frequently involves narrative conventions that require the onscreen unmasking of one's identity. Such revelations are often delayed, and prompt discomfort, fear, or even disgust in the cisgender characters' reactions to this discovery (Miller 2017). Many current programs rely on this narrative device: *Transparent*'s primary storyline in season one centers on Maura Pfefferman's struggle to disclose her trans identity to her friends and family, and while *Orange Is the New Black* introduces Sophia Burset as a transgender woman, the series uses flashbacks to demonstrate how her transition impacted her relationship with her wife and son.

Michael Lovelock (2017) argues that this conflation of trans identities with gender transition frames televisual representations of trans subjectivity within a "wrong body discourse" and over-emphasizes a trans character's feelings of being born or trapped in the "wrong body." This framing defines trans people by their bodies, particularly through the rhetoric of lack and difference; sex assigned at birth, and specifically, one's genitals, is invariably used to signify a trans person's gender identity and to dispossess a trans person's autonomy to name one's self (Funk and Funk 2016). As a result, television's preoccupation with transition narratives excludes other representations of trans life and subjectivity. Trans characters are rarely depicted within romantic storylines, or portrayed in erotic or sexual relationships (Abbott 2013). For example, *Transparent*'s Maura is only given a love interest in season two, and while Sophia from *Orange Is the New Black* is married, she is never shown being sexually intimate.

In contrast to queer televisual trajectories, transgender scholarship and critical reviews have also highlighted the limited employment opportunities facing transgender people within the entertainment industry. Many have cited the frequent casting of cisgender actors in transgender roles, as well as an overwhelming emphasis on whiteness: Jaye Davidson in *The Crying Game* (1992), Hilary Swank in *Boys Don't Cry* (1999), Felicity Huffman in *Transamerica* (2005), Kerry Washington in *Life Is Hot in Cracktown* (2009), Jared Leto in *Dallas Buyers Club* (2013), Jeffrey Tambor in *Transparent* (2014–2019), Eddie Redmayne in *The Danish Girl* (2015), and, most recently in 2018, the initial casting of Scarlet Johansson as a trans man in the forthcoming production *Rub and Tug* before she withdrew from the project due to the backlash she faced. The director of GLAAD's Transgender Media Program, Nick Adams, asserts that the casting of cisgender actors in the roles of trans women sends viewers two "strong and wrong messages: 1. that being transgender is an act, a performance, just a matter of playing dress-up; and 2. that underneath all that artifice, a transgender woman really is a man" (Adams 2016). These casting decisions continue to define trans people by their bodies and through a rhetoric of lack and difference. Again, sex assigned at birth is used to signify a trans person's gender identity (Funk and Funk 2016, 881).

Jen Richards has also commented extensively about the issue of self-representation of transgender people:

> With the rapid changes in trans visibility, the community has become increasingly vocal about how it's portrayed. Trans activists and their allies refuse to be quiet as their stories are exploited for drama and pathos by artists who know little to nothing about their experiences, as cis[gender] actors reap rewards for the bravery of the performances while failing to acknowledge the actual current struggles of trans people. (Richards 2014)

For Richards, series depicting trans characters do a "superlative job of mining the particular," but it is a particular she describes being "largely exhausted by" (2014). Indeed, many of these series portray yet another story about a transitioning, middle-class, usually white transwoman with a family, which has long been the default depiction of trans people—that is, when they are not portrayed as victimized, evil, deceptive, or pathological. These accounts raise critical questions surrounding trans representation: who can and should tell transgender stories, and how ought trans narratives be told? Although trans lives are being spotlighted on television, in almost all these cases, these stories continue to be told by cisgender creators and portrayed by white cisgender actors. The issue of self-representation has thus become a cornerstone of transgender politics, particularly in film and television analyses, and serves as a critical departure from queer televisual trajectories.

Her Story is acutely aware of this history of trans visibility and it reflects a political commitment to the self-representation of queer and trans folks. Richards sees *Her Story* as both an intervention within and a critical departure from these limited portrayals and emphasizes the authenticity of these trans characters alongside the importance of self-representation. As journalist Mary Emily O'Hara suggests in an interview with Richards, "people all over the world have learned some basics about trans issues thanks to the hyper-presence of people like Caitlyn Jenner in the media, a show like [*Her Story*] lays the path going forward" (2015). Then she adds that the series reminds us that there are many more stories left to be told.

Her Story is written by and for the communities it represents. It depicts an ensemble cast and foregrounds two trans women, Violet (Jen Richards) and Paige (Angelica Ross), who are already living in their affirmed gender identities. Moving beyond transition narratives, *Her Story* highlights the dating and romantic lives of these women, which is something rarely seen on television, as previously mentioned. It also addresses a number of complex themes, such as the friendship between a Black and a white trans woman, transgender lesbians, and the challenges associated with disclosing one's trans identity both within dating and professional work contexts, particularly when one is not easily read as trans. Additionally, many of the series' characters, scenes, and dialogue sequences are drawn from the lived experiences of actual transgender people, including the showrunners themselves (Lang 2016). Such representations challenge current media coverage of trans people, focused on the fights over bathroom access and the high rates of homicides against trans people in the United States, and therefore they make a critical departure from other transgender media projects (Stafford 2016).

As a series about subjects and identities that are invisible in mainstream media, *Her Story* is tasked with the responsibility to introduce viewers to complex trans characters and themes. The combination of *Her Story*'s characters, representations, and storylines, which I define as *Her Story*'s character proxy structure, thus serves a pedagogical role. By engaging with and responding to a larger body of mediated transgender narratives created and acted by cisgender people, *Her Story* provides alternative modes of trans (self-) representation. The idea that television can be entertaining and educating is well covered by Jonathan Gray in his book *Television Entertainment* (2008). The author emphasizes the medium as a form of travel. The episodic nature of regularly scheduled programming encourages viewers to tune in once a week, "[introducing] us to people we might otherwise never meet, and [introducing] us to lives and ideas foreign to us" (2008, 55).

However, the show's pedagogical potential is significant because of the ways its character proxy structure addresses a wide array of spectators.

ADDRESSING DIFFERENT AUDIENCES THROUGH A CHARACTER PROXY STRUCTURE

In this section, I elucidate *Her Story*'s character proxy structure. My textual analysis demonstrates how this device folds audiences into the series' content by representing multiple perspectives on trans issues and, in doing so, educates LGBTQ and non-LGBTQ viewers about the complexities of trans life. Finally, I conclude by assessing the possible implications of this device for queer, trans, and other spectators.

To begin with, Violet's and Paige's storylines center on more universal and seemingly everyday themes like dating, romance, love, and friendship. For Jen Richards, this move is essential for trans representation:

> There is real power in seeing yourself represented. It's something that a lot of people can take for granted—they grew up and can always identify with the heroes of stories. When you grow up in media and you are only ever a tragedy or a joke, it's hard not to see your own life as a tragic joke. I think for us to show this other model of possibility, to show what it's like for trans women to have friendships and to be in relationships, to laugh, to have joy, very human dramas, that include but can't be reduced to their trans-ness. (Richards interviewed in Rude 2015)

Laura Zak adds:

> I think the lesbian community and gay male community have had their moment[s] where they got their *Queer as Folk* moment or *The L Word* moment where there's a more mainstream show about love lives and dating lives and hopefully, this [show] could be something like that. (Zak interviewed in Rude 2015)

As both producers suggest, all viewers, regardless of how they identify, can relate to the series' larger themes. *Her Story* acknowledges its broad-based viewership by providing viewers with familiar narrative entry points: the show's queer and trans characters address what it means to be a "woman" or a "lesbian" through their experiences navigating the intersections of desire, love, and label identity.

Allie and Violet

Although *Her Story*'s writers and producers are committed to self-representation of queer and trans people, they maintain that the series is "about people rather than politics" (Carrera 2015). *Her Story*'s showrunners emphasize how the series' diverse characters and modes of narrative storytelling address trans issues without being polemical: the characters offer a spectrum of perspectives and allow viewers to formulate their own positions on issues raised by the show. Allie's role is explicitly pedagogical. As a journalist who is writing about trans women in the LGBTQ community, her job is to ask Violet questions: Allie's article is the central plot device used to introduce her character (and by extension the audience) to Violet and Paige. As a white, upper-middle class, and cisgender lesbian, Allie invites viewers to identify with her whiteness, class privilege, femininity, and queerness. By anchoring these identities, Allie centers Violet's perspective and educates viewers about transgender issues.

Allie's exchanges with Violet reference and contest stereotypes about trans people, and they give viewers a chance to see what kinds of relationships queer and trans women can have with one another. Allie often stumbles through these conversations with Violet, and she either apologizes or corrects herself when she says something potentially offensive or inappropriate. For example, when Allie first introduces herself to Violet, the camera work and editing invite viewers to adopt Allie's eye-line as their own. A shot-reverse-shot changes the viewer's gaze to the look of the camera as if it were Allie's point of view and it enables the viewer to see what Allie sees: Violet. Following this suturing effect, Allie asks Violet: "Ok, sorry, I'm not actually sure how to ask this, so I apologize in advance if I say anything inappropriate. So, I'm working on a story, and … shit, I'm just going to ask. Are you transgender?" Caught off-guard by Allie's question, although not entirely surprised, a resigned Violet affirms her identity before Allie blurts out: "Sorry, was that rude of me to ask?" Violet reassures Allie and expresses how she wishes her trans identity "wasn't so obvious" but that Allie's decision to ask is ultimately "better than assuming."

Implicit in Allie's role is an address to cisgender audiences: her discomfort is palpable and, alongside the suturing of her gaze to the look of the camera, Allie's position mirrors that of the viewer who is unfamiliar with how to navigate these encounters. The conversation exemplifies the types of invasive questioning trans people experience, and the scene tactfully addresses the effects of passing privilege as related to the supposed readability of trans identity. Allie's (and by extension, the audience's) introduction to Violet addresses the effects of passing privilege and the supposed readability of trans identity. As Anne Enke (2012, 69) suggests, because cisgender is positioned as non-trans, trans identity must be made visible and marked on the body through a narrow set of narrative and visual signifiers. This process requires trans people to repeatedly perform their marginalized status through a series of disclosures, like Violet's to Allie. The scene demonstrates how trans people must frequently explain, defend, or answer for their gender identity to others because being cisgender is taken as the norm. Violet's repeated disclosure of her history places considerable strain on her interactions with others, particularly when she is meeting new people.

A similar exchange occurs in the second episode when Allie interviews Violet for her article. Allie asks some very personal questions, including if Violet was "a gay man before" her transition. Violet bursts out laughing in response, and a sheepish Allie, who is unsure how to interpret Violet's laughter, immediately apologies: "Sorry, is that too personal?" The scene continues with Violet explaining how she dated women before transition, and, upon hearing this news, Allie eagerly questions if this kind of "switch" is common amongst trans people. Violet explains:

> It's not *un*common. There's really no normal. In fact, the most common reaction I got when I told people I was transitioning was, "Oh, I didn't know you were gay." I mean, to be fair, I had dated men. It just never felt right, not until I was seen as a woman … It's not about them. It's about *me*. When I'm with a man, I have no doubt about my womanhood. My body, next to theirs, is so obviously feminine.

The scene once again demonstrates a complex negotiation of trans identity within *Her Story*'s pedagogical form. Allie's interview questions reference some of the misconceptions, incorrect ideas, and biases against trans people (e.g., that one's gender identity solely defines one's sexuality and sexual orientation), but they ultimately work to center Violet's perspective. Violet is invited to answer and share her experience, and, in doing so, she exemplifies the importance of trans people having the autonomy to name themselves. By explicitly offering viewers a transgender perspective on a trans issue, the scene challenges the stereotypes embedded in Allie's comments, and it posits alternative modes of trans representation by revealing how such representations are currently absent from television. Although Violet's open and frank responses make Allie uncomfortable, Allie provides a model for viewers and educates them through her own learning: (1) she listens carefully and recognizes the limits of her knowledge, for example, when she admits to Violet that she doesn't "know shit about transgender issues," (2) she apologizes and corrects herself when she makes a mistake, (3) she doesn't react defensively to Violet's comments, and (4) she avoids re-centring the conversation around herself and her experience. Watching Allie work through her feelings of discomfort on screen gives viewers a chance to work through theirs while simultaneously gaining practical tips on how to navigate these types of conversations.

Allie's friendships also present a spectrum of queer women's perspectives on trans issues to tackle transphobia. An example is in the second episode when Allie's friends tease her for crushing on Violet. In this scene, viewers can see the group fold laundry together, an act meant to emphasize the everydayness of both their conversation and their lives as lesbian and queer women. In the meantime, the friends discuss whether trans women can really be lesbians:

> **Jenna:** Did you have a date?
> **Lisa:** With a tranny!

Allie:	I'm not bi, guys.
Lisa:	Why are you being all weird? You like him. I can totally tell.
Allie:	Oh my god. It wasn't a date. I'm writing a feature on trans women, and it was just an interview. And yeah, I like *her* ...
Jenna:	Come on, seriously. Could you guys ever consider dating a transsexual?
Kat:	Well, yeah.
Jenna:	Really? You're going to give a blowjob? How long has it been?
Kat:	Seven years.
Jenna:	Right? Not unless you want to stop claiming the term "lesbian," and I'm not losing my gold star.
Kat:	Seriously though, these girls, they can be, like, really fine.
Lisa:	These girls? They represent the exact opposite of what feminism has worked so hard to achieve.
Allie:	Thank you! [With sarcasm] Thank you, Madam Chairwoman, for speaking for all of us.
Lisa:	It's not like I'm the first person to say this shit. A lot of people feel this way.
Jenna:	Can transsexuals even be lesbians?
Lisa:	Nope. Babe, if there's a cock involved, it's not a dyke.
Kat:	Says the queen of strap-ons.
Lisa:	If a guy wants to throw on a skirt and call himself Veronica, that's fine. I mean, I don't think he has to chop his dick off, but I don't think I have to share a bathroom with him.

The exchange between Allie and her friends is a didactic tool for exploring discrimination within the queer community: the scene not only complicates what it means to be a "woman" and a "lesbian," but also informs viewers about the kinds of relationships queer and transgender women can have both within and across LGBTQ spaces. Lisa's and Jenna's comments introduce viewers to a fear of trans people within the LGBTQ community. Their comments reproduce the idea that gender is reducible to sex characteristics, and their position perpetuates the transphobic premise that trans women are not women.

Lisa's character is intentionally antagonistic, and she speaks to a "radical feminist perspective" that "doesn't accept trans women as part of their community" (Ennis 2015). As Zak explains:

> We portrayed [Lisa] as someone who feels their identity has been hard-won, has gone through a lot of suffering and discrimination for her lesbian identity, and isn't terribly open to other perspectives that she feels might challenge that. [...] But especially for people outside the LGBTQ communities, that may be something that is not even known, that there are so many riffs even within the queer and trans communities. (Zak quoted in Ennis 2015)

Kat's and Allie's positions contrast and interrogate the ideological assumptions inflected in Lisa's and Jenna's statements. Kat's comment about strap-ons complicates the idea that the categories "woman" or "lesbian" can be reduced to questions of biology, anatomy, or penetrative sex. The scene ends with Allie abruptly exiting the conversation and confiding in Kat if it would be less "lesbian" of her to like a trans woman, to which Kat reassures her: "Last time I checked, 'lesbian' means loving women. So what's the problem?" Allie and her friends represent a myriad of perspectives, and although the exchange centers cisgender women's reactions to trans people, the contrasting perspectives introduce viewers to a transphobic bias within the LGBTQ community. By speaking to queer and lesbian cisgender women who may be unaware of the marginalization of trans people within their own communities, the scene collectively highlights a growing rejection against the exclusion of trans women from lesbian and feminist spaces.

Paige and James

Allie's anchoring of white, queer, and lesbian cisgender women's identities allows Paige's character to educate viewers about the specificity of her experience as a Black transgender woman who is not so easily read as trans. Paige's storyline is explored and developed through her struggle to disclose her identity to her date James (Christian Ochoa), a Mexican American, cisgender, and heterosexual man. Although previous narratives like *The Crying Game* and *Dallas Buyer's Club* emphasize cisgender men's reactions to the revelation of a trans woman's history, Paige's storyline flips this script. Her narrative engages these conventions to ultimately subvert them and to re-center her perspective. For example, on Paige's and James' first date, he playfully asks her to tell him everything about herself, to which she scoffs: "Everything, about what?" Because viewers are already aware of Paige's trans identity, something which James is not yet privy to, her sarcastic remark reflects her trepidation in disclosing her history. The scene intertextually references a larger body of works that rely on the delayed revelation of a character's transgender identity, a narrative trope accompanied by an onscreen unmasking that prompts fear and disgust in others' reactions to this discovery (Miller 2017). James' attraction to Paige motivates him to know everything about her, but in an ironic twist, viewers understand that the disclosure of Paige's past may become a deal-breaker. Indeed, fear and disgust are very much positioned as plausible reactions from James, should Paige choose to make this disclosure.

Paige's history is eventually disclosed to James in episode six where she is publicly outed by Lisa before she can share this information with him. When Paige and James meet to discuss this revelation, the scene opens with James sternly telling Paige "you should have told me." The line is suggestive, and it leads viewers to believe that this discovery is likely to be a problem for James; it calls forth the narrative trope wherein the delayed revelation of a trans character's history elicits fear, anger, or repulsion on behalf of the (male) cisgender character. However, the conversation takes an unexpected turn. James instead confesses to Paige that he has a gambling problem, and, much like Paige, he was struggling to find an appropriate time to share this information with her. Paige is taken aback by James' confession, and after a long pause, the scene closes with James stating how much he really likes Paige. Rather than highlighting the reactions of cisgender folks, Paige's relationship with James re-writes this disclosure narrative from her perspective as a trans woman. This alternative representation exposes the historical absence of these narratives: the tension builds because viewers anticipate that James will react violently toward Paige. But when audiences are given an unexpected release, they are invited to question why they assumed the scene would play out in the way that they initially imagined.

The camera work and editing also center Paige's perspective. For example, when Paige first notices James checking her out in the second episode, a shot-reverse-shot sutures the viewer's gaze to the look of the camera, from Paige's point of view as she glances lustfully at James. This scene is one of the few moments in the entire series where audiences are invited to explicitly adopt the eye-line of one of its trans characters. For straight and/or cisgender viewers, the effect is distancing. They can "look with, rather than at, the transgender body" (Halberstam 2005, 92) and participate in the sexualization and objectification of someone who is like them (in this case, James). For trans viewers, however, Paige creates a position for a desiring transgender subject fortified by the traditional (white and male) operation of the gaze, something rarely seen on TV (Halberstam 2005, 89).

In addition to centering Paige's perspective within narratives of disclosure, Paige's character addresses racialization in relation to trans identities. *Her Story* does not shy away from Paige's Blackness: her dialogue is peppered with colloquial phrases like "Mmmhmm," "Girl," and "Naw bitch," and on her first date with James, Paige is depicted asking the server at an upscale restaurant for hot sauce, stating that she's "not gonna eat white people food without a little help." Paige's typification as a sassy Black woman continues throughout the series, and it is used to educate white viewers (anchored initially by Allie) about intersections between race and gender. For example, when James is surprised to find out that Paige is a lawyer on their first date, she firmly interjects: "Is it because I'm Black?" Paige's comment performs a double work: it interrogates the racialized implications behind James' statement and, as a result, it demonstrates how such representations of Black trans women are still largely absent from television. Although viewers are not shown the discrimination Paige has undoubtedly experienced, the narrative ellipsis suggests that Paige has worked hard to get to where she is now as a young, successful, and Black transgender lawyer.

A similar exchange occurs between Paige and Lisa in episode six, this time with Paige mobilizing her Blackness to call out Lisa's transphobia as an effect of her privilege as a white lesbian woman. In this scene, Paige confronts Lisa for publicly outing her at work in front of a client, a trans woman who was denied access to a women's shelter. Lisa expresses how trans women are "biologically male" and are therefore different from women. Paige immediately shuts her down:

> You know how many times I run into people like you? That talk about racial inequality without a Black girl in sight. Write your little economic inequality pieces, but you've never been poor. This is about women who you've decided aren't women, and you are wrong.

Here, Paige's call out educates viewers on the multiple dimensions of trans discrimination within the LGBTQ community. However, it does so at risk of stereotyping Paige as an angry Black woman. In spite of that, the series departs from previous representations of trans people by depicting Paige as a successful, career-minded lawyer, which differs from the historical portrayals of trans people of color as villains, sex workers, and sexual deviants, if they were represented at all.

CONCLUSION

Her Story's character proxy structure is essential to its pedagogical role. Although the device folds viewers into the series' content with the purpose of engaging cisgender viewers who are unfamiliar with trans issues, it has a very different effect for trans audiences. Throughout the series, there continues to be a tacit fetishization and pathologization of trans identities at the service of educating others: the series includes problematic and age-old tropes in order to contest and subvert them through narrative storytelling, such as Lisa's antagonism and Paige's disclosure storyline. But these moments unintentionally reify stereotypes of trans people. For example, Violet's backstory includes sex work and drug addiction, which aligns with the historical framing of trans people as criminals and sexual deviants. Additionally, the man Violet is living with, Mark (Josh Wingate), is disturbingly possessive, and he is uncomfortable with Violet identifying herself as trans in front of others. He even tells Violet not to do the interview with Allie, and he becomes abusive toward her when he finds out that she went against his suggestion. In Paige's case, her story arc remains secondary: she is introduced to viewers through her friendship with Violet, which is an entry point only made possible by Allie's initial positioning as viewers' introduction to the series. This secondary positioning of Paige's narrative tacitly implies that her difference as a Black trans woman may distance larger audiences. In a similar way that Violet's storyline must be introduced and told through Allie, a white cisgender lesbian, Paige's Black trans subjectivity is secondary to the series' white trans representations. *Her Story*'s character proxy structure thus reveals how the transformative and pedagogical nature of the show as a queer crossover series is meant for white cisgender audiences, rather than for the transgender communities the series intends to represent.

Her Story does attempt to complicate these problematic representations. Violet is given a rich narrative that centers her life after recovery, and her scenes with Mark focus on her feelings and reactions rather than his: they frame her arrangement with Mark as one born out of necessity, and thus Violet is framed as being sympathetic in her plight. With Paige, her career as a young attorney suggests to viewers that there can be successful Black trans women, as much as the interventions her character makes regarding the racialization of trans identity rely on prevailing stereotypes of Black women. Although the series engages these narrative and representational tropes to subvert and re-tell them from the perspective of its trans characters, what is evident is the fact that the series cannot simply begin with either Violet or Paige. *Her Story* may be written by and for people who are queer and trans with the express purpose of intervening within a body of transgender media projects created and acted by cisgender people, but the didactic function of its character proxy structure necessitates an address to white cisgender audiences, first and foremost. Thus, *Her Story* may center trans characters and themes, but its character proxy structure demonstrates how the series must continue to make specific assumptions about who is watching and who needs to be educated.

REFERENCES

Abbott, Traci B. 2013. "The Trans/Romance Dilemma in Transamerica and Other Films." *The Journal of American Culture* 36, no. 1: 32–41.

Adams, Nick. 2016. "Men Who Play Transgender Women Send a 'Toxic and Dangerous' Message." *The Hollywood Reporter*, September 1, 2016. https://www.hollywoodreporter.com/news/matt-bomer-transgender-movie-anything-guest-column-925170

Ahmed, Sara. 2004. *The Cultural Politics of Emotion*. New York: Routledge.

Bonney, Grace. 2016. "Her Story: An Interview with Executive Producer Katherine Fisher." *Design Sponge*, January 27, 2016. http://www.designsponge.com/2016/01/her-story-an-interview-with-producer-kate-fisher

Booth, Tristian E. 2015. "The Provisional Acknowledgment of Identity Claims in Televised Documentary." *Transgender Communication: History, Trends, and Trajectories*, 111–26. Lanham, MD: Lexington Books.

Capuzza, Jamie C. and Leland G. Spencer. 2017. "Regressing, Progressing, or Transgressing on the Small Screen? Transgender Characters on U.S. Scripted Television Series." *Communication Quarterly* 65, no. 2: 214–30.

Carrera, Lianna. 2015. "*Her Story* Follows a Cisgender Lesbian and a Trans Woman Finding Love." *AfterEllen*, August 19, 2015. https://www.afterellen.com/tv/448863-herstory-follows-cisgender-lesbian-trans-woman-finding-love

Cavalcante, Andre. 2016. "'I Did It All Online': Transgender Identity and the Management of Everyday Life." *Critical Studies in Media Communication* 33, no. 1: 109–22.
Dame, Avery. 2013. "'I'm Your Hero? Like me?': The Category of 'Expert' in the Trans Male Vlog." *Journal of Language and Sexuality* 2, no. 1: 40–69.
Enke, Anne. 2012. *Transfeminist Perspectives in and beyond Transgender and Gender Studies*. Philadelphia, PA: Temple University Press.
Ennis, Dawn. 2015. "*Her Story* Explores the Dating Lives of Trans Women." *Advocate*, November 16, 2015. https://www.advocate.com/arts-entertainment/2015/11/16/her-story-explores-dating-lives-transgender-women-us-us
Farr, Daniel and Nathalie Degroult. 2008. "Understand the Queer World of the L-esbian Body: Using *Queer as Folk* and *The L Word* to Address the Construction of the Lesbian Body." *Journal of Lesbian Studies* 12, no. 4: 423–34.
Funk, Steven and Jaydi Funk. 2016. "Transgender Dispossession in *Transparent*: Coming Out as a Euphemism for Honesty." *Sexuality and Culture* 20: 879–905.
Gamson, Joshua. 1998. "Publicity Traps: Television Talk Shows and Lesbian, Gay, Bisexual, and Transgender Visibility." *Sexualities* 1, no. 1: 11–41.
———. 2001. *Queer Families, Queer Politics: Challenging Culture and the State*. New York: Columbia University Press.
Gray, Jonathan. 2008. *Television Entertainment*. New York: Routledge.
Halberstam, Jack. 2005. *In a Queer Time and Place: Transgender Bodies, Subcultural Lives*. New York: New York University Press.
Hall, Stuart. 1997. "The Work of Representation." In *Representation: Cultural Representations and Signifying Practices*, 13–75. London: SAGE.
Her Story. 2016. Created by Jen Richards and Laura Zak. Directed by Sydney Freeland, 2016.
Horak, Laura. 2014. "Trans on YouTube: Intimacy, Visibility, Temporality." *Transgender Studies Quarterly* 1, no. 4: 572–85.
Jusino, Teresa. 2015. "The Mary Sue Interview: *Her Story*'s Jen Richards Talks Bringing Trans and Queer Women's Stories to Life." *The Mary Sue*, August 27, 2015. https://www.themarysue.com/tms-interview-her-story-jen-richards/
Kohnen, Melanie. 2016. *Queer Representation, Visibility, and Race in American Film and Television: Screening the Closet*. New York: Routledge.
Lang, Nico. 2016. "The Only Emmy-Nominated Show Starring Trans Actors Is the One You're Not Watching." *Esquire*, September 15, 2016. https://www.esquire.com/entertainment/tv/a48589/her-story-emmys-jen-richards-trans-stories/
Lovelock, Michael. 2017. "'I Am … ': Caitlyn Jenner, Jazz Jennings, and the Cultural Politics of Transgender Celebrity." *Feminist Media Studies* 17, no. 5: 737–54.
Miller, Lucy J. 2017. "Fear and the Cisgender Audience: Transgender Representation and Audience Identification in *Sleepaway Camp*." *The Spectator* 37, no. 2: 40–7.
Namaste, Viviane K. 2005. *Sex Change, Social Change: Reflections on Identity, Institutions, and Imperialism*, 41–59. Toronto: Women's Press.
Ng, Eve. 2015. "A 'Post-Gay' Era? Media Gaystreaming, Homonormativity, and the Politics of LGBT Integration." *Communication, Culture, and Critique* 6, no. 2: 258–83.
O'Hara, Mary E. 2015. "*Her Story* is something new for Hollywood with Trans Actresses in Trans Roles." *The Daily Dot*, October 27, 2015. https://www.dailydot.com/irl/her-story-premiere-new-york/?tw=dd

Raley, Amber and Jennifer L. Lucas. 2006. "Stereotype or Success? Prime-time Television's Portrayal of Gay Male, Lesbian, and Bisexual Characters." *Journal of Homosexuality* 51, no. 2: 19–38.

Richards, Jen. 2014. "Behind the Scenes with the Trans Advisors of Amazon's *Transparent*." *The Kernel*, September 26, 2014. https://kernelmag.dailydot.com/issue-sections/features-issue-sections/13433/transparent-amazon-trans-advisors/

Rose, Gillian. 2008. *Visual Methodologies: An Introduction to the Interpretation of Visual Materials*, 2nd edition. London: SAGE.

Rude, Mey. 2015. "*Her Story* Stars Wanna Tell Real Trans Love Stories." *Autostraddle*, September 8, 2015. https://www.autostraddle.com/her-story-stars-wanna-tell-real-trans-love-stories-305274/

Serano, Julia. 2007. *Whipping Girl: A Transsexual Woman on Sexism and the Scapegoating of Femininity*. Emeryville, CA: Seal Press.

Siebler, Kay. 2012. "Transgender Transitions: Sex/Gender Binaries in the Digital Age." *Journal of Gay and Lesbian Mental Health* 16, no. 1: 74–99.

Stafford, Zach. 2016. "*Her Story*: The Transgender-Themed Web Series up for a 'Shock' Emmy." *The Guardian*, August 10, 2016. https://www.theguardian.com/tv-and-radio/2016/aug/10/her-story-jen-richards-emmys-transgender-women

Steinmetz, Katy. 2014. "The Transgender Tipping Point." *Time*, May 29, 2014, http://time.com/135480/transgender-tipping-point/

Villarejo, Amy. 2013. *Ethereal Queer: Television Historicity, Desire*. Durham: Duke University Press.

List of Contributors

Charles Goehring is an Assistant Professor in the School of Communication at San Diego State University. He earned his Ph.D. in Communication Studies from the University of Iowa. He teaches a wide variety of undergraduate and graduate courses, including rhetorical criticism, rhetorical theory, and gender and communication.

Debra Hope received her Ph.D. in Clinical Psychology from the University at the Albany-State University of New York in 1990, when she joined the Psychology Department at the University of Nebraska-Lincoln. Co-founder of Trans Collaborations and director of the Rainbow Clinic, she is currently Aaron Douglas Professor in the department.

Emma A. Jane (formerly published as Emma Tom) is an Associate Professor in the School of Arts and Media at the University of New South Wales in Sydney, Australia. Her tenth book, *Misogyny Online: A Short (and Brutish) History*, was published by SAGE in 2017. Her next book, *Diagnosis Normal*, will be published by Penguin Random House in March, 2022.

Erika M. Thomas earned her Ph.D. in Communication from Wayne State University in 2011. She is an Associate Professor in the Department of Human Communication Studies and Queer Studies Minor Affiliated Faculty at California

State University, Fullerton. Her areas of study include rhetorical criticism and theory and media representations of gender, sex, and sexuality.

Jennifer Huemmer is an Assistant Professor of Strategic Communication in the Roy H. Park School of Communications at Ithaca College. Her research examines media as a process of meaning-making that is interpreted, negotiated, and resisted through the actions and interactions of individuals and communities.

Katerina Symes is a Ph.D. candidate in the Department of Communication Studies at Concordia University in Montreal, Canada. She is an instructor in Humanities at Vanier College. Her research engages questions of spectatorship, desire, identity, and identification. Her current project examines how digital television has contributed to the popularization of queer and transgender content.

Magalí Daniela Pérez Riedel is a Doctor in Communication from the Universidad Nacional de La Plata, Argentina. She has eight years of teaching and research experience, specializing in media and LGBTQ representation. She is the author of the book *Género y diversidad sexual en el blog Boquitas pintadas* (2014).

Mary E. Brooks is an Assistant Professor in the Department of Communication at West Texas A&M University. Her research interests include the representation of marginalized groups in media with a specific focus on the ageing population.

Nathian Shae Rodriguez, Ph.D. is an Associate Professor of Digital Media in the School of Journalism and Media Studies at San Diego State University. He specializes in critical-cultural and digital media studies, critical communication pedagogy, and pop culture pedagogy. His research focuses on minority representation in media, specifically LGBTQ and Latinx portrayals and intersectional identity negotiation, as well as pop culture, identity, radio broadcasting, and issues of masculinity/mascing.

Patricia Di Risio completed her Ph.D. in Screen Studies at the University of Melbourne. She has taught at the University of Melbourne and Monash University in Australia. She is currently a lecturer in media, film, and journalism at Monash College (Monash University). Her research focuses on the representation of women and femininity in Hollywood cinema.

Richard Mocarski is the Assistant Vice Chancellor for Research and graduate faculty of Communication at the University of Nebraska at Kearney. He is a co-founder of Trans Collaborations, an academic-community partnership dedicated to reducing health disparities in the transgender and gender diverse communities.

Robyn Myers holds a B.A. in Psychology and earned her School Psychology Education Specialist degree through the University of Nebraska at Kearney. Robyn worked as a Graduate Research Assistant at Trans Collaborations for two years.

Sarah F. Price is an Assistant Professor in the department of Communication and Philosophy at Florida Gulf Coast University. Her research focuses on transgender and gender diverse identity, representation, and access to healthcare, and she has worked with Trans Collaborations for the past four years.

Sim Butler is an Assistant Professor of Communication Studies at the University of Alabama. His research interests include power, rhetoric, and health disparities.

Index

20/20 121–124

A

Adventure Time (TV show) 7, 78–93
age 5, 8, 27, 30–31, 132–133
agency 6, 18, 28, 32, 37–52, 126, 133
Amazon Prime Video 16, 42, 144
America's Next Top Model (TV show) 7, 97–116

B

Basic Instinct (film) 60
beyond transition narratives 149
biological sex 19, 62, 64, 67, 101, 156
bisexuality 60–61, 64, 91, 114
Black transgender women 2, 9, 154–155
Bono, Chaz 7, 15, 97–116

Bornstein, Kate 90
Boys Don't Cry (film) 6, 55, 57–58, 64–67, 69, 70
breakout texts 58
broadcast television 3, 7, 19, 77, 81, 128
Burset, Sophia (fictional character) 21–23, 25–30, 32, 77, 147–148
Butler, Judith 17–19, 58, 66, 80, 88, 101, 116

C

cable television 3, 7, 81
canonical films 6, 55–72
capitalism 56, 68
Capuzza and Spencer 4, 10, 15, 40–41, 44, 57, 72, 98–99, 147
Cartoon Network 7, 85
casting 33, 60, 82, 97, 100, 103, 105, 115, 148
Catastrophe (TV show) 6, 38, 42–52

INDEX

Cavalcante, Andre 58, 81–82, 91–92, 124–125, 145
celebrity status 8, 23–24, 99, 109, 124, 129, 131–136
"cisgender gaze" 6, 18, 32, 151, 155
cisnormativity 2–4, 58, 62, 68, 72, 84
coming out 8, 16, 49, 59, 82, 89, 121, 129, 133–136, 147
commercial cinema 5, 55–61, 71–72
communication, definition of 2–3
confession 70, 121–124, 135–136, 155
conflating gender identity with sexual orientation 57, 59–60
Connell, Raewyn 17, 19
contemporary television 4–7, 37–52, 77–93
Cox, Laverne 21, 30, 77–78, 83–84, 91, 98, 123, 129, 133, 147
Crenshaw, Kimberlé 5, 18, 32, 125–126, 134–136
criminal behavior 1, 6, 30, 57, 59–61, 69
critical rhetorical analysis 20, 42, 102
cross-dressing 10, 57, 59, 62–63, 66, 69–70, 112, 124
Crying Game, The (film) 6, 55, 57, 61–64, 66, 71–72, 148, 154

D

Dancing with the Stars (TV show) 7, 15, 97–116
Danish Girl, The (film) 6, 55, 58, 68–72, 148
dating 8, 28, 47–48, 141–142, 149–158
death 4, 6, 59, 61, 64, 66, 72, 82–83
deception 30, 58, 63
deviance 1, 3–6, 15–16, 21–22, 25–26, 29–31, 60, 123, 127, 146, 156
digital television 143–157
disclosing 8, 25, 147–149, 151–156
discourses of power 17–19, 32, 123
discrimination 1–2, 8, 24, 44, 50, 83, 100, 126, 132, 155

disgust 46, 61, 63, 67, 82, 147, 154
Dr. Jekyll and Sister Hyde (film) 58, 60
Dressed to Kill (film) 59–60
DSM-V (*Diagnostic and Statistical Manual of Mental Disorders*) 68

E

Elbe, Lili 68–72
everydayness 65, 81, 91–93, 152

F

fame 24, 84, 122, 130–136
family 29–31, 40, 48, 64, 66–68, 87, 89, 109, 124, 146–148
fear 1, 4, 41, 58–59, 61, 63, 65, 68, 87, 90, 99, 110–115, 124, 147, 152–155
femininity 4, 7, 19, 40, 67, 102, 110, 114–115, 151
fetishization 6, 8, 37–52, 91, 156
fictional characters 6–9, 33, 43–46, 70, 90, 141
Figure 6.1 Timeline of events surrounding Caitlyn Jenner's mediated transition 129
film genres
  docudrama see *Boys Don't Cry, Glen or Glenda?*
  drama see *M. Butterfly, Danish Girl, Transamerica*
  horror see *Dr. Jekyll and Sister Hyde, The Silence of the Lambs, Psycho*
  thriller see *Basic Instinct, Dressed to Kill, The Crying Game*
Foucault, Michel 6, 17–19, 55–58, 70, 123, 137
framing 7–8, 31, 77–79, 83, 88–91, 97–116, 121–136, 147, 156
Freud, Sigmund 41, 46
FTM (Female to Male) 40, 59, 64

G

gender ambiguity 57, 60, 63, 72, 97
gender bias 17–18
gender confirmation procedures *see* gender confirmation surgery, hormones
gender confirmation surgery 4, 6, 20, 24–26, 30, 45, 47–48, 50, 55, 57, 62, 64, 67–72, 82–83, 99, 105, 109, 113
"gender dysphoria" 68, 86. *See also* wrong body discourse
gender ideology 2
gender outlaws 90
gender performativity 18–19, 62, 89, 97–116, 134
gender *status quo* 2, 6, 90, 101
GLAAD (Gay and Lesbian Alliance Against Defamation) 16, 81, 148
Glen or Glenda? (film) 58–59

H

Halberstam, Jack 58, 65–66, 80–82, 91, 98, 124–126, 155
Hall, Stuart 41, 79–81, 84, 91, 145
hate crimes 2, 64–67, 69–72, 124–125. *See also* Teena, Brandon
hegemonic gender binary 17, 19–21, 25, 31–32, 115
  hegemonic femininity 102
  hegemonic masculinity 19–20, 99, 108, 115
Her Story (TV show) 8, 141–157
hermaphrodites 56
heteronormativity 16, 19–20, 30, 99, 126, 132, 143
heterosexual ideology 56, 68
HIV/AIDS 1, 4, 39, 47, 49–50
Hollywood 4, 6–7, 55–72, 124
homoeroticism 89
homonormativity 20, 92, 126
homophobia 1

homosexuality 1–2, 8, 20, 56, 59–60, 62, 65–68, 70–73, 87, 91, 97, 114, 123, 127, 141–156
hormones 24–26, 109, 112

I

I am Cait (TV show) 5, 8, 16, 20–33, 121–136, 144
I am Jazz (TV show) 5, 16, 20, 22, 24, 26, 28, 30
identity politics 38–40
institutionalization 56, 87, 127
intelligibility 8, 18, 31, 115
intersectionality 5, 18, 22, 32, 125–129, 134–136
invisibility 37–38, 57, 72, 146
irrelevance 84–85

J

Jenner, Caitlyn 8, 16, 23–24, 27, 29–30, 91, 98–99, 121–136, 144, 147, 149
Jennings, Jazz 16, 23–28, 98–99

K

Kardashian family 121, 129
King, Isis 7, 97–116

L

legitimacy of transgender identities 2, 61, 111, 115
LGBTQ rights 1–2, 123, 127–128

M

M. Butterfly (film) 63
mainstream audience 115, 141–157

mainstream media 2, 5, 123, 133, 149
male privilege 8, 84, 90, 130–136
marginalization 3, 38, 44, 56, 147, 154
Marxist theory 40
masculinity 4, 7, 10, 19–20, 40–41, 45–47, 63, 65, 99, 102–104, 108, 111, 115
media studies 3, 9, 124
medical discourses 6, 26, 55–57, 68
medical transition 23–26, 29, 109, 112. *See also* hormones
misrepresentation 51, 92
Mocarski, Richard 4, 16, 99, 103–104, 109, 115
moral panic 1, 65, 91
MTF (Male To Female) 40, 69
murder 6, 59–61, 64, 66, 69, 82–83

N

narratives 3–8, 20, 26, 30–33, 37–38, 51, 57, 72, 83, 90, 99, 124, 145–149, 154–157
Netflix 4, 16, 77, 144
Nomi (fictional character) 20, 28–31
non-binary 81, 87, 102, 128
normalization 20, 146

O

objectification 37, 42, 46, 52, 132, 155. *See also* fetishization, sexualization
oppression 5, 18, 21, 23, 84, 134–139
Orange Is the New Black (TV show) 5, 16, 20–33, 77–78, 147–148
otherness 59, 73, 89, 91, 124

P

"passing" 65–67, 86, 151
pathologization 6, 8, 50, 55, 59, 64, 69–71, 83, 148, 156
pedagogy 8, 84, 126, 142, 144–145, 149–157

performance theory 7, 18–19, 101
perverse implantation 6, 55–61, 64–72
Pfefferman, Maura (fictional character) 21, 24–29, 32, 45–47, 147–148
Phelan, Peggy 38–42
political ideologies 130, 132–136
politics of representation 84
popular media texts 2–3, 5–7, 10, 38, 40, 42, 60, 67, 77, 79, 85, 92, 123–124
pornography 61
Pose (TV show) 9, 33
post-classical Hollywood films 57
prison 9, 20–34, 64, 77, 86, 147
pronouns 87, 106
proxy structure 8, 141–157
psychiatric discourses 55–57, 60, 68–70, 87
Psycho (film) 57, 59–60, 69
psychoanalysis 41
psychological disorders 56, 60, 68–70
public culture 97

Q

quality coding 79
queer cinema 65
queer crossover program 8, 143, 157
queer family 68
queer television studies 145–146

R

race 5–6, 10, 16, 18, 20–33, 41, 79–80, 124–129
reality television show 8, 16, 27, 97–116
rhetoric 97, 102, 135, 147
romance 6, 25, 40, 50–51, 64, 66, 68, 71–72, 85, 87, 142, 148–150

S

sameness 92, 99
Sawyer, Diane 121–123, 129–136

INDEX | 169

self-representation 145, 149–150
Sense8 (TV show) 5, 16, 20, 26–33
Serano, Julia 3–4, 81, 146
sex worker 4, 43–48, 50–51, 146. 156
sex, lack of 6, 25–29, 32, 40–41, 64, 68, 71
sexual deviance 4, 29
sexualization 6, 52, 155. *See also* fetishization
Siebler, Kay 37, 39–40, 99, 102, 106, 109, 115, 147
Silence of the Lambs, The (film) 60
social acceptance 8, 24, 31, 44, 51, 56–57, 59, 99–100, 103, 124, 133
social androgyny 87, 89
social media 8, 121–136. *See also* Twitter
socioeconomic status 5, 18, 21–25, 32, 124, 126, 129. *See also* wealth
spectatorship 8–9, 16–17, 22–33, 65–66, 121–123, 150
stereotypes 5–6, 9, 9, 24, 29, 32, 38, 51, 79
stigmatization 18, 24, 29, 47–48, 71, 86, 146
streaming services 4–5, 7, 16, 42, 77, 81, 144. *See also* Amazon Prime Video, Netflix
"structuring absences" 85
Stryker, Susan 80, 87–89, 97, 101, 125
suicide 31, 82–83, 86, 89

T

Teena, Brandon 64–66, 69, 72, 124–125
television genres
    animated series see *Adventure Time*
    comedy see *Catastrophe*
    drama see *Her Story, Orange Is the New Black, Pose, Transparent*
    reality television shows see *20/20, America's Next Top Model, Dancing with the Stars, I am Cait, I am Jazz*
    sci-fi see *Sense 8*
textual analysis 8, 58, 79, 90, 97, 102, 129, 145
"trans chasers" 46, 51

trans reality star *see* Chaz Bono, Isis King
"trans ridicule" 4, 40, 42–44, 70–71, 82, 115
Transamerica (film) 6, 55, 58, 67–72, 148
transgender body 6, 37–38, 40–43, 46–47, 50–52, 81, 124–125, 155
transgender gaze 65–66
transgender media studies 3, 9, 124
transgender men 4, 9–10, 40, 64–65, 81–82, 148
"Transgender Tipping Point" 77, 83–84, 91
transgender, definitions of 2, 57, 80, 125
transitioning 21, 24, 26, 40, 57, 71–72, 99, 109, 147, 152
transmisogyny 4
trans-ness 84–85, 90, 91, 150
transnormativity 16–17, 20–21, 29–33
transordinary 7, 90–92
Transparent (TV show) 5–6, 16, 20–21, 24, 26–29, 38–52, 78, 86, 147–148
transphobia 1, 4, 43, 91, 100, 152, 156. *See also* hate crimes
transsexuals 56–57, 59, 62–63, 67–69, 105, 124, 153
transvestism 57, 59
tropes 6–7, 30–32, 69, 78, 82–87
    tragic trope 82–83, 87
    trailblazer trope 83–85
Twitter 8, 121–136

U

unscripted television shows 98–100, 114–116
Us Weekly 122

V

violence 1–2, 40, 44, 49, 61–62, 65–66, 71, 83, 128, 133–134
visibility 2–6, 16, 37–46, 51–52, 57, 71–72, 84, 97–102, 114–116, 133–136, 145–149

W

wealth 8, 20, 23–26, 32, 99, 125, 130–136, 151
white privilege 8, 21–23, 30, 99, 127, 130–136, 146, 148, 151, 156
wrong body discourse 6, 57, 67–68, 83, 105, 147

Y

YouTube 144

Cultural Media Studies

Leandra Hernandez and Amanda R. Martinez
Series Editors

In the past few years, our political, cultural, and media landscapes have cultivated a sharp, notable rise of media activism, more representations of diverse groups and characters, and the need for intersectional approaches to media studies. The #MeToo campaign, the 2017 and 2018 Women's Marches, Black Lives Matter marches, cross-border anti-feminicide activist marches, immigration marches, and increased representation of diverse sexual identities, racial/ethnic groups, and gender identities are evidence of the need for continued research on cultural media studies topics.

The Peter Lang Cultural Media Studies book series is accepting book proposals for both proposed book and fully developed manuscripts on a rolling basis for media studies books that explore media production, media consumption, media effects, and media representations of feminism(s), race/ethnicity, gender, sexuality, and related topics.

For additional information about this series or for the submission of manuscripts, please contact:

editorial@peterlang.com

To order other books in this series, please contact our Customer Service Department:

peterlang@presswarehouse.com (within the U.S.)
orders@peterlang.com (outside the U.S.)

Or browse online by series:

www.peterlang.com

www.ingramcontent.com/pod-product-compliance
Lightning Source LLC
Chambersburg PA
CBHW052023290426
44112CB00014B/2352